The Waste Land

Study Edition

The Waste Land

T. S. Eliot

Study edition, including:

From Ritual to Romance, by Jessie L. Weston

The Adonis, Attis, and Osiris chapters from the abridged edition of *The Golden Bough,* by Sir James G. Frazer

Waking Lion Press

Cover: *Klosterfriedhof im Schnee [Cloister Cemetery in Snow]*, painting by Caspar David Friedrich, about 1818.

The views expressed in this book are the responsibility of the author and do not necessarily represent the position of the publisher. The reader alone is responsible for the use of any ideas or information provided by this book.

ISBN 978-1-4341-0240-9

Published by Waking Lion Press, an imprint of The Editorium

Any additions to original text (editor's notes, etc.) © 2007 by The Editorium. All rights reserved. Printed in the United States of America.

Waking Lion Press™, the Waking Lion Press logo, and The Editorium™ are trademarks of The Editorium, LLC

The Editorium, LLC
West Valley City, UT 84128-3917
wakinglionpress.com
wakinglion@editorium.com

Contents

The Waste Land	1
I. The Burial of the Dead	5
II. A Game of Chess	8
III. The Fire Sermon	12
IV. Death by Water	18
V. What the Thunder Said	19
From Ritual to Romance	25
Publisher's Preface	27
Preface	29
I. Introductory	33
II. The Task of the Hero	41
III. The Freeing of the Waters	51
IV. Tammuz and Adonis	58
V. Medieval and Modern Forms of Nature Ritual	72
VI. The Symbols	82
VII. The Sword Dance	94
VIII. The Medicine Man	109
IX. The Fisher King	119
X. The Secret of the Grail (1)	136

Contents

XI. The Secret of the Grail (2)	145
XII. Mithra and Attis	156
XIII. The Perilous Chapel	164
XIV. The Author	174

The Adonis, Attis, and Osiris Chapters from The Golden Bough — *189*

XXIX. The Myth of Adonis	191
XXX. Adonis in Syria	196
XXXI. Adonis in Cyprus	199
XXXII. The Ritual of Adonis	207
XXXIII. The Gardens of Adonis	214
XXXIV. The Myth and Ritual of Attis	222
XXXV. Attis as a God of Vegetation	229
XXXVI. Human Representatives of Attis	231
XXXVII. Oriental Religions in the West	235
XXXVIII. The Myth of Osiris	243
XXXIX. The Ritual of Osiris	250
XL. The Nature of Osiris	262

The Waste Land [1]

---

[1]. Not only the title, but the plan and a good deal of the incidental symbolism of the poem were suggested by Miss Jessie L. Weston's book on the Grail legend: *From Ritual to Romance* (Macmillan). Indeed, so deeply am I indebted, Miss Weston's book will elucidate the difficulties of the poem much better than my notes can do; and I recommend it (apart from the great interest of the book itself) to any who think such elucidation of the poem worth the trouble. To another work of anthropology I am indebted in general, one which has influenced our generation profoundly; I mean *The Golden Bough;* I have used especially the two volumes *Adonis, Attis, Osiris.* Anyone who is acquainted with these works will immediately recognize in the poem certain references to vegetation ceremonies. [Editor's notes (not Eliot's) are given in brackets, as here.]

Nam Sibyllam quidem Cumis ego ipse oculis meis vidi in ampulla pendere, et cum illi pueri dicerent: Σίβυλλα τί θέλεις· *respondebat illa:* ἀποθανεῖν θέλω.[1]

For Ezra Pound
il miglior fabbro.[2]

---

    1. ["For once I myself saw with my own eyes the Sibyl at Cumae hanging in a cage, and when the boys said to her: 'Sibyl, what do you want?' she replied, 'I want to die.' " Petronius' *Satyricon* (1st century A.D.)]
    2. [The better craftsman.]

I. The Burial of the Dead

April is the cruellest month, breeding
Lilacs out of the dead land, mixing
Memory and desire, stirring
Dull roots with spring rain.
Winter kept us warm, covering
Earth in forgetful snow, feeding
A little life with dried tubers.
Summer surprised us, coming over the Starnbergersee
With a shower of rain; we stopped in the colonnade,
And went on in sunlight, into the Hofgarten,
And drank coffee, and talked for an hour.
Bin gar keine Russin, stamm' aus Litauen, echt deutsch.[1]
And when we were children, staying at the archduke's,
My cousin's, he took me out on a sled,
And I was frightened. He said, Marie,
Marie, hold on tight. And down we went.
In the mountains, there you feel free.
I read, much of the night, and go south in the winter.

    What are the roots that clutch, what branches grow
Out of this stony rubbish? Son of man,[2]
You cannot say, or guess, for you know only
A heap of broken images, where the sun beats,
And the dead tree gives no shelter, the cricket no relief,[3]
And the dry stone no sound of water. Only
There is shadow under this red rock,
(Come in under the shadow of this red rock),

---

    1. ["I am not Russian at all; I come from Lithuania, a true German."]
    2. Cf. Ezekiel 2:7.
    3. Cf. Ecclesiastes 12:5.

I. The Burial of the Dead

And I will show you something different from either
Your shadow at morning striding behind you
Or your shadow at evening rising to meet you;
I will show you fear in a handful of dust.

>*Frisch weht der Wind*
>*Der Heimat zu.*
>*Mein Irisch Kind,*
>*Wo weilest du?*[4]

'You gave me hyacinths first a year ago;
'They called me the hyacinth girl.'
—Yet when we came back, late, from the Hyacinth garden,
Your arms full, and your hair wet, I could not
Speak, and my eyes failed, I was neither
Living nor dead, and I knew nothing,
Looking into the heart of light, the silence.
Od' und leer das Meer.[5]

    Madame Sosostris, famous clairvoyante,
Had a bad cold, nevertheless
Is known to be the wisest woman in Europe,
With a wicked pack of cards. Here, said she,[6]
Is your card, the drowned Phoenician Sailor,
(Those are pearls that were his eyes. Look!)
Here is Belladonna, the Lady of the Rocks,
The lady of situations.
Here is the man with three staves, and here the Wheel,
And here is the one-eyed merchant, and this card,
Which is blank, is something he carries on his back,
Which I am forbidden to see. I do not find

---

    4. ["Fresh blows the wind / to the homeland; / my Irish child, / where are you waiting?"] V. *Tristan und Isolde*, i, verses 5–8.

    5. ["Waste and empty, the sea."] Id. iii, verse 24.

    6. I am not familiar with the exact constitution of the Tarot pack of cards, from which I have obviously departed to suit my own convenience. The Hanged Man, a member of the traditional pack, fits my purpose in two ways: because he is associated in my mind with the Hanged God of Frazer, and because I associate him with the hooded figure in the passage of the disciples to Emmaus in Part V. The Phoenician Sailor and the Merchant appear later; also the 'crowds of people,' and Death by Water is executed in Part IV. The Man with Three Staves (an authentic member of the Tarot pack) I associate, quite arbitrarily, with the Fisher King himself.

I. The Burial of the Dead

The Hanged Man. Fear death by water.
I see crowds of people, walking round in a ring.
Thank you. If you see dear Mrs. Equitone,
Tell her I bring the horoscope myself:
One must be so careful these days.

   Unreal City,[7]
Under the brown fog of a winter dawn,
A crowd flowed over London Bridge, so many,
I had not thought death had undone so many.[8]
Sighs, short and infrequent, were exhaled,[9]
And each man fixed his eyes before his feet.
Flowed up the hill and down King William Street,
To where Saint Mary Woolnoth kept the hours
With a dead sound on the final stroke of nine.[10]
There I saw one I knew, and stopped him, crying 'Stetson!
'You who were with me in the ships at Mylae!
'That corpse you planted last year in your garden,
'Has it begun to sprout? Will it bloom this year?
'Or has the sudden frost disturbed its bed?
'Oh keep the Dog far hence, that's friend to men,[11]
'Or with his nails he'll dig it up again!
'You! hypocrite lecteur!—mon semblable,—mon frère!'[12]

---

7. Cf. Baudelaire:
Fourmillante cité, cité pleine de rêves,
Où le spectre en plein jour raccroche le passant.
[Swarming city, city full of dreams, / Where the specter in broad daylight accosts the passer-by.]
8. Cf. *Inferno*, iii. 55-7:
           si lunga tratta
di gente, ch'io non avrei mai creduto
che morte tanta n'avesse disfatta.
[So long a train / of people, that I should never have believed / that death had undone so many.]
9. Cf. *Inferno*, iv. 25-27:
Quivi, secondo che per ascoltare,
non avea pianto, ma' che di sospiri,
che l'aura eterna facevan tremare.
[Here there was no plaint, / that could be heard, except of sighs, / which caused the eternal air to tremble.]
10. A phenomenon which I have often noticed.
11. Cf. the Dirge in Webster's *White Devil*.
12. ["Hypocrite reader!—my double!—my brother!"] V. Baudelaire, Preface to *Fleurs du Mal*.

II. A Game of Chess

The Chair she sat in, like a burnished throne,[1]
Glowed on the marble, where the glass
Held up by standards wrought with fruited vines
From which a golden Cupidon peeped out
(Another hid his eyes behind his wing)
Doubled the flames of sevenbranched candelabra
Reflecting light upon the table as
The glitter of her jewels rose to meet it,
From satin cases poured in rich profusion;
In vials of ivory and coloured glass
Unstoppered, lurked her strange synthetic perfumes,
Unguent, powdered, or liquid—troubled, confused
And drowned the sense in odours; stirred by the air
That freshened from the window, these ascended
In fattening the prolonged candle-flames,
Flung their smoke into the laquearia,[2]
Stirring the pattern on the coffered ceiling.
Huge sea-wood fed with copper
Burned green and orange, framed by the coloured stone,
In which sad light a carvèd dolphin swam.
Above the antique mantel was displayed
As though a window gave upon the sylvan scene[3]
The change of Philomel, by the barbarous king[4]
So rudely forced; yet there the nightingale[5]

---

    1. Cf. *Antony and Cleopatra*, II. ii. 190.
    2. Laquearia. V. *Aeneid*, I. 726:
dependent lychni laquearibus aureis incensi, et noctem flammis funalia vincunt.
[Blazing torches hang from the gold-paneled ceiling, and torches vanquish the night with flames.]
    3. Sylvan scene. V. Milton, *Paradise Lost*, iv. 140.
    4. V. Ovid, *Metamorphoses*, vi, Philomela.
    5. Cf. Part III, 1. 204.

II. A Game of Chess

Filled all the desert with inviolable voice
And still she cried, and still the world pursues,
'Jug Jug' to dirty ears.
And other withered stumps of time
Were told upon the walls; staring forms
Leaned out, leaning, hushing the room enclosed.
Footsteps shuffled on the stair.
Under the firelight, under the brush, her hair
Spread out in fiery points
Glowed into words, then would be savagely still.

   'My nerves are bad to-night. Yes, bad. Stay with me.
'Speak to me. Why do you never speak. Speak.
    'What are you thinking of? What thinking? What?
'I never know what you are thinking. Think.'

   I think we are in rats' alley[6]
Where the dead men lost their bones.

   'What is that noise?'
                     The wind under the door.[7]
'What is that noise now? What is the wind doing?'
                  Nothing again nothing.
                                    'Do
'You know nothing? Do you see nothing? Do you remember
'Nothing?'

     I remember
Those are pearls that were his eyes.
'Are you alive, or not? Is there nothing in your head?'[8]
                                         But

O O O O that Shakespeherian Rag—
It's so elegant
So intelligent
'What shall I do now? What shall I do?'
'I shall rush out as I am, and walk the street

---

6. Cf. Part III, l. 195.
7. Cf. Webster: 'Is the wind in that door still?'
8. Cf. Part I, l. 37, 48.

II. A Game of Chess

'With my hair down, so. What shall we do to-morrow?
'What shall we ever do?'
                                    The hot water at ten.
And if it rains, a closed car at four.
And we shall play a game of chess,
Pressing lidless eyes and waiting for a knock upon the door.[9]

    When Lil's husband got demobbed, I said—
I didn't mince my words, I said to her myself,
HURRY UP PLEASE IT'S TIME
Now Albert's coming back, make yourself a bit smart.
He'll want to know what you done with that money he gave you
To get yourself some teeth. He did, I was there.
You have them all out, Lil, and get a nice set,
He said, I swear, I can't bear to look at you.
And no more can't I, I said, and think of poor Albert,
He's been in the army four years, he wants a good time,
And if you don't give it him, there's others will, I said.
Oh is there, she said. Something o' that, I said.
Then I'll know who to thank, she said, and give me a straight look.
HURRY UP PLEASE IT'S TIME
If you don't like it you can get on with it, I said.
Others can pick and choose if you can't.
But if Albert makes off, it won't be for lack of telling.
You ought to be ashamed, I said, to look so antique.
(And her only thirty-one.)
I can't help it, she said, pulling a long face,
It's them pills I took, to bring it off, she said.
(She's had five already, and nearly died of young George.)
The chemist said it would be alright, but I've never been the same.
You *are* a proper fool, I said.
Well, if Albert won't leave you alone, there it is, I said,
What you get married for if you don't want children?
HURRY UP PLEASE IT'S TIME
Well, that Sunday Albert was home, they had a hot gammon,
And they asked me in to dinner, to get the beauty of it hot—
HURRY UP PLEASE IT'S TIME

---

9. Cf. the game of chess in Middleton's *Women beware Women*.

II. A Game of Chess

Hurry up please it's time
Goonight Bill. Goonight Lou. Goonight May. Goonight.
Ta ta. Goonight. Goonight.
Good night, ladies, good night, sweet ladies, good night, good night.

III. The Fire Sermon

The river's tent is broken: the last fingers of leaf
Clutch and sink into the wet bank. The wind
Crosses the brown land, unheard. The nymphs are departed.
Sweet Thames, run softly, till I end my song.[1]
The river bears no empty bottles, sandwich papers,
Silk handkerchiefs, cardboard boxes, cigarette ends
Or other testimony of summer nights. The nymphs are departed.
And their friends, the loitering heirs of city directors;
Departed, have left no addresses.
By the waters of Leman I sat down and wept . . .
Sweet Thames, run softly till I end my song,
Sweet Thames, run softly, for I speak not loud or long.
But at my back in a cold blast I hear
The rattle of the bones, and chuckle spread from ear to ear.
A rat crept softly through the vegetation
Dragging its slimy belly on the bank
While I was fishing in the dull canal
On a winter evening round behind the gashouse
Musing upon the king my brother's wreck
And on the king my father's death before him.[2]
White bodies naked on the low damp ground
And bones cast in a little low dry garret,
Rattled by the rat's foot only, year to year.
But at my back from time to time I hear[3]
The sound of horns and motors, which shall bring[4]
Sweeney to Mrs. Porter in the spring.

---

  1. V. Spenser, *Prothalamion*.
  2. Cf. *The Tempest*, I. ii.
  3. Cf. Marvell, "To His Coy Mistress."
  4. Cf. Day, *Parliament of Bees:*
  When of the sudden, listening, you shall hear,

III. The Fire Sermon

O the moon shone bright on Mrs. Porter⁵
And on her daughter
They wash their feet in soda water
*Et O ces voix d'enfants, chantant dans la coupole!*⁶

   Twit twit twit
Jug jug jug jug jug jug
So rudely forc'd.
Tereu

   Unreal City
Under the brown fog of a winter noon
Mr. Eugenides, the Smyrna merchant
Unshaven, with a pocket full of currants⁷
C.i.f. London: documents at sight,
Asked me in demotic French
To luncheon at the Cannon Street Hotel
Followed by a weekend at the Metropole.

   At the violet hour, when the eyes and back
Turn upward from the desk, when the human engine waits
Like a taxi throbbing waiting,
I Tiresias, though blind, throbbing between two lives,⁸

  A noise of horns and hunting, which shall bring
  Actaeon to Diana in the spring,
  Where all shall see her naked skin . . .'
    5. I do not know the origin of the ballad from which these lines are taken: it was reported to me from Sydney, Australia.
    6. [And O those children's voices, singing in the dome!] V. Verlaine, *Parsifal*.
    7. The currants were quoted at a price 'carriage and insurance free to London'; and the Bill of Lading, etc., were to be handed to the buyer upon payment of the sight draft.
    8. Tiresias, although a mere spectator and not indeed a 'character,' is yet the most important personage in the poem, uniting all the rest. Just as the one-eyed merchant, seller of currants, melts into the Phoenician Sailor, and the latter is not wholly distinct from Ferdinand Prince of Naples, so all the women are one woman, and the two sexes meet in Tiresias. What Tiresias sees, in fact, is the substance of the poem. The whole passage from Ovid is of great anthropological interest:
  . . . Cum Iunone iocos et 'maior vestra profecto est
  Quam, quae contingit maribus,' dixisse, 'voluptas.'
  Illa negat; placuit quae sit sententia docti
  Quaerere Tiresiae: venus huic erat utraque nota.
  Nam duo magnorum viridi coeuntia silva
  Corpora serpentum baculi violaverat ictu
  Deque viro factus, mirabile, femina septem
  Egerat autumnos; octavo rursus eosdem
  Vidit et 'est vestrae si tanta potentia plagae,'

III. The Fire Sermon

Old man with wrinkled female breasts, can see
At the violet hour, the evening hour that strives
Homeward, and brings the sailor home from sea,⁹
The typist home at teatime, clears her breakfast, lights
Her stove, and lays out food in tins.
Out of the window perilously spread
Her drying combinations touched by the sun's last rays,
On the divan are piled (at night her bed)
Stockings, slippers, camisoles, and stays.
I Tiresias, old man with wrinkled dugs
Perceived the scene, and foretold the rest—

    Dixit 'ut auctoris sortem in contraria mutet,
Nunc quoque vos feriam!' percussis anguibus isdem
Forma prior rediit genetivaque venit imago.
Arbiter hic igitur sumptus de lite iocosa
Dicta Iovis firmat; gravius Saturnia iusto
Nec pro materia fertur doluisse suique
Iudicis aeterna damnavit lumina nocte,
At pater omnipotens (neque enim licet inrita cuiquam
Facta dei fecisse deo) pro lumine adempto
Scire futura dedit poenamque levavit honore.
[. . . Jove, they say, was happy
And feeling pretty good (with wine) forgetting
Anxiety and care, and killing time
Joking with Juno. "I maintain," he told her
"You females get more pleasure out of loving
Than we poor males do, ever." She denied it,
So they decided to refer the question
To wise Tiresias' judgment: he should know
What love was like, from either point of view.
Once he had come upon two serpents mating
In the green woods, and struck them from each other,
And thereupon, from man was turned into woman,
And was a woman seven years, and saw
The serpents once again, and once more struck them
Apart, remarking: "If there is such magic
In giving you blows, that man is turned into woman,
It may be that woman is turned to man. Worth trying."
And so he was a man again; as umpire,
He took the side of Jove. And Juno
Was a bad loser, and she said that umpires
Were always blind, and made him so forever.
No god can over-rule another's action,
But the Almighty Father, out of pity,
In compensation, gave Tiresias power
To know the future, so there was some honor
Along with punishment.
(Translation by Rolphe Humphries.)]
    9. This may not appear as exact as Sappho's lines, but I had in mind the 'longshore' or 'dory' fisherman, who returns at nightfall.

III. The Fire Sermon

I too awaited the expected guest.
He, the young man carbuncular, arrives,
A small house agent's clerk, with one bold stare,
One of the low on whom assurance sits
As a silk hat on a Bradford millionaire.
The time is now propitious, as he guesses,
The meal is ended, she is bored and tired,
Endeavours to engage her in caresses
Which still are unreproved, if undesired.
Flushed and decided, he assaults at once;
Exploring hands encounter no defence;
His vanity requires no response,
And makes a welcome of indifference.
(And I Tiresias have foresuffered all
Enacted on this same divan or bed;
I who have sat by Thebes below the wall
And walked among the lowest of the dead.)
Bestows one final patronising kiss,
And gropes his way, finding the stairs unlit ...

   She turns and looks a moment in the glass,
Hardly aware of her departed lover;
Her brain allows one half-formed thought to pass:
'Well now that's done: and I'm glad it's over.'
When lovely woman stoops to folly and[10]
Paces about her room again, alone,
She smoothes her hair with automatic hand,
And puts a record on the gramophone.

   'This music crept by me upon the waters'[11]
And along the Strand, up Queen Victoria Street.
O City city, I can sometimes hear
Beside a public bar in Lower Thames Street,
The pleasant whining of a mandoline
And a clatter and a chatter from within
Where fishmen lounge at noon: where the walls

---

10. V. Goldsmith, the song in *The Vicar of Wakefield*.
11. V. *The Tempest*, as above.

III. The Fire Sermon

Of Magnus Martyr hold[12]
Inexplicable splendour of Ionian white and gold.

    The river sweats[13]
Oil and tar
The barges drift
With the turning tide
Red sails
Wide
To leeward, swing on the heavy spar.
The barges wash
Drifting logs
Down Greenwich reach
Past the Isle of Dogs.
        Weialala leia
        Wallala leialala

    Elizabeth and Leicester[14]
Beating oars
The stern was formed
A gilded shell
Red and gold
The brisk swell
Rippled both shores
Southwest wind
Carried down stream
The peal of bells
White towers
        Weialala leia
        Wallala leialala

    'Trams and dusty trees.

---

12. The interior of St. Magnus Martyr is to my mind one of the finest among Wren's interiors. See *The Proposed Demolition of Nineteen City Churches* (P. S. King & Son, Ltd.).

13. The Song of the (three) Thames-daughters begins here. From line 292 to 306 inclusive they speak in turn. V. Götterdammerung, III. i: The Rhine-daughters.

14. V. Froude, Elizabeth, vol. I, ch. iv, letter of De Quadra to Philip of Spain:

In the afternoon we were in a barge, watching the games on the river. (The queen) was alone with Lord Robert and myself on the poop, when they began to talk nonsense, and went so far that Lord Robert at last said, as I was on the spot there was no reason why they should not be married if the queen pleased.

III. The Fire Sermon

Highbury bore me. Richmond and Kew[15]
Undid me. By Richmond I raised my knees
Supine on the floor of a narrow canoe.'

'My feet are at Moorgate, and my heart
Under my feet. After the event
He wept. He promised "a new start."
I made no comment. What should I resent?'

'On Margate Sands.
I can connect
Nothing with nothing.
The broken fingernails of dirty hands.
My people humble people who expect
Nothing.'
       la la

To Carthage then I came[16]

Burning burning burning burning[17]
O Lord Thou pluckest me out[18]
O Lord Thou pluckest

burning

---

15. Cf. *Purgatorio*, V. 133:
'Ricorditi di me, che son la Pia;
Siena mi fe,' disfecemi Maremma.'
[Remember me! I am called Pia; / Siena gave me life, Maremma death.]
16. V. St. Augustine's *Confessions:* 'to Carthage then I came, where a cauldron of unholy loves sang all about mine ears.'
17. The complete text of the Buddha's Fire Sermon (which corresponds in importance to the Sermon on the Mount) from which these words are taken, will be found translated in the late Henry Clarke Warren's *Buddhism in Translation* (Harvard Oriental Series). Mr. Warren was one of the great pioneers of Buddhist studies in the Occident.
18. From St. Augustine's *Confessions again.* The collocation of these two representatives of eastern and western asceticism, as the culmination of this part of the poem, is not an accident.

IV. Death by Water

Phlebas the Phoenician, a fortnight dead,
Forgot the cry of gulls, and the deep seas swell
And the profit and loss.
                        A current under sea
Picked his bones in whispers. As he rose and fell
He passed the stages of his age and youth
Entering the whirlpool.
                        Gentile or Jew
O you who turn the wheel and look to windward,
Consider Phlebas, who was once handsome and tall as you.

V. What the Thunder Said[1]

After the torchlight red on sweaty faces
After the frosty silence in the gardens
After the agony in stony places
The shouting and the crying
Prison and palace and reverberation
Of thunder of spring over distant mountains
He who was living is now dead
We who were living are now dying
With a little patience

    Here is no water but only rock
Rock and no water and the sandy road
The road winding above among the mountains
Which are mountains of rock without water
If there were water we should stop and drink
Amongst the rock one cannot stop or think
Sweat is dry and feet are in the sand
If there were only water amongst the rock
Dead mountain mouth of carious teeth that cannot spit
Here one can neither stand nor lie nor sit
There is not even silence in the mountains
But dry sterile thunder without rain
There is not even solitude in the mountains
But red sullen faces sneer and snarl
From doors of mudcracked houses
                            If there were water
   And no rock
   If there were rock

---

    1. In the first part of Part V three themes are employed: the journey to Emmaus, the approach to the Chapel Perilous (see Miss Weston's book), and the present decay of eastern Europe.

V. What the Thunder Said

And also water
And water
A spring
A pool among the rock
If there were the sound of water only
Not the cicada
And dry grass singing
But sound of water over a rock
Where the hermit-thrush sings in the pine trees
Drip drop drip drop drop drop drop[1]
But there is no water

Who is the third who walks always beside you?
When I count, there are only you and I together[2]
But when I look ahead up the white road
There is always another one walking beside you
Gliding wrapt in a brown mantle, hooded
I do not know whether a man or a woman
—But who is that on the other side of you?

What is that sound high in the air
Murmur of maternal lamentation[3]
Who are those hooded hordes swarming
Over endless plains, stumbling in cracked earth
Ringed by the flat horizon only
What is the city over the mountains

---

1. This is Turdus aonalaschkae pallasii, the hermit-thrush which I have heard in Quebec County. Chapman says (*Handbook of Birds in Eastern North America*) 'it is most at home in secluded woodland and thickety retreats.... Its notes are not remarkable for variety or volume, but in purity and sweetness of tone and exquisite modulation they are unequalled.' Its 'water-dripping song' is justly celebrated.

2. The following lines were stimulated by the account of one of the Antarctic expeditions (I forget which, but I think one of Shackleton's): it was related that the party of explorers, at the extremity of their strength, had the constant delusion that there was one more member than could actually be counted.

3. This line and the following nine lines, cf. Hermann Hesse, *Blick ins Chaos:*
'Schon ist halb Europa, schon ist zumindest der halbe Osten Europas auf dem Wege zum Chaos, fährt betrunken im heiligen Wahn am Abgrund entlang und singt dazu, singt betrunken und hymnisch wie Dmitri Karamasoff sang. Ueber diese Lieder lacht der Bürger beleidigt, der Heilige und Seher hört sie mit Tränen.'
['Already half of Europe, already at least half of Eastern Europe, on the way to Chaos, drives drunk in sacred infatuation along the edge of the precipice, sings drunkenly, as though hymn singing, as Dmitri Karamazov (in Dostoyevski's *Brothers Karamazov*) sang. The offended bourgeois laughs at the songs; the saint and the seer hear them with tears.']

V. What the Thunder Said

Cracks and reforms and bursts in the violet air
Falling towers
Jerusalem Athens Alexandria
Vienna London
Unreal

A woman drew her long black hair out tight
And fiddled whisper music on those strings
And bats with baby faces in the violet light
Whistled, and beat their wings
And crawled head downward down a blackened wall
And upside down in air were towers
Tolling reminiscent bells, that kept the hours
And voices singing out of empty cisterns and exhausted wells.

   In this decayed hole among the mountains
In the faint moonlight, the grass is singing
Over the tumbled graves, about the chapel
There is the empty chapel, only the wind's home.
It has no windows, and the door swings,
Dry bones can harm no one.
Only a cock stood on the rooftree
Co co rico co co rico
In a flash of lightning. Then a damp gust
Bringing rain

   Ganga was sunken, and the limp leaves
Waited for rain, while the black clouds
Gathered far distant, over Himavant.
The jungle crouched, humped in silence.
Then spoke the thunder
D A
Datta: what have we given?[4]
My friend, blood shaking my heart
The awful daring of a moment's surrender
Which an age of prudence can never retract

---

   4. 'Datta, dayadhvam, damyata' (Give, sympathize, control). The fable of the meaning of the Thunder is found in the Brihadaranyaka—Upanishad, 5, 1. A translation is found in Deussen's Sechzig *Upanishads des Veda*, p. 489.

V. What the Thunder Said

By this, and this only, we have existed
Which is not to be found in our obituaries
Or in memories draped by the beneficent spider[5]
Or under seals broken by the lean solicitor
In our empty rooms
DA
Dayadhvam: I have heard the key[6]
Turn in the door once and turn once only
We think of the key, each in his prison
Thinking of the key, each confirms a prison
Only at nightfall, aetherial rumours
Revive for a moment a broken Coriolanus
DA
Damyata: The boat responded
Gaily, to the hand expert with sail and oar
The sea was calm, your heart would have responded
Gaily, when invited, beating obedient
To controlling hands

                         I sat upon the shore
Fishing, with the arid plain behind me[7]
Shall I at least set my lands in order?
London Bridge is falling down falling down falling down
Poi s'ascose nel foco che gli affina[8]
Quando fiam uti chelidon[9] —O swallow swallow

---

    5. Cf. Webster, *The White Devil*, V, vi:
                . . . they'll remarry
Ere the worm pierce your winding-sheet, ere the spider
Make a thin curtain for your epitaphs.
    6. Cf. *Inferno*, xxxiii. 46:
ed io sentii chiavar l'uscio di sotto
all'orribile torre.
[And from below I heard them driving nails / into the dreadful tower's door.]
    Also F. H. Bradley, *Appearance and Reality*, p. 346:
"My external sensations are no less private to myself than are my thoughts or my feelings. In either case my experience falls within my own circle, a circle closed on the outside; and, with all its elements alike, every sphere is opaque to the others which surround it. . . ." In brief, regarded as an existence which appears in a soul, the whole world for each is peculiar and private to that soul.
    7. V. Weston, *From Ritual to Romance;* chapter on the Fisher King.
    8. ["He hid himself in the fire which refines them."] V. *Purgatorio*, xxvi. 148.
'Ara vos prec per aquella valor
'que vos guida al som de l'escalina,
'sovegna vos a temps de ma dolor.'
["Now I pray you, by that virtue / which guides you to the summit of the stairway, / be mindful in due time of my pain."]
    9. ["When shall I be as the swallow?"] V. *Pervigilium Veneris*. Cf. Philomela in Parts II and III.

V. What the Thunder Said

Le Prince d' Aquitaine à la tour abolie[10]
These fragments I have shored against my ruins
Why then Ile fit you. Hieronymo's mad againe.[11]
Datta. Dayadhvam. Damyata.
                Shantih   shantih   shantih[12]

---

10. ["The Prince of Aquitaine at the ruined tower."] V. Gerard de Nerval, *Sonnet El Desdichado*.
11. V. Kyd's *Spanish Tragedy*.
12. Shantih. Repeated as here, a formal ending to an Upanishad. 'The Peace which passeth understanding' is our equivalent to this word.

From Ritual to Romance

Publisher's Preface

Jessie Laidlay Weston (1850–1928) was an independent scholar who specialized in medieval Arthurian texts. In 1920, at the age of seventy, she published *From Ritual to Romance,* which examines the roots of the King Arthur legends, exploring the connections between early pagan elements and later Christian influences. Its revolutionary theory holds that the basic elements of the Grail story are remnants of ancient fertility rites designed to heal the "broken land."

Poet T. S. Eliot acknowledged the book as crucial to understanding his poem *The Waste Land,* noting, "Not only the title, but the plan and a good deal of the incidental symbolism of the poem were suggested by Miss Jessie L. Weston's book on the Grail legend: *From Ritual to Romance* (Cambridge). Indeed, so deeply am I indebted, Miss Weston's book will elucidate the difficulties of the poem much better than my notes can do; and I recommend it (apart from the great interest of the book itself) to any who think such elucidation of the poem worth the trouble."[1]

Drawing on *The Golden Bough,* Sir James George Frazer's seminal work on folklore, magic, and religion, Weston examines the mystical elements of the Quest—the Wasteland, the Fisher King, the Chapel Perilous, and the Grail itself—tying them to the symbols and rites of the ancient mystery religions. She writes, "The study and the criticism of the Grail literature will possess an even deeper interest, a more absorbing fascination, when it is definitely recognized that we possess in that literature a unique example of the restatement of an ancient and august Ritual in terms of imperishable Romance."

---

1. Although this edition of *From Ritual to Romance* does not preserve the pagination of the original, it does include the original page numbers in brackets for easy reference. (For example, [p17] designates the beginning of page 17.) It also includes Weston's exhaustive notes as footnotes rather than endnotes.

Publisher's Preface

Although her style is formal and academic, the information she presents is riveting—mandatory reading for anyone interested in exploring mythology, the Arthurian legend, and the roots of religion.

Preface

In the introductory Chapter the reader will find the aim and object of these studies set forth at length. In view of the importance and complexity of the problems involved it seemed better to incorporate such a statement in the book itself, rather than relegate it to a Preface which all might not trouble to read. Yet I feel that such a general statement does not adequately express my full debt of obligation.

Among the many whose labour has been laid under contribution in the following pages there are certain scholars whose published work, or personal advice, has been specially illuminating, and to whom specific acknowledgment is therefore due. Like many others I owe to Sir J. G. Frazer the initial inspiration which set me, as I may truly say, on the road to the Grail Castle. Without the guidance of *The Golden Bough* I should probably, as the late M. Gaston Paris happily expressed it, still be wandering in the forest of Broceliande!

During the Bayreuth Festival of 1911 I had frequent opportunities of meeting, and discussion with, Professor von Schroeder. I owe to him not only the introduction to his own work, which I found most helpful, but references which have been of the greatest assistance; *e.g.* my knowledge of Cumont's *Les Religions Orientales,* and Scheftelowitz's valuable study on *Fish Symbolism,* both of which have furnished important links in the chain of evidence, is due to Professor von Schroeder.

The perusal of Miss J. E. Harrison's *Themis* opened my eyes to the extended importance of these Vegetation rites. In view of the evidence there adduced I asked myself whether beliefs which had found expression not only in social institution, and popular custom, but, as set forth in Sir G. Murray's study on Greek Dramatic Origins, attached to the work, also in Drama and Literature, might not reasonably—even inevitably—be expected to have left their mark on Romance? The one seemed to me a necessary corollary of the other, and I felt that I had gained, as the result of Miss Harrison's work, a wider, and more assured basis for my own researches. I was no longer engaged merely in enquiring into the sources of a fascinating legend, but on the identification of another field of activity for forces whose potency as agents of evolution we were only now beginning rightly to appreciate.

Finally, a casual reference, in Anrich's work on the Mysteries, to the *Naassene Document,* caused me to apply to Mr G. R. S. Mead, of whose knowledge of the mysterious border-land between Christianity and Paganism, and willingness to place that knowledge at the disposal of others, I had, for some years past, had pleasant experience. Mr Mead referred me to his own translation and analysis of the text in question, and there, to my satisfaction, I found, not only the final link that completed the chain of evolution from Pagan Mystery to Christian Ceremonial, but also proof of that wider significance I was beginning to apprehend. The problem involved was not one of Folk-lore, not even one of Literature, but of Comparative Religion in its widest sense.

Thus, while I trust that my co-workers in the field of Arthurian research will accept these studies as a permanent contribution to the elucidation of the Grail problem, I would fain hope that those scholars who labour in a wider field, and to whose works I owe so much, may find in the results here set forth elements that may prove of real value in the study of the evolution of religious belief.

J. L. W.
Paris,
October, 1919.

"Animus ad amplitudinem Mysteriorum pro modulo suo dilatetur, non Mysteria ad angustias animi constringantur." (Bacon.)

"Many literary critics seem to think that an hypothesis about obscure and remote questions of history can be refuted by a simple demand for the production of more evidence than in fact exists.—But the true test of an hypothesis, if it cannot be shewn to conflict with known truths, is the number of facts that it correlates, and explains." (Cornford, Origins of Attic Comedy.*)*

I. Introductory

Nature of the Grail problem. Unsatisfactory character of results achieved. Objections to Christian Legendary origin; to Folk-lore origin. Elements in both theories sound. Solution to be sought in a direction which will do justice to both. Sir J. G. Frazer's Golden Bough *indicates possible line of research. Sir W. Ridgeway's criticism of* Vegetation *theory examined. Dramas and Dramatic Dances. The Living and not the Dead King the factor of importance. Impossibility of proving human origin for Vegetation Deities. Not Death but Resurrection the essential centre of Ritual.* Muharram *too late in date and lacks Resurrection feature. Relation between defunct heroes and special localities. Sanctity possibly antecedent to connection.* Mana *not necessarily a case of relics. Self-acting weapons frequent in Medieval Romance. Sir J. G. Frazer's theory holds good. Remarks on method and design of present Studies.*

In view of the extensive literature to which the Grail legend has already given birth it may seem that the addition of another volume to the already existing *corpus* calls for some words of apology and explanation. When the student of the subject contemplates the countless essays and brochures, the volumes of studies and criticism, which have been devoted to this fascinating subject, the conflicting character of their aims, their hopelessly contradictory results, he, or she, may well hesitate before adding another element to such a veritable witches' cauldron of apparently profitless study. And indeed, were I not convinced that the theory advocated in the following pages contains in itself the element that will resolve these conflicting ingredients into one harmonious compound I should hardly feel justified in offering a further contribution to the subject.

But it is precisely because upwards of thirty years' steady and persevering study of the Grail texts has brought me gradually and inevitably to certain very definite conclusions, has placed me in possession of evidence hitherto ignored, or unsuspected, that I venture to offer the result in these studies, trusting that they may be accepted as, what I believe them to be, a genuine *Elucidation* of the Grail problem.

I. Introductory

My fellow-workers in this field know all too well the essential elements of that problem; I do not need here to go over already well-trodden ground; it will be sufficient to point out certain salient features of the position.

[p2] The main difficulty of our research lies in the fact that the Grail legend consists of a congeries of widely differing elements—elements which at first sight appear hopelessly incongruous, if not completely contradictory, yet at the same time are present to an extent, and in a form, which no honest critic can afford to ignore.

Thus it has been perfectly possible for one group of scholars, relying upon the undeniably Christian-Legendary elements, preponderant in certain versions, to maintain the thesis that the Grail legend is a*b initio* a Christian, and ecclesiastical, legend, and to analyse the literature on that basis alone.

Another group, with equal reason, have pointed to the strongly marked Folk-lore features preserved in the tale, to its kinship with other themes, mainly of Celtic *provenance,* and have argued that, while the later versions of the cycle have been worked over by ecclesiastical writers in the interests of edification, the story itself is non-Christian, and Folk-lore in origin.

Both groups have a basis of truth for their arguments: the features upon which they rely are, in each case, undeniably present, yet at the same time each line of argument is faced with certain insuperable difficulties, fatal to the claims advanced.

Thus, the theory of Christian origin breaks down when faced with the awkward fact that there is no Christian legend concerning Joseph of Arimathea and the Grail. Neither in Legendary, nor in Art, is there any trace of the story; it has no existence outside the Grail literature, it is the creation of romance, and no genuine tradition.

On this very ground it was severely criticized by the Dutch writer Jacob van Maerlant, in 1260. In his *Merlin* he denounces the whole Grail history as lies, asserting that the Church knows nothing of it—which is true.

[p3] In the same way the advocate of a Folk-lore origin is met with the objection that the section of the cycle for which such a source can be definitely proved, *i.e.*, the *Perceval* story, has originally nothing whatever to do with the Grail; and that, while parallels can be found for this or that feature of the legend, such parallels are isolated in character and involve the breaking up of the tale into a composite of mutually

I. Introductory

independent themes. A prototype, containing the main features of the Grail story—the Waste Land, the Fisher King, the Hidden Castle with its solemn Feast, and mysterious Feeding Vessel, the Bleeding Lance and Cup—does not, so far as we know, exist. None of the great collections of Folk-tales, due to the industry of a Cosquin, a Hartland, or a Campbell, has preserved specimens of such a type; it is not such a story as, *e.g.*, *The Three Days Tournament*, examples of which are found all over the world. Yet neither the advocate of a Christian origin, nor the Folk-lorist, can afford to ignore the arguments, and evidence of the opposing school, and while the result of half a century of patient investigation has been to show that the origin of the Grail story must be sought elsewhere than in ecclesiastical legend, or popular tale, I hold that the result has equally been to demonstrate that neither of these solutions should be ignored, but that the ultimate source must be sought for in a direction which shall do justice to what is sound in the claims of both.

Some years ago, when fresh from the study of Sir J. G. Frazer's epoch-making work, *The Golden Bough,* I was struck by the resemblance existing between certain features of the Grail story, and characteristic details of the Nature Cults described. The more closely I analysed the tale, the more striking became the resemblance, and I finally asked myself whether it were not possible that in this mysterious legend—mysterious alike in its character, its sudden appearance, the importance apparently assigned to it, followed by as [p4] sudden and complete a disappearance—we might not have the confused record of a ritual, once popular, later surviving under conditions of strict secrecy? This would fully account for the atmosphere of awe and reverence which even under distinctly non-Christian conditions never fails to surround the Grail, It may act simply as a feeding vessel, It is none the less *toute sainte cose;* and also for the presence in the tale of distinctly popular, and Folk-lore, elements. Such an interpretation would also explain features irreconcilable with orthodox Christianity, which had caused some scholars to postulate a heterodox origin for the legend, and thus explain its curiously complete disappearance as a literary theme. In the first volume of my *Perceval* studies, published in 1906, I hinted at this possible solution of the problem, a solution worked out more fully in a paper read before the Folk-lore Society in December of the same year, and published in Volume XVIII. of the Journal of the Society. By the time my second volume of studies was ready for publication in 1909, further evidence had come into my hands; I was then certain that I was upon the right

I. Introductory

path, and I felt justified in laying before the public the outlines of a theory of evolution, alike of the legend, and of the literature, to the main principles of which I adhere to-day.

But certain links were missing in the chain of evidence, and the work was not complete. No inconsiderable part of the information at my disposal depended upon personal testimony, the testimony of those who knew of the continued existence of such a ritual, and had actually been initiated into its mysteries—and for such evidence the student of the letter has little respect. He worships the written word; for the oral, living, tradition from which the word derives force and vitality he has little use. Therefore the written word had to be found. It has taken me some [p5] nine or ten years longer to complete the evidence, but the chain is at last linked up, and we can now prove by printed texts the parallels existing between each and every feature of the Grail story and the recorded symbolism of the Mystery cults. Further, we can show that between these Mystery cults and Christianity there existed at one time a close and intimate union, such a union as of itself involved the practical assimilation of the central rite, in each case a 'Eucharistic' Feast, in which the worshippers partook of the Food of Life from the sacred vessels.

In face of the proofs which will be found in these pages I do not think any fair-minded critic will be inclined to dispute any longer the origin of the 'Holy' Grail; after all it is as august and ancient an origin as the most tenacious upholder of Its Christian character could desire.

But I should wish it clearly to be understood that the aim of these studies is, as indicated in the title, to determine the *origin* of the Grail, not to discuss the *provenance* and interrelation of the different versions. I do not believe this latter task can be satisfactorily achieved unless and until we are of one accord as to the character of the subject matter. When we have made up our minds as to what the Grail really was, and what it stood for, we shall be able to analyse the romances; to decide which of them contains more, which less, of the original matter, and to group them accordingly. On this point I believe that the table of descent, printed in Volume II. of my *Perceval* studies is in the main correct, but there is still much analytical work to be done, in particular the establishment of the original form of the *Perlesvaus* is highly desirable. But apart from the primary object of these studies, and the results therein obtained, I would draw attention to the manner in which the evidence set forth in the chapters on the Mystery cults, and especially

I. Introductory

that on *The Naassene Document,* a text of extraordinary [p6] value from more than one point of view, supports and complements the researches of Sir J. G. Frazer. I am, of course, familiar with the attacks directed against the 'Vegetation' theory, the sarcasms of which it has been the object, and the criticisms of what is held in some quarters to be the exaggerated importance attached to these Nature cults. But in view of the use made of these cults as the medium of imparting high spiritual teaching, a use which, in face of the document above referred to, can no longer be ignored or evaded, are we not rather justified in asking if the true importance of the rites has as yet been recognized? Can we possibly exaggerate their value as a factor in the evolution of religious consciousness?

Such a development of his researches naturally lay outside the range of Sir J. G. Frazer's work, but posterity will probably decide that, like many another patient and honest worker, he 'built better than he knew.'

I have carefully read Sir W. Ridgeway's attack on the school in his *Dramas and Dramatic Dances,* and while the above remarks explain my position with regard to the question as a whole, I would here take the opportunity of stating specifically my grounds for dissenting from certain of the conclusions at which the learned author arrives. I do not wish it to be said: "This is all very well, but Miss Weston ignores the arguments on the other side." I do not ignore, but I do not admit their validity. It is perfectly obvious that Sir W. Ridgeway's theory, reduced to abstract terms, would result in the conclusion that all religion is based upon the cult of the Dead, and that men originally knew no gods but their grandfathers, a theory from which as a student of religion I absolutely and entirely dissent. I can understand that such Dead Ancestors can be looked upon as Protectors, or as Benefactors, but I see no ground for supposing that they have ever been [p7] regarded as Creators, yet it is precisely as vehicle for the most lofty teaching as to the Cosmic relations existing between God and Man, that these Vegetation cults were employed. The more closely one studies pre-Christian Theology, the more strongly one is impressed with the deeply, and daringly, spiritual character of its speculations, and the more doubtful it appears that such teaching can depend upon the unaided processes of human thought, or can have been evolved from such germs as we find among the supposedly 'primitive' peoples, such as *e.g.* the Australian tribes. Are they really primitive? Or are we dealing, not with the primary elements of religion, but with the *disjecta membra* of a vanished civilization? Certain it is that so far as historical evidence goes our earliest records point to the recognition of a spiritual, not of a material, origin of the human race; the Sumerian and Babylonian Psalms were not composed by men who believed themselves the descendants of 'witchetty grubs.' The Folk practices and ceremonies studied in these pages, the Dances, the rough Dramas, the local and seasonal celebrations, do not represent the material out of which the Attis-Adonis cult was formed, but surviving fragments of a worship from which the higher significance has vanished.

Sir W. Ridgeway is confident that Osiris, Attis, Adonis, were all at one time human beings, whose tragic fate gripped hold of popular imagination, and led to their ultimate deification. The first-named cult stands on a somewhat different basis from the others, the beneficent activities of Osiris being more widely diffused, more universal in their operation. I should be inclined to regard the Egyptian deity primarily as a Culture Hero, rather than a Vegetation God.

With regard to Attis and Adonis, whatever their original character (and it seems to me highly improbable that there should have been two youths each beloved by a goddess, each [p8] victim of a similar untimely fate), long before we have any trace of them both have become so intimately identified with the processes of Nature that they have ceased to be men and become gods, and as such alone can we deal with them. It is also permissible to point out that in the case of Tammuz, Esmun, and Adonis, the title is not a proper name, but a vague appellative, denoting an abstract rather than a concrete origin. Proof of this will be found later. Sir W. Ridgeway overlooks the fact that it is not the tragic death of Attis-Adonis which is of importance for these cults, but their subsequent restoration to life, a feature which cannot be postulated of any ordinary mortal.

And how are we to regard Tammuz, the prototype of all these deities? Is there any possible ground for maintaining that he was ever a man? Prove it we cannot, as the records of his cult go back thousands of years before our era. Here, again, we have the same dominant feature; it is not merely the untimely death which is lamented, but the restoration to life which is celebrated.

Throughout the whole study the author fails to discriminate between the activities of the living, and the dead, king. The Dead king may, as I have said above, be regarded as the Benefactor, as the Protector, of his

I. Introductory

people, but it is the Living king upon whom their actual and continued prosperity depends. The detail that the ruling sovereign is sometimes regarded as the re-incarnation of the original founder of the race strengthens this point—the king never dies—*Le Roi est mort, Vive le Roi* is very emphatically the motto of this Faith. It is the insistence on Life, Life continuous, and ever-renewing, which is the abiding characteristic of these cults, a characteristic which differentiates them utterly and entirely from the ancestral worship with which Sir W. Ridgeway would fain connect them.

Nor are the arguments based upon the memorial rites of [p9] definitely historical heroes, of comparatively late date, such as Hussein and Hossein, of any value here. It is precisely the death, and not the resurrection, of the martyr which is of the essence of the Muharram. No one contends that Hussein rose from the dead, but it is precisely this point which is of primary importance in the Nature cults; and Sir W. Ridgeway must surely be aware that Folk-lorists find in this very Muharram distinct traces of borrowing from the earlier Vegetation rites.

The author triumphantly asserts that the fact that certain Burmese heroes and heroines are after death reverenced as tree spirits 'sets at rest for ever' the belief in abstract deities. But how can he be sure that the process was not the reverse of that which he postulates, *i.e.*, that certain natural objects, trees, rivers, etc., were not regarded as sacred *before* the Nats became connected with them? That the deified human beings were not after death assigned to places already held in reverence? Such a possibility is obvious to any Folk-lore student, and local traditions should in each case be carefully examined before the contrary is definitely asserted.

So far as the origins of Drama are concerned the Ode quoted later from the Naassene Document is absolute and definite proof of the close connection existing between the Attis Mystery ritual, and dramatic performances, *i.e.*, Attis regarded in his deified, Creative, 'Logos,' aspect, not Attis, the dead youth.

Nor do I think that the idea of 'Mana' can be lightly dismissed as 'an ordinary case of relics.' The influence may well be something entirely apart from the continued existence of the ancestor, an independent force, assisting him in life, and transferring itself after death to his successor. A 'Magic' Sword or Staff is not necessarily a relic; Medieval romance supplies numerous instances of self-acting weapons whose virtue in no wise depends upon their previous owner, as *e.g.* the Sword in *Le*

Chevalier à l'Épée, [p10] or the Flaming Lance of the *Chevalier de la Charrette*. Doubtless the cult of Ancestors plays a large *rôle* in the beliefs of certain peoples, but it is not a sufficiently solid foundation to bear the weight of the super-structure Sir W. Ridgeway would fain rear upon it, while it differs too radically from the cults he attacks to be used as an argument against them; the one is based upon Death, the other on Life.

Wherefore, in spite of all the learning and ingenuity brought to bear against it, I avow myself an impenitent believer in Sir J. G. Frazer's main theory, and as I have said above, I hold that theory to be of greater and more far-reaching importance than has been hitherto suspected.

I would add a few words as to the form of these studies—they may be found disconnected. They have been written at intervals of time extending over several years, and my aim has been to prove the essentially archaic character of *all* the elements composing the Grail story rather than to analyse the story as a connected whole. With this aim in view I have devoted chapters to features which have now either dropped out of the existing versions, or only survive in a subordinate form, *e.g.* the chapters on *The Medicine Man,* and *The Freeing of the Waters*. The studies will, I hope, and believe, be accepted as offering a definite contribution towards establishing the fundamental character of our material; as stated above, when we are all at one as to what the Holy Grail really was, and is, we can then proceed with some hope of success to criticize the manner in which different writers have handled the inspiring theme, but such success seems to be hopeless so long as we all start from different, and often utterly irreconcilable, standpoints and proceed along widely diverging roads. One or another may, indeed, arrive at the goal, but such unanimity of opinion as will lend to our criticism authoritative weight is, on such lines, impossible of achievement. [p11]

II. The Task of the Hero

Essential to determine the original nature of the task imposed upon the hero. Versions examined. The GAWAIN forms—Bleheris, Diû Crône. *PERCEVAL versions*—Gerbert, prose Perceval, Chrétien de Troyes, Perlesvaus, Manessier, Peredur, Parzival. GALAHAD—Queste. *Result, primary task healing of Fisher King and removal of curse of Waste Land. The two inter-dependent. Illness of King entails misfortune on Land. Enquiry into nature of King's disability.* Sone de Nansai. *For elucidation of problem necessary to bear in mind close connection between Land and Ruler. Importance of Waste Land motif for criticism.*

As a first step towards the successful prosecution of an investigation into the true nature and character of the mysterious object we know as the Grail it will be well to ask ourselves whether any light may be thrown upon the subject by examining more closely the details of the Quest in its varying forms; *i.e.*, what was the precise character of the task undertaken by, or imposed upon, the Grail hero, whether that hero were Gawain, Perceval, or Galahad, and what the results to be expected from a successful achievement of the task. We shall find at once a uniformity which assures us of the essential identity of the tradition underlying the varying forms, and a diversity indicating that the tradition has undergone a gradual, but radical, modification in the process of literary evolution. Taken in their relative order the versions give the following result.

GAWAIN (*Bleheris*). Here the hero sets out on his journey with no clear idea of the task before him. He is taking the place of a knight mysteriously slain in his company, but whither he rides, and why, he does not know, only that the business is important and pressing. From the records of his partial success we gather that he ought to have enquired concerning the nature of the Grail, and that this enquiry would have resulted in the restoration to fruitfulness of a Waste Land, the desolation of which is, in some manner, not clearly explained, connected with the death of a knight whose name and identity are never disclosed. [p12]

"Great is the loss that ye lie thus, 'tis even the destruction of kingdoms, God grant that ye be avenged, so that the folk be once more joyful and the land repeopled which by ye and this sword are wasted and made void."[1] The fact that Gawain does ask concerning the Lance assures the partial restoration of the land; I would draw attention to the special terms in which this is described: "for so soon as Sir Gawain asked of the Lance . . . the waters flowed again thro' their channel, and all the woods were turned to verdure."[2]

Diû Crône. Here the question is more general in character; it affects the marvels beheld, not the Grail alone; but now the Quester is prepared, and knows what is expected of him. The result is to break the spell which retains the Grail King in a semblance of life, and we learn, by implication, that the land is restored to fruitfulness: "yet had the land been waste, but by his coming had folk and land alike been delivered."[3] Thus in the earliest preserved, the GAWAIN form, the effect upon the land appears to be the primary result of the Quest.

PERCEVAL. The *Perceval* versions, which form the bulk of the existing Grail texts, differ considerably the one from the other, alike in the task to be achieved, and the effects resulting from the hero's success, or failure. The distinctive feature of the Perceval version is the insistence upon the sickness, and disability of the ruler of the land, the Fisher King. Regarded first as the direct cause of the wasting of the land, it gradually assumes overwhelming importance, the task of the Quester becomes that of healing the King, the restoration of the land not only falls into the background but the operating cause of its desolation is changed, and [p13] finally it disappears from the story altogether. One version, alone, the source of which is, at present, undetermined, links the PERCEVAL with the GAWAIN form; this is the version preserved in the Gerbert continuation of the *Perceval* of Chrétien de Troyes. Here the hero having, like Gawain, partially achieved the task, but again like Gawain, having failed satisfactorily to resolder the broken sword, wakes, like the earlier hero, to find that the Grail Castle has disappeared, and he is alone in a flowery meadow. He pursues his way through a land fertile, and well-peopled and marvels much, for the day before it had been a waste desert. Coming to a castle he is received by a solemn procession, with great rejoicing; through him the folk have regained the land and goods

---

1. MS. Bibl. Nat., f. Franç. 12576, fo. 90.
2. *Ibid.* fo. 90vo, 91.
3. *Diû Crône* (ed. Stoll, Stuttgart, 1852). Cf. *Sir Gawain of the Grail Castle* for both versions.

II. The Task of the Hero

which they had lost. The mistress of the castle is more explicit. Perceval had asked concerning the Grail:

"par coi amendé
Somes, en si faite maniére
Qu'en ceste regne n'avoit riviére
Qui ne fust gaste, ne fontaine.
E la terre gaste et soutaine."

Like Gawain he has 'freed the waters' and thus restored the land.[4]

In the prose *Perceval* the *motif* of the Waste Land has disappeared, the task of the hero consists in asking concerning the Grail, and by so doing, to restore the Fisher King, who is suffering from extreme old age, to health, and youth.[5]

"Se tu eusses demandé quel'en on faisoit, que li rois ton aiol fust gariz de l'enfermetez qu'il a, et fust revenu en sa juventé."

When the question has been asked: "Le rois péschéor estoit gariz et tot muez de sa nature." "Li rois peschiére estoit mués de se nature et estoit garis de se maladie, et [p14] estoit sains comme pissons."[6] Here we have the introduction of a new element, the restoration to youth of the sick King.

In the *Perceval* of Chrétien de Troyes we find ourselves in presence of certain definite changes, neither slight, nor unimportant, upon which it seems to me insufficient stress has hitherto been laid. The question is changed; the hero no longer asks what the Grail is, but (as in the prose *Perceval*) whom it serves? a departure from an essential and primitive simplicity—the motive for which is apparent in Chrétien, but not in the prose form, where there is no enigmatic personality to be served apart. A far more important change is that, while the malady of the Fisher King is antecedent to the hero's visit, and capable of cure if the question be asked, the failure to fulfil the prescribed conditions of itself entails disaster upon the land. Thus the sickness of the King, and the desolation of the land, are not necessarily connected as cause and effect, but, a point which seems hitherto unaccountably to have been overlooked, the latter is directly attributable to the Quester himself.[7]

---

4. Cf. MS. B.N. 12576, fo. 154.
5. *Perceval,* ed. Hucher, p. 466; Modena, p. 61.
6. Cf. Hucher, p. 482; Modena, p. 82.
7. *Percevel li Gallois*, ed. Potvin, ll. 6048-52.

II. The Task of the Hero

"Car se tu demandé l'eusses
Li rice roi qui moult s'esmaie
Fust or tost garis de sa plaie
Et si tenist sa tière en pais
Dont il n'en tenra point jamais,"

but by Perceval's failure to ask the question he has entailed dire misfortune upon the land:

"Dames en perdront lor maris,
Tiéres en seront essiliés,
Et pucielles desconselliés
Orfenes, veves, en remanront
Et maint chevalier en morront."[8]

[p15] This idea, that the misfortunes of the land are not antecedent to, but dependent upon, the hero's abortive visit to the Grail Castle, is carried still further by the compiler of the *Perlesvaus,* where the failure of the predestined hero to ask concerning the office of the Grail is alone responsible for the illness of the King and the misfortunes of the country. "Une grans dolors est avenue an terre novelement par un jeune chevalier qui fu herbergiez an l'ostel au riche roi Peschéor, si aparut à lui li saintimes Graaus, et la lance de quoi li fiers seigne par la poignte; ne demanda de quoi ce servoit, ou dont ce venoit, et por ce qu'il ne demanda sont toutes les terres comméues an guerre, ne chevalier n'ancontre autre au forest qu'il ne li core sus, et ocie s'il peut."[9]

"Li Roi Pecheors de qui est grant dolors, quar il est cheüz en une douleureuse langour—ceste langour li est venue par celui qui se heberga an son ostel, à qui li seintimes Graaus s'aparut, por ce que cil ne vost demander de qu'il an servoit, toutes les terres an furent comméues en gerre."[10]

"Je suis cheüz an langour dès cele oure que li chevaliers se herberga çoianz dont vous avez oï parler; par un soule parole que il déloia a dire me vint ceste langour."[11]

---

8. *Ib.* ll. 6056–60.
9. Potvin, Vol. I. p. 15.
10. *Ib.* p. 26.
11. *Ib.* p. 86.

From this cause the Fisher King dies before the hero has achieved the task, and can take his place. "Li bons Rois Peschiéres est morz."[12] There is here no cure of the King or restoration of the land, the specific task of the Grail hero is never accomplished, he comes into his kingdom as the result of a number of knightly adventures, neither more nor less significant than those found in non-Grail romances.

The *Perlesvaus,* in its present form, appears to be a later, and more fully developed, treatment of the *motif* noted in Chrétien, *i.e.,* that the misfortunes of King and country are [p16] directly due to the Quester himself, and had no antecedent existence; this, I would submit, alters the whole character of the story, and we are at a loss to know what, had the hero put the question on the occasion of his first visit, could possibly have been the result achieved. It would not have been the cure of the King: he was, apparently, in perfect health; it would not have been the restoration to verdure of the Land: the Land was not Waste; where, as in the case of Gawain, there is a Dead Knight, whose death is to be avenged, *something* might have been achieved, in the case of the overwhelming majority of the *Perceval* versions, which do not contain this feature, the dependence of the Curse upon the Quester reduces the story to incoherence. In one *Perceval* version alone do we find a *motif* analogous to the earlier *Gawain Bleheris* form. In Manessier the hero's task is not restricted to the simple asking of a question, but he must also slay the enemy whose treachery has caused the death of the Fisher King's brother; thereby healing the wound of the King himself, and removing the woes of the land. What these may be we are not told, but, apparently, the country is not 'Waste.'[13]

In *Peredur* we have a version closely agreeing with that of Chrétien; the hero fails to enquire the meaning of what he sees in the Castle of Wonders, and is told in consequence: "Hadst thou done so the King would have been restored to health, and his dominions to peace, whereas from henceforth he will have to endure battles and conflicts, and his knights will perish, and wives will be widowed, and maidens will be left portionless, and all this because of thee."[14] This certainly seems to imply that, while the illness of the Fisher King may be antecedent to, and independent of, the visit and failure of the hero, the misfortunes which fall on the land have been directly caused thereby.

---

12. *Ib.* pp. 176, 178.
13. MS. B.N. 12576, ff. 221–222vo.
14. *Mabinogion,* ed. Nutt, p. 282.

II. The Task of the Hero

[p17] The conclusion which states that the Bleeding Head seen by the hero "was thy cousin's, and he was killed by the Sorceresses of Gloucester, who also lamed thine uncle—and there is a prediction that thou art to avenge these things—" would seem to indicate the presence in the original of a 'Vengeance' theme, such as that referred to above.[15]

In *Parzival* the stress is laid entirely on the sufferings of the King; the question has been modified in the interests of this theme, and here assumes the form "What aileth thee, mine uncle?" The blame bestowed upon the hero is solely on account of the prolonged sorrow his silence has inflicted on King and people; of a Land laid Waste, either through drought, or war, there is no mention.

"Iuch solt' iur wirt erbarmet hân,
An dem Got wunder hât getân,
Und het gevrâget sîner nôt,
Ir lebet, und sît an saelden tôt."[16]

"Dô der trûrege vischaere
Saz âne fröude und âne trôst
War umb' iren niht siufzens hât erlôst."[17]

The punishment falls on the hero who has failed to put the question, rather than on the land, which, indeed, appears to be in no way affected, either by the wound of the King, or the silence of the hero. The divergence from Chrétien's version is here very marked, and, so far, seems to have been neglected by critics. The point is also of importance in view of the curious parallels which are otherwise to be found between this version and *Perlesvaus;* here the two are in marked contradiction with one another.

[p18] The question finally asked, the result is, as indicated in the prose version, the restoration of the King not merely to health, but also to youth—

"Swaz der Frânzoys heizet flô'rî'
Der glast kom sinem velle bî,
Parzival's schoen' was nu ein wint;

---

15. Cf. *Peredur* (ed. Nutt), pp. 282, 291-92.
16. *Parzival*, Book v. ll. 947-50.
17. *Ib.* Book VI. ll. 1078-80.

II. The Task of the Hero

> Und Absalôn Dâvîdes kint,
> Von Askalûn Vergulaht
> Und al den schoene was geslaht,
> Und des man Gahmurete jach
> Dô man'n in zogen sach
> Ze Kanvoleis sô wünneclîch,
> Ir dechéines schoen' was der gelîch,
> Die Anfortas ûz siecheit truoc.
> Got noch künste kan genuoc."[18]

GALAHAD. In the final form assumed by the story, that preserved in the *Queste*, the achievement of the task is not preceded by any failure on the part of the hero, and the advantages derived therefrom are personal and spiritual, though we are incidentally told that he heals the Fisher King's father, and also the old King, Mordrains, whose life has been preternaturally prolonged. In the case of this latter it is to be noted that the mere fact of Galahad's being the predestined winner suffices, and the healing takes place *before* the Quest is definitely achieved.

There is no Waste Land, and the wounding of the two Kings is entirely unconnected with Galahad. We find hints, in the story of Lambar, of a knowledge of the earlier form, but for all practical purposes it has disappeared from the story.[19]

[p19] Analysing the above statements we find that the results may be grouped under certain definite headings:

(*a*) There is a general consensus of evidence to the effect that the main object of the Quest is the restoration to health and vigour of a King suffering from infirmity caused by wounds, sickness, or old age;

(*b*) and whose infirmity, for some mysterious and unexplained reason, reacts disastrously upon his kingdom, either depriving it of vegetation, or exposing it to the ravages of war.

(*c*) In two cases it is definitely stated that the King will be restored to youthful vigour and beauty.

(*d*) In both cases where we find Gawain as the hero of the story, and in one connected with Perceval, the misfortune which has fallen upon the country is that of a prolonged drought, which has destroyed vegetation, and left the land Waste; the effect of the hero's question is to

---

18. Parzival, Book XVI, ll. 275–86.
19. Cf. *Morte Arthure*, Malory, Book XVII. Chap. 18. Note the remark of Mordrains that his flesh which has waxen old shall become young again.

II. The Task of the Hero

restore the waters to their channel, and render the land once more fertile.

(e) In three cases the misfortunes and wasting of the land are the result of war, and directly caused by the hero's failure to ask the question; we are not dealing with an antecedent condition. This, in my opinion, constitutes a marked difference between the two groups, which has not hitherto received the attention it deserves. One aim of our present investigation will be to determine which of these two forms should be considered the elder.

But this much seems certain, the aim of the Grail Quest is two-fold; it is to benefit (a) the King, (b) the land. The first of these two is the more important, as it is the infirmity of the King which entails misfortune on his land, the condition of the one reacts, for good or ill, upon the other; how, or why, we are left to discover for ourselves.

Before proceeding further in our investigation [p20] it may be well to determine the precise nature of the King's illness, and see whether any light upon the problem can be thus obtained.

In both the *Gawain* forms the person upon whom the fertility of the land depends is dead, though, in the version of *Diû Crône* he is, to all appearance, still in life. It should be noted that in the *Bleheris* form the king of the castle, who is not referred to as the Fisher King, is himself hale and sound; the wasting of the land was brought about by the blow which slew the knight whose body Gawain sees on the bier.

In both the *Perlesvaus,* and the prose *Perceval* the King has simply 'fallen into languishment,' in the first instance, as noted above, on account of the failure of the Quester, in the second as the result of extreme old age.

In Chrétien, Manessier, *Peredur,* and the *Parzival,* the King is suffering from a wound the nature of which, euphemistically disguised in the French texts, is quite clearly explained in the German.[20]

But the whole position is made absolutely clear by a passage preserved in *Sone de Nansai* and obviously taken over from an earlier poem. This romance contains a lengthy section dealing with the history of Joseph 'd'Abarimathie,' who is represented as the patron Saint of the kingdom of Norway; his bones, with the sacred relics of which he had the charge, the Grail and the Lance, are preserved in a monastery on an island in the interior of that country. In this version Joseph himself is

---

20. *Parzival*, Bk. IX. ll. 1388–92.

the Fisher King; ensnared by the beauty of the daughter of the Pagan King of Norway, whom he has slain, he baptizes her, though she is still an unbeliever at heart, and makes her his wife, thus drawing the wrath of Heaven upon himself. God punishes him for his sin:

"Es rains et desous l'afola
De coi grant dolor endura."[21]

[p21] Then, in a remarkable passage, we are told of the direful result entailed by this punishment upon his land:

"Sa tierre ert a ce jour nommée
Lorgres, ch'est verités prouvée,
Lorgres est uns nons de dolour
Nommés en larmes et en plours,
Bien doit iestre en dolour nommés
Car on n'i seme pois ne blés
Ne enfes d'omme n'i nasqui
Ne puchielle n'i ot mari,
Ne arbres fueille n'i porta
Ne nus prés n'i raverdïa,
Ne nus oysiaus n'i ot naon
Ne se n'i ot beste faon,
Tant que li rois fu mehaigniés
Et qu'il fu fors de ses pechiés,
Car Jesu-Crist fourment pesa
Qu'à la mescréant habita."[22]

Now there can be no possible doubt here, the condition of the King is sympathetically reflected on the land, the loss of virility in the one brings about a suspension of the reproductive processes of Nature on the other. The same effect would naturally be the result of the death of the sovereign upon whose vitality these processes depended.

To sum up the result of the analysis, I hold that we have solid grounds for the belief that the story postulates a close connection between the vitality of a certain King, and the prosperity of his kingdom; the forces

---

21. *Sone de Nansai* (ed. Goldschmidt, Stuttgart, 1899), ll. 4775-76.
22. *Sone de Nansai*, ll. 4841-56.

of the ruler being weakened or destroyed, by wound, sickness, old age, or death, the land becomes Waste, and the task of the hero is that of restoration.[23]

[p22] It seems to me, then, that, if we desire to elucidate the perplexing mystery of the Grail romances, and to place the criticism of this important and singularly fascinating body of literature upon an assured basis, we shall do so most effectually by pursuing a line of investigation which will concentrate upon the persistent elements of the story, the character and significance of the achievement proposed, rather than upon the varying details, such as Grail and Lance, however important may be their *rôle*. If we can ascertain, accurately, and unmistakably, the meaning of the whole, we shall, I think, find less difficulty in determining the character and office of the parts, in fact, the question *solvitur ambulando*, the 'complex' of the problem being solved, the constituent elements will reveal their significance.

As a first step I propose to ask whether this 'Quest of the Grail' represents an isolated, and unique achievement, or whether the task allotted to the hero, Gawain, Perceval, or Galahad, is one that has been undertaken, and carried out by heroes of other ages, and other lands. In the process of our investigation we must retrace our steps and turn back to the early traditions of our Aryan forefathers, and see whether we cannot, even in that remote antiquity, lay our hand upon a clue, which, like the fabled thread of Ariadne, shall serve as guide through the mazes of a varying, yet curiously persistent, tradition. [p23]

---

23. It is evidently such a version as that of *Sone de Nansai*, and *Parzival*, which underlies the curious statement of the *Merlin* MS. B.N. f. Fr. 337, where the wife of the Fisher King is known as 'la Veve Dame,' while her husband is yet in life, though sorely wounded.

III. The Freeing of the Waters

Enquiry may commence with early Aryan tradition. The Rig-Veda. *Extreme importance assigned to Indra's feat of "Freeing the Waters." This also specific achievement of Grail heroes. Extracts from* Rig-Veda. *Dramatic poems and monologues. Professor von Schroeder's theory.* Mysterium und Mimus. Rishyaçriñga *drama. Parallels with* Perceval *story. Result, the specific task of the Grail hero not a literary invention but an inheritance of Aryan tradition.*

'To begin at the beginning,' was the old story-telling formula, and it was a very sound one, if 'the beginning' could only be definitely ascertained! As our nearest possible approach to it I would draw attention to certain curious parallels in the earliest literary monuments of our race. I would at the same time beg those scholars who may think it 'a far cry' from the romances of the twelfth century of our era to some 1000 years B.C. to suspend their judgment till they have fairly examined the evidence for a tradition common to the Aryan race in general, and persisting with extraordinary vitality, and a marked correspondence of characteristic detail, through all migrations and modifications of that race, down to the present day.

Turning back to the earliest existing literary evidence, the *Rig-Veda*, we become aware that, in this vast collection of over 1000 poems (it is commonly known as *The Thousand and One Hymns* but the poems contained in it are more than that in number) are certain parallels with our Grail stories which, if taken by themselves, are perhaps interesting and suggestive rather than in any way conclusive, yet which, when they are considered in relation to the entire body of evidence, assume a curious significance and importance. We must first note that a very considerable number of the *Rig-Veda* hymns depend for their initial inspiration on the actual bodily needs and requirements of a mainly agricultural population, *i.e.,* of a people that [p24] depend upon the fruits of the earth for their subsistence, and to whom the regular and ordered sequence of the processes of Nature was a vital necessity.

III. The Freeing of the Waters

Their hymns and prayers, and, as we have strong reason to suppose, their dramatic ritual, were devised for the main purpose of obtaining from the gods of their worship that which was essential to ensure their well-being and the fertility of their land—warmth, sunshine, above all, sufficient water. That this last should, in an Eastern land, under a tropical sun, become a point of supreme importance, is easily to be understood. There is consequently small cause for surprise when we find, throughout the collection, the god who bestows upon them this much desired boon to be the one to whom by far the greater proportion of the hymns are addressed. It is not necessary here to enter into a discussion as to the original conception of Indra, and the place occupied by him in the early Aryan Pantheon, whether he was originally regarded as a god of war, or a god of weather; what is important for our purpose is the fact that it is Indra to whom a disproportionate number of the hymns of the *Rig-Veda* are addressed, that it is from him the much desired boon of rain and abundant water is besought, and that the feat which above all others redounded to his praise, and is ceaselessly glorified both by the god himself, and his grateful worshippers, is precisely the feat by which the Grail heroes, Gawain and Perceval, rejoiced the hearts of a suffering folk, *i.e.*, the restoration of the rivers to their channels, the 'Freeing of the Waters.' Tradition relates that the seven great rivers of India had been imprisoned by the evil giant, Vritra, or Ahi, whom Indra slew, thereby releasing the streams from their captivity.

The *Rig-Veda* hymns abound in references to this feat; it will only be necessary to cite a few from among the numerous passages I have noted.

[p25] 'Thou hast set loose the seven rivers to flow.'
'Thou causest water to flow on every side.'
'Indra set free the waters.'
'Thou, Indra, hast slain Vritra by thy vigour, thou hast set free the rivers.'
'Thou hast slain the slumbering Ahi for the release of the waters, and hast marked out the channels of the all-delighting rivers.'
'Indra has filled the rivers, he has inundated the dry land.'
'Indra has released the imprisoned waters to flow upon the earth.'[1]

---

1. Cf. *Rig-Veda Sanhita*, trans. H. H. Wilson, 6 vols. 1854-1888. Vol. I. p. 88, v. 12. 172, v. 8 206, v. 10 Vol. III. p. 157, vv. 2, 5, 7, 8.

III. The Freeing of the Waters

It would be easy to fill pages with similar quotations, but these are sufficient for our purpose.

Among the *Rig-Veda* hymns are certain poems in Dialogue form, which from their curious and elliptic character have been the subject of much discussion among scholars. Professor Oldenberg, in drawing attention to their peculiarities, had expressed his opinion that these poems were the remains of a distinct type of early Indian literature, where verses forming the central, and illuminating, point of a formal ceremonial recital had been 'farced' with illustrative and explanatory prose passages; the form of the verses being fixed, that of the prose being varied at the will of the reciter.[2]

This theory, which is technically known as the 'Âkhyâna' theory (as it derived its starting point from the discussion of the Supar*n*âkhyâna text), won considerable support, but was contested by M. Sylvain Lévi, who asserted that, in these hymns, we had the remains of the earliest, and oldest, Indian dramatic creations, the beginning of the [p26] Indian Drama; and that the fragments could only be satisfactorily interpreted from the point of view that they were intended to be spoken, not by a solitary reciter, but by two or more *dramatis personae*.[3]

J. Hertel (*Der Ursprung des Indischen Dramas und Epos*) went still further, and while accepting, and demonstrating, the justice of this interpretation of the 'Dialogue' poems, suggested a similar origin for certain 'Monologues' found in the same collection.[4]

Professor Leopold von Schroeder, in his extremely interesting volume, *Mysterium und Mimus im Rig-Veda*,[5] has given a popular and practical form to the results of these researches, by translating and publishing, with an explanatory study, a selection of these early 'Culture' Dramas, explaining the speeches, and placing them in the mouth of the respective actors to whom they were, presumably, assigned. Professor von Schroeder holds the entire group to be linked together by one common intention, *viz.*, the purpose of stimulating the processes of Nature, and of obtaining, as a result of what may be called a Ritual Culture Drama, an abundant return of the fruits of the earth. The whole book is rich in parallels drawn from ancient and modern sources, and is of extraordinary interest to the Folk-lore student.

---

2. *Zeitschrift der Deutschen Morgenlandischen Geschichte*, Vols. XXXVII. and XXXIX.
3. Cf. *Le Théâtre Indien*, Paris, 1890.
4. Cf. *Wiener Zeitsch, für die Kunde des Morgenlandes*, Vol. XVIII. 1904.
5. Leipzig, 1908.

III. The Freeing of the Waters

In the light thrown by Professor von Schroeder's researches, following as they do upon the illuminating studies of Mannhardt, and Frazer, we become strikingly aware of the curious vitality and persistence of certain popular customs and beliefs; and while the two last-named writers have rendered inestimable service to the study of Comparative Religion by linking the practices of Classical [p27] and Medieval times with the Folk-customs of to-day, we recognize, through von Schroeder's work, that the root of such belief and custom is imbedded in a deeper stratum of Folk-tradition than we had hitherto realized, that it is, in fact, a heritage from the far-off past of the Aryan peoples.

For the purposes of our especial line of research *Mysterium und Mimus* offers much of value and interest. As noted above, the main object of these primitive Dramas was that of encouraging, we may say, ensuring, the fertility of the Earth; thus it is not surprising that more than one deals with the theme of which we are treating, the Freeing of the Waters, only that whereas, in the quotations given above, the worshippers praise Indra for his beneficent action, here Indra himself, *in propria persona* appears, and vaunts his feat.

"Ich schlug den *V*ritra mit der Kraft des Indra!
Durch eignen Grimm war ich so stark geworden!
Ich machte für die Menschen frei die Wasser."[6]

And the impersonated rivers speak for themselves.

"Indra, den Blitz im Arm, brach uns die Bahnen,
Er schlug den *V*ritra, die Ströme einschloss."[7]

There is no need to insist further on the point that the task of the Grail hero is in this special respect no mere literary invention, but a heritage from the achievements of the prehistoric heroes of the Aryan race.

But the poems selected by Professor von Schroeder for discussion offer us a further, and more curious, parallel with the Grail romances.

In Section VIII. of the work referred to the author discusses the story of *R*ishyaçriñga, as the *Mahâbhârata* names the hero; here we find a young Brahmin brought up by his father, Vibhâ*n*daka, in a lonely forest

---

6. *Op. cit.* p. 105.
7. *Ib.* p. 230.

III. The Freeing of the Waters

hermitage[8] absolutely [p28] ignorant of the outside world, and even of the very existence of beings other than his father and himself. He has never seen a woman, and does not know that such a creature exists.

A drought falls upon a neighbouring kingdom, and the inhabitants are reduced to great straits for lack of food. The King, seeking to know by what means the sufferings of his people may be relieved, learns that so long as *R*ishyaçri*n*ga continues chaste so long will the drought endure. An old woman, who has a fair daughter of irregular life, undertakes the seduction of the hero. The King has a ship, or raft (both versions are given), fitted out with all possible luxury, and an apparent Hermit's cell erected upon it. The old woman, her daughter and companions, embark; and the river carries them to a point not far from the young Brahmin's hermitage.

Taking advantage of the absence of his father, the girl visits *R*ishyaçri*n*ga in his forest cell, giving him to understand that she is a Hermit, like himself, which the boy, in his innocence, believes. He is so fascinated by her appearance and caresses that, on her leaving him, he, deep in thought of the lovely visitor, forgets, for the first time, his religious duties.

On his father's return he innocently relates what has happened, and the father warns him that fiends in this fair disguise strive to tempt hermits to their undoing. The next time the father is absent the temptress, watching her opportunity, returns, and persuades the boy to accompany her to her 'Hermitage' which she assures him, is far more beautiful than his own. So soon as *R*ishyaçri*n*ga is safely on board the ship sails, the lad is carried to the capital of the rainless land, the King gives him his daughter as wife, and so soon as the marriage is consummated the spell is broken, and rain falls in abundance.

[p29] Professor von Schroeder points out that there is little doubt that, in certain earlier versions of the tale, the King's daughter herself played the *rôle* of temptress.

There is no doubt that a ceremonial 'marriage' very frequently formed a part of the 'Fertility' ritual, and was supposed to be specially efficacious in bringing about the effect desired.[9] The practice subsists in Indian ritual to this hour, and the surviving traces in European Folk-custom have been noted in full by Mannhardt in his exhaustive work

---

8. *Ib.* p. 292, for sources, and variants of tale.
9. On this point cf. Cornford, *Origin of Attic Comedy*, pp. 8, 78, for importance of this feature.

III. The Freeing of the Waters

on *Wald und Feld-Kulte;* its existence in Classic times is well known, and it is certainly one of the living Folk-customs for which a well-attested chain of descent can be cited. Professor von Schroeder remarks that the efficacy of the rite appears to be enhanced by the previous strict observance of the rule of chastity by the officiant.[10]

What, however, is of more immediate interest for our purpose is the fact that the Rishyaçriñga story does, in effect, possess certain curious points of contact with the Grail tradition.

Thus, the lonely upbringing of the youth in a forest, far from the haunts of men, his absolute ignorance of the existence of human beings other than his parent and himself, present a close parallel to the accounts of Perceval's youth and woodland life, as related in the Grail romances.[11]

In Gerbert's continuation we are told that the marriage of the hero is an indispensable condition of achieving the Quest, a detail which must have been taken over from an earlier version, as Gerbert proceeds to stultify himself by describing the solemnities of the marriage, and the ceremonial blessing of the nuptial couch, after which hero and [p30] heroine simultaneously agree to live a life of strict chastity, and are rewarded by the promise that the Swan Knight shall be their descendant—a tissue of contradictions which can only be explained by the *mal-à-droit* blending of two versions, one of which knew the hero as wedded, the other, as celibate. There can be no doubt that the original *Perceval* story included the marriage of the hero.[12]

The circumstances under which Rishyaçriñga is lured from his Hermitage are curiously paralleled by the account, found in the *Queste* and Manessier, of Perceval's temptation by a fiend, in the form of a fair maiden, who comes to him by water in a vessel hung with black silk, and with great riches on board.[13]

In pointing out these parallels I wish to make my position perfectly clear; I do not claim that either in the *Rig-Veda*, or in any other early Aryan literary monument, we can hope to discover the direct sources of the Grail legend, but what I would urge upon scholars is the fact that, in adopting the hypothesis of a Nature Cult as a possible origin,

---

10. *Op. cit.* pp. 161-170, for general discussion of question, and summary of authorities. Also pp. 297 *et seq.*
11. Cf. *Legend of Sir Perceval*, Vol. I. Chapter 3.
12. MS. Bibl. Nat., f. Fr. 12576, fo. 173. Cf. also *Legend of Sir Perceval*, I. Chap. 4.
13. Malory, *Le Morte Arthure*, Book XIV. Chaps. 8 and 9. Potvin, ll. 40420 *et seq.*

III. The Freeing of the Waters

and examining the history of these Cults, their evolution, and their variant forms, we do, in effect, find at every period and stage of development undoubted points of contact, which, though taken separately, might be regarded as accidental, in their *ensemble* can hardly be thus considered. When every parallel to our Grail story is found within the circle of a well-defined, and carefully studied, sequence of belief and practice, when each and all form part of a well-recognized body of tradition the descent of which has been abundantly demonstrated, then I submit such parallels stand on a sound basis, and it is not unreasonable to conclude [p31] that the body of tradition containing them belongs to the same family and is to be interpreted on the same principles as the closely analogous rites and ceremonies.

I suspend the notice and discussion of other poems contained in Prof. von Schroeder's collection till we have reached a later stage of the tradition, when their correspondence will be recognized as even more striking and suggestive. [p32]

IV. Tammuz and Adonis

General objects to be attained by these Nature Cults. Stimulation of Fertility, Animal and Vegetable. Principle of Life ultimately conceived of in anthropomorphic form. This process already advanced in Rig-Veda. *Greek Mythology preserves intermediate stage. The* Eniautos Daimon. *TAMMUZ—earliest known representative of Dying God. Character of the worship. Origin of the name. Lament for Tammuz. His death affects not only Vegetable but Animal life. Lack of artistic representation of Mysteries. Mr Langdon's suggestion. Ritual possibly dramatic. Summary of evidence. ADONIS—Phoenician-Greek equivalent of Tammuz. Probably most popular and best known form of Nature Cult. Mythological tale of Adonis. Enquiry into nature of injury. Importance of recognizing true nature of these cults and of the ritual observed. Varying dates of celebration. Adonis probably originally* Eniautos Daimon. *Principle of Life in general, hence lack of fixity in date. Details of the ritual. Parallels with the Grail legend examined. Dead Knight or Disabled King. Consequent misfortunes of Land. The Weeping Women. The Hairless Maiden. Position of Castle. Summing up. Can incidents of such remote antiquity be used as criticism for a Medieval text?*

Part I. Tammuz

In the previous chapter we considered certain aspects of the attitude assumed by our Aryan forefathers towards the great processes of Nature in their ordered sequence of Birth, Growth, and Decay. We saw that while on one hand they, by prayer and supplication, threw themselves upon the mercy of the Divinity, who, in their belief, was responsible for the granting, or withholding, of the water, whether of rain, or river, the constant supply of which was an essential condition of such ordered sequence, they, on the other hand, believed that, by their own actions, they could stimulate and assist the Divine activity. Hence the dramatic representations to which I have referred, the performance, for instance, of such a drama as the *Rishyaçriñga*, the ceremonial 'marriages,' and other exercises of what we now call sympathetic

IV. Tammuz and Adonis

magic. To quote a well-known passage from Sir J. G. Frazer: "They commonly believed that the tie between the animal and vegetable world was even closer than it really is—to them the principle of life and fertility, whether animal or vegetable, was one and indivisible. Hence actions that induced fertility in the animal world were held to be equally efficacious in stimulating the reproductive energies of the vegetable."[1] How deeply this idea was rooted in the minds of our ancestors we, their descendants, may learn from its survival to our own day.

[p33] The ultimate, and what we may in a general sense term the classical, form in which this sense of the community of the Life principle found expression was that which endowed the vivifying force of Nature with a distinct personality, divine, or semi-divine, whose experiences, in virtue of his close kinship with humanity, might be expressed in terms of ordinary life.

At this stage the progress of the seasons, the birth of vegetation in spring, or its revival after the autumn rains, its glorious fruition in early summer, its decline and death under the maleficent influence either of the scorching sun, or the bitter winter cold, symbolically represented the corresponding stages in the life of this anthropomorphically conceived Being, whose annual progress from birth to death, from death to a renewed life, was celebrated with a solemn ritual of corresponding alternations of rejoicing and lamentation.

Recent research has provided us with abundant material for the study of the varying forms of this Nature Cult, the extraordinary importance of which as an evolutionary factor in what we may term the concrete expression of human thought and feeling is only gradually becoming realized.[2]

Before turning our attention to this, the most important, section of our investigation, it may be well to consider one characteristic difference between the Nature ritual of the *Rig-Veda*, and that preserved to us in the later monuments of Greek antiquity.

In the *Rig-Veda*, early as it is, we find the process of religious [p34] evolution already far advanced; the god has separated himself from his worshippers, and assumed an anthropomorphic form. Indra, while still

---

1. Cf. Frazer, Adonis, Attis, Osiris, p. 5.
2. In this connection not only the epoch-making works of Mannhardt and Frazer, which are more specifically devoted to an examination of Folk-belief and practice should be studied, but also works such as The Mediaeval Stage, E. K. Chambers; Themis, J. E. Harrison; The Origin of Attic Comedy, F. Cornford; and Sir Gilbert Murray's essay on the evolution of the Greek Drama, published in Miss Harrison's Themis. The cumulative evidence is most striking.

retaining traces of his 'weather' origin, is no longer, to borrow Miss Harrison's descriptive phrase, 'an automatic explosive thunder-storm,' he wields the thunderbolt certainly, but he appears in heroic form to receive the offerings made to him, and to celebrate his victory in a solemn ritual dance. In Greek art and literature, on the other hand, where we might expect to find an even more advanced conception, we are faced with one seemingly more primitive and inchoate, *i.e.*, the idea of a constantly recurring cycle of Birth, Death, and Resurrection, or Re-Birth, of all things in Nature, this cycle depending upon the activities of an entity at first vaguely conceived of as the 'Luck of the Year,' the *Eniautos Daimon*. This Being, at one stage of evolution theriomorphic—he might assume the form of a bull, a goat, or a snake (the latter, probably from the close connection of the reptile with the earth, being the more general form)—only gradually, and by distinctly traceable stages, assumed an anthropomorphic shape.[3] This gives to the study of Greek antiquity a special and peculiar value, since in regard to the body of religious belief and observance with which we are here immediately concerned, neither in what we may not improperly term its ultimate (early Aryan), nor in what has been generally considered its proximate (Syro-Phoenician), source, have these intermediate stages been preserved; in each case the ritual remains are illustrative of a highly developed cult, distinctly anthropomorphic in conception. I offer no opinion as to the critical significance of this fact, but I would draw the attention of scholars to its existence.

[p35] That the process of evolution was complete at a very early date has been proved by recent researches into the Sumerian-Babylonian civilization. We know now that the cult of the god Tammuz, who, if not the direct original of the Phoenician-Greek Adonis, is at least representative of a common parent deity, may be traced back to 3000 B.C., while it persisted among the Sabeans at Harran into the Middle Ages.[4]

While much relating to the god and his precise position in the Sumerian-Babylonian Pantheon still remains obscure, fragmentary cuneiform texts connected with the religious services of the period have been discovered, and to a considerable extent deciphered, and we are

---

3. A full study of this evolutionary process will be found in Miss Harrison's Themis, A Study of Greek Social Origins, referred to above.

4. Baudissin, in his exhaustive study of these cults, Adonis und Esmun, comes to the conclusion that Tammuz and Adonis are different gods, owing their origin to a common parent deity. Where the original conception arose is doubtful; whether in Babylon, in Canaan, or in a land where the common ancestors of Phoenicians and Babylonian Semites formed an original unit.

IV. Tammuz and Adonis

thus in a position to judge, from the prayers and invocations addressed to the deity, what were the powers attributed to, and the benefits besought from, him. These texts are of a uniform character; they are all 'Lamentations,' or 'Wailings,' having for their exciting cause the disappearance of Tammuz from this upper earth, and the disastrous effects produced upon animal and vegetable life by his absence. The woes of the land and the folk are set forth in poignant detail, and Tammuz is passionately invoked to have pity upon his worshippers, and to end their sufferings by a speedy return. This return, we find from other texts, was effected by the action of a goddess, the mother, sister, or paramour, of Tammuz, who, descending into the nether world, induced the youthful deity to return with her to earth. It is perfectly clear from the texts which have been deciphered that Tammuz is not to be regarded merely as representing the Spirit of Vegetation; his influence is operative, not only [p36] in the vernal processes of Nature, as a Spring god, but in all its reproductive energies, without distinction or limitation, he may be considered as an embodiment of the Life principle, and his cult as a Life Cult.

Mr Stephen Langdon inclines to believe that the original Tammuz typified the vivifying waters; he writes: "Since, in Babylonia as in Egypt, the fertility of the soil depended upon irrigation, it is but natural to expect that the youthful god who represents the birth and death of nature, would represent the beneficent waters which flooded the valleys of the Tigris and Euphrates in the late winter, and which ebbed away, and nearly disappeared, in the canals and rivers in the period of Summer drought. We find therefore that the theologians regarded this youthful divinity as belonging to the cult of Eridu, centre of the worship of Ea, lord of the nether sea."[5] In a note to this passage Mr Langdon adds: "He appears in the great theological list as *Dami-zi, ab-zu,* 'Tammuz of the nether sea,' *i.e.,* 'the faithful son of the fresh waters which come from the earth.'"[6]

---

5. Cf. Tammuz and Ishtar, S. Langdon, p. 5.
6. It may be well to note here the 'Life' deity has no proper name; he is only known by an appellative; Damu-zi, Damu, 'faithful son,' or 'son and consort,' is only a general epithet, which designates the dying god in a theological aspect, just as the name Adōni, 'my lord,' certainly replaced a more specific name for the god of Byblos. Esmun of Sidon, another type of Adonis, is a title only, and means simply, 'the name.' Cf. Langdon, op. cit. p. 7. Cf. this with previous passages on the evolution of the Greek idea from a nameless entity to a definite god. Mr Langdon's remarks on the evolution of the Tammuz cult should be carefully studied in view of the theory maintained by Sir W. Ridgeway—that the Vegetation deities were all of them originally men.

IV. Tammuz and Adonis

This presents us with an interesting analogy to the citations given in the previous chapter from the *Rig-Veda;* the Tammuz cult is specially valuable as providing us with evidence of the gradual evolution of the Life Cult from the early conception of the vivifying power of the waters, to the wider recognition of a common principle underlying all manifestations of Life.

[p37] This is very clearly brought out in the beautiful Lament for Tammuz, published by Mr Langdon in *Tammuz and Ishtar,* and also in *Sumerian and Babylonian Psalms.*[7]

> "In Eanna, high and low, there is weeping,
> Wailing for the house of the lord they raise.
> The wailing is for the plants; the first lament is 'they grow not.'
> The wailing is for the barley; the ears grow not.
> For the habitations and flocks it is; they produce not.
> For the perishing wedded ones, for perishing children it is; the dark-headed people create not.
> The wailing is for the great river; it brings the flood no more.
> The wailing is for the fields of men; the gunū grows no more.
> The wailing is for the fish-ponds; the dasuḫur fish spawn not.
> The wailing is for the cane-brake; the fallen stalks grow not.
> The wailing is for the forests; the tamarisks grow not.
> The wailing is for the highlands; the masgam trees grow not.
> The wailing is for the garden store-house; honey and wine are produced not.
> The wailing is for the meadows; the bounty of the garden, the siḫtū plants grow not.
> The wailing is for the palace; life unto distant days is not."

Can anything be more expressive of the community of life animating the whole of Nature than this poignantly worded lament?

A point which differentiates the worship of Tammuz from the kindred, and better known, cult of Adonis, is the fact that we have no liturgical record of the celebration of the resurrection of the deity; it certainly took place, for the effects are referred to:

> "Where grass was not, there grass is eaten,

---

7. From a liturgy employed at Nippur in the period of the Isin dynasty. Langdon, op. cit. p. 11. Also, Sumerian and Babylonian Psalms, p. 338.

IV. Tammuz and Adonis

Where water was not, water is drunk,
Where the cattle sheds were not, cattle sheds are built."[8]

[p38] While this distinctly implies the revival of vegetable and animal life, those features (*i.e.*, resurrection and sacred marriage), which made the Adonis ritual one of rejoicing as much as of lamentation, are absent from liturgical remains of the Tammuz cult.[9]

A detail which has attracted the attention of scholars is the lack of any artistic representation of this ritual, a lack which is the more striking in view of the important position which these 'Wailings for Tammuz' occupy in the extant remains of Babylonian liturgies. On this point Mr Langdon makes an interesting suggestion: "It is probable that the service of wailing for the dying god, the descent of the mother, and the resurrection, were attended by mysterious rituals. The actual mysteries may have been performed in a secret chamber, and consequently the scenes were forbidden in Art. This would account for the surprising dearth of archaeological evidence concerning a cult upon which the very life of mankind was supposed to depend."[10]

In view of the fact that my suggestion as to the possible later development of these Life Cults as Mysteries has aroused considerable opposition, it is well to bear in mind that such development is held by those best acquainted with the earliest forms of the ritual to have been not merely possible, but to have actually taken place, and that at a very remote date. Mr Langdon quotes a passage referring to "Kings who in their day played the *rôle* of Tammuz in the mystery of this cult"; he considers that here we have to do with kings who, by a symbolic act, escaped [p39] the final penalty of sacrifice as representative of the Dying God.[11]

The full importance of the evidence above set forth will become more clearly apparent as we proceed with our investigation; here I would simply draw attention to the fact that we now possess definite proof that, at a period of some 3000 years B.C., the idea of a Being upon

---

8. Cf. Langdon, Tammuz and Ishtar, p. 23.
9. What we have been able to ascertain of the Sumerian-Babylonian religion points to it rather as a religion of mourning and supplication, than of joy and thanksgiving. The people seem to have been in perpetual dread of their gods, who require to be appeased by continual acts of humiliation. Thus the 9th, 15th, 19th, 28th, and 29th of the month were all days of sack-cloth and ashes, days of wailing; the 19th especially was 'the day of the wrath of Gulu.'
10. Cf. Langdon, op. cit. p. 24.
11. Cf. Langdon, op. cit. p. 26.

IV. Tammuz and Adonis

whose life and reproductive activities the very existence of Nature and its corresponding energies was held to depend, yet who was himself subject to the vicissitudes of declining powers and death, like an ordinary mortal, had already assumed a fixed, and practically final, form; further, that this form was specially crystallized in ritual observances. In our study of the later manifestations of this cult we shall find that this central idea is always, and unalterably, the same, and is, moreover, frequently accompanied by a remarkable correspondence of detail. The chain of evidence is already strong, and we may justly claim that the links added by further research strengthen, while they lengthen, that chain.

Part II. Adonis

While it is only of comparatively recent date that information as to the exact character of the worship directed to Tammuz has been available and the material we at present possess is but fragmentary in character, the corresponding cult of the Phoenician-Greek divinity we know as Adonis has for some years been the subject of scholarly research. Not only have the details of the ritual been examined and discussed, and the surviving artistic evidence described and illustrated, but from the anthropological side attention has been forcibly directed to its importance as a factor in the elucidation of certain widespread Folk-beliefs and practices.[12]

[p40] We know now that the worship of Adonis, which enjoyed among the Greeks a popularity extending to our own day, was originally of Phoenician origin, its principal centres being the cities of Byblos, and Aphaka. From Phoenicia it spread to the Greek islands, the earliest evidence of the worship being found in Cyprus, and from thence to the mainland, where it established itself firmly. The records of the cult go back to 700 B.C., but it may quite possibly be of much earlier date. Mr Langdon suggests that the worship of the divinity we know as Adonis,

---

12. The most complete enquiry into the nature of the god is to be found in Baudissin, *Adonis und Esmun*. For the details of the cult cf. Farnell, *Cults of the Greek States*, Vol. II.; Vellay, *Adonis* (Annales du Musée Guimet). For the Folk-lore evidence cf. Mannhardt, *Wald un Feld-Kulte*; Frazer, *The Golden Bough*, and *Adonis, Attis and Osiris*. These remarks apply also to the kindred cult of Attis, which as we shall see later forms an important link in our chain of evidence. The two cults are practically identical and scholars are frequently at a loss to which group surviving fragments of the ritual should be assigned.

IV. Tammuz and Adonis

may, under another name, reach back to an antiquity equal with that we can now ascribe to the cult of Tammuz. In its fully evolved classical form the cult of Adonis offers, as it were, a halfway house, between the fragmentary relics of Aryan and Babylonian antiquity, and the wealth of Medieval and Modern survivals to which the ingenuity and patience of contemporary scholars have directed our attention.

We all know the mythological tale popularly attached to the name of Adonis; that he was a fair youth, beloved of Aphrodite, who, wounded in the thigh by a wild boar, died of his wound. The goddess, in despair at his death, by her prayers won from Zeus the boon that Adonis be allowed to return to earth for a portion of each year, and henceforward the youthful god divides his time between the goddess of Hades, Persephone, and Aphrodite. But the importance assumed by the story, the elaborate ceremonial with which the death of Adonis was mourned, and his restoration to [p41] life fêted, the date and character of the celebrations, all leave no doubt that the personage with whom we are dealing was no mere favourite of a goddess, but one with whose life and well-being the ordinary processes of Nature, whether animal or vegetable, were closely and intimately concerned. In fact the central figure of these rites, by whatever name he may be called, is the somewhat elusive and impersonal entity, who represents in anthropomorphic form the principle of animate Nature, upon whose preservation, and unimpaired energies, the life of man, directly, and indirectly, depends.[13]

Before proceeding to examine these rites there is one point, to which I have alluded earlier, in another connection, upon which our minds must be quite clear, *i.e.,* the nature of the injury suffered. Writers upon the subject are of one accord in considering the usual account to be but a euphemistic veiling of the truth, while the close relation between the stories of Adonis and Attis, and the practices associated with the cult, place beyond any shadow of a doubt the fact that the true reason for this universal mourning was the cessation, or suspension, by injury or

---

13. In this connection note the extremely instructive remarks of Miss Harrison in the chapter on Herakles in the work referred to above. She points out that the Eniautos Daimon never becomes entirely and Olympian, but always retains traces of his 'Earth' origin. This principle is particularly well illustrated by Adonis, who, though, admitted to Olympus as the lover of Aphrodite, is yet by this very nature forced to return to the earth, and descend to the realm of Persephone. This agrees well with the conclusion reached by Baudissin (Adonis und Esmun, p. 71) that Adonis belongs to "einer Klasse von Wesen sehr unbestimmter Art, die wohl über den Menschen aber unter den grossen Göttern stehen."

IV. Tammuz and Adonis

death, of the reproductive energy of the god upon whose virile activity vegetable life directly, and human life indirectly, depended.¹⁴ [p42] What we have need to seize and to insist upon is the overpowering influence which the sense of Life, the need for Life, the essential Sanctity of the Life-giving faculty, exercised upon primitive religions. Vellay puts this well when he says: "En réalité c'est sur la conception de la vie physique, considérée dans son origine, et dans son action, et dans le double principe qui l'anime, que repose tout le cycle religieux des peuples Orientaux de l'Antiquité."¹⁵

Professor von Schroeder says even more precisely and emphatically: "In der Religion der Arischen Urzeit ist Alles auf Lebensbejahung gerichtet, Mann kann den Phallus als ihr Beherrschendes Symbol betrachten."¹⁶ And in spite of the strong opposition to this cult manifested in Indian literature, beginning with the *Rig-Veda,* and ripening to fruition in the *Upanishads,* in spite of the rise of Buddhism, with its opposing dictum of renunciation, the 'Life-Cult' asserted its essential vitality against all opposition, and under modified forms represents the 'popular' religion of India to this day.

Each and all of the ritual dramas, reconstructed in the pages of *Mysterium und Mimus* bear, more or less distinctly, the stamp of their 'Fertility' origin,¹⁷ while outside India the pages of Frazer and Mannhardt, and numerous other writers on Folk-lore and Ethnology, record the widespread, and persistent, survival of these rites, and their successful defiance of the spread of civilization.

It is to this special group of belief and practice [p43] that the Adonis (and more especially its Phrygian counterpart the Attis) worship belong, and even when transplanted to the more restrained and cultured environment of the Greek mainland, they still retained their primitive character. Farnell, in his *Cults of the Greek States,* refers to the worship of Adonis as "a ritual that the more austere State religion of Greece

---

14. Cf. Vellay, op. cit. p. 93. Dulaure, Des Divinités Génératrices. If Baudissin is correct, and the introduction of the Boar a later addition to the story, it would seem to indicate the intrusion of a phallic element into ritual which at first, like that of Tammuz, dealt merely with the death of the god. The Attis form, on the contrary, appears to have been phallic from the first. Cf. Baudissin, Adonis und Esmun, p. 160.

15. Op. cit. p. 83.

16. Cf. L. von Schroeder, Vollendung den Arischen Mysterium, p. 14.

17. It may be well to explain the exact meaning attached to these terms by the author. In Professor von Schroeder's view Mysterium may be held to connote a drama in which the gods themselves are actors; Mimus on the contrary, is the term applied to a drama which treats of the doings of mortals.

IV. Tammuz and Adonis

probably failed to purify, the saner minds, bred in a religious atmosphere that was, on the whole, genial, and temperate, revolted from the din of cymbals and drums, the meaningless ecstasies of sorrow and joy, that marked the new religion."[18]

It is, I submit, indispensable for the purposes of our investigation that the essential character and significance of the cults with which we are dealing should not be evaded or ignored, but faced, frankly admitted and held in mind during the progress of our enquiry.

Having now determined the general character of the ritual, what were the specific details?

The date of the feast seems to have varied in different countries; thus in Greece it was celebrated in the Spring, the moment of the birth of Vegetation; according to Saint Jerome, in Palestine the celebration fell in June, when plant life was in its first full luxuriance. In Cyprus, at the autumnal equinox, *i.e.,* the beginning of the year in the Syro-Macedonian calendar, the death of Adonis falling on the 23rd of September, his resurrection on the 1st of October, the beginning of a New Year. This would seem to indicate that here Adonis was considered, as Vellay suggests, less as the god of Vegetation than as the superior and nameless Lord of Life (Adonis = Syriac *Adôn*, Lord), under whose protection the year was placed.[19] He is the *Eniautos Daimon*.

[p44] In the same way as the dates varied, so, also, did the order of the ritual; generally speaking the elaborate ceremonies of mourning for the dead god, and committing his effigy to the waves, preceded the joyous celebration of his resurrection, but in Alexandria the sequence was otherwise; the feast began with the solemn and joyous celebration of the nuptials of Adonis and Aphrodite, at the conclusion of which a Head, of papyrus, representing the god, was, with every show of mourning, committed to the waves, and borne within seven days by a current (always to be counted upon at that season of the year) to Byblos, where it

---

18. Op. cit. Vol. II. p. 647.
19. Op. cit. p. 115. Much of the uncertainty as to date is doubtless due to the reflective influence of other forms of the cult; the Tammuz celebrations were held from June 20th, to July 20th, when the Dog-star Sirius was in the ascendant, and vegetation failed beneath the heat of the summer sun. In other, and more temperate, climates the date would fall later. Where, however, the cult was an off-shoot of a Tammuz original (as might be the case through emigration) the tendency would be to retain the original date.

IV. Tammuz and Adonis

was received and welcomed with popular rejoicing.[20] The duration of the feast varied from two days, as at Alexandria, to seven or eight.

Connected with the longer period of the feast were the so-called 'Gardens of Adonis,' baskets, or pans, planted with quick growing seeds, which speedily come to fruition, and as speedily wither. In the modern survivals of the cult three days form the general term for the flowering of these gardens.[21]

The most noticeable feature of the ritual was the prominence assigned to women; "ce sont les femmes qui le pleurent, et qui l'accompagnent à sa tombe. Elles sanglotent éperdument pendant les nuits,—c'est leur dieu plus [p45] que tout autre, et seules elles veulent pleurer sa mort, et chanter sa résurrection."[22]

Thus in the tenth century the festival received the Arabic name of *El-Bûgat,* or 'The Festival of the Weeping Women.'[23]

One very curious practice during these celebrations was that of cutting off the hair in honour of the god; women who hesitated to make this sacrifice must offer themselves to strangers, either in the temple, or on the market-place, the gold received as the price of their favours being offered to the goddess. This obligation only lasted for one day.[24] It was also customary for the priests of Adonis to mutilate themselves in imitation of the god, a distinct proof, if one were needed, of the traditional cause of his death.[25]

Turning from a consideration of the Adonis ritual, its details, and significance, to an examination of the Grail romances, we find that their *mise-en-scène* provides a striking series of parallels with the Classical celebrations, parallels, which instead of vanishing, as parallels have occasionally an awkward habit of doing, before closer investigation, rather gain in force the more closely they are studied.

---

20. Cf. Vellay, op. cit. p. 55; Mannhardt, Vol. II. pp. 277-78, for a description of the feast. With regard to the order and sequence of the celebration cf. Miss Harrison's remark, Themis, p. 415: "In the cyclic monotony of the Eniautos Daimon it matters little whether Death follows Resurrection, or Resurrection, Death."
21. Cf. Mannhardt, supra, p. 279.
22. Cf. Vellay, op. cit. p. 103. This seems also to have been the case with Tammuz, cf. Ezekiel, Chap. viii. v. 14.
23. Cf. Frazer, The Golden Bough, under heading Adonis.
24. Vellay, p. 130, Mannhardt, Vol. II. p. 287; note the writer's suggestion that the women here represent the goddess, the stranger, the risen Adonis.
25. Cf. Vellay, p. 93.

IV. Tammuz and Adonis

Thus the central figure is either a dead knight on a bier (as in the *Gawain* versions), or a wounded king on a litter; when wounded the injury corresponds with that suffered by Adonis and Attis.[26]

Closely connected with the wounding of the king is the destruction which has fallen on the land, which will be removed when the king is healed. The version of *Sone de Nansai* is here of extreme interest; the position is stated with so much [p46] clearness and precision that the conclusion cannot be evaded—we are face to face with the dreaded calamity which it was the aim of the Adonis ritual to avert, the temporary suspension of all the reproductive energies of Nature.[27]

While the condition of the king is the cause of general and vociferous lamentation, a special feature, never satisfactorily accounted for, is the presence of a weeping woman, or several weeping women. Thus in the interpolated visit of Gawain to the Grail castle, found in the C group of *Perceval* MSS., the Grail-bearer weeps piteously, as she does also in *Diû Crône*.[28]

In the version of the prose *Lancelot* Gawain, during the night, sees twelve maidens come to the door of the chamber where the Grail is kept, kneel down, and weep bitterly, in fact behave precisely as did the classical mourners for Adonis—"Elles sanglotent éperdument pendant la nuit."[29]— [p47] behaviour for which the text, as it now stands, provides no shadow of explanation or excuse. The Grail is here the most revered of Christian relics, the dwellers in the castle of Corbenic have all that heart can desire, with the additional prestige of being the

---

26. Vide supra, pp. 20. 21.
27. Supra, p. 21.
28. Cf. Potvin, appendix to Vol. III.; Sir Gawain and the Grail Castle, pp. 41, 44, and note.
29. My use of this parallel has been objected to on the ground that the prose Lancelot is a late text, and therefore cannot be appealed to as evidence for original incidents. But the Lancelot in its original form was held by so competent an authority as the late M. Gaston Paris to have been one of the earliest, if not the very earliest, of French prose texts. (Cf. M. Paris's review of Suchier and Birch-Hirschfield's Geschichte der Franz. Litt.) The adventure in question is a 'Gawain' adventure; we do not know whence it was derived, and it may well have been included in an early version of the romance. Apart from the purely literary question, from the strictly critical point of view the adventure is here obviously out of place, and entirely devoid of raison d'être. If the origins of the Grail legend is really to be found in these cults, which are not a dead but a living tradition (how truly living, the exclusively literary critic has little idea), we are surely entitled to draw attention to the obvious parallels, no matter in which text they appear. I am not engaged in reconstructing the original form of the Grail story, but in endeavoring to ascertain the ultimate source, and it is surely justifiable to point out that, in effect, no matter what version we take, we find in that version points of contact with one special group of popular belief and practice. If I be wrong in my conclusions my critics have only to suggest another origin for this particular feature of the romance—as a matter of fact, they have failed to do so.

IV. Tammuz and Adonis

guardians of the Grail; if the feature be not a belated survival, which has lost its meaning, it defies any explanation whatsoever.

In *Diû Crône* alone, where the Grail-bearer and her maidens are the sole living beings in an abode of the Dead, is any explanation of the 'Weeping Women' attempted, but an interpolated passage in the Heralds' College MS. of the *Perceval* states that when the Quest is achieved, the hero shall learn the cause of the maiden's grief, and also the explanation of the Dead Knight upon the bier:

"del graal q'vient aprés
E purquei plure tut adés
La pucele qui le sustient
De la biere qu'aprés vient
Savera la vérité adonques
Ceo que nul ne pot saveir onques
Pur nule rien qui avenist." fo. 180*vo*-181.

Of course in the *Perceval* there is neither a Weeping Maiden, nor a Bier, and the passage must therefore be either an unintelligent addition by a scribe familiar with the *Gawain* versions, or an interpolation from a source which did contain the features in question. So far as the texts at our disposal are concerned, both features belong exclusively to the *Gawain*, and not to the *Perceval* Quest. The interpolation is significant as it indicates a surviving sense of the importance of this feature.

In the *Perlesvaus* we have the curious detail of a maiden who has lost her hair as a result of the hero's failure to ask the question, and the consequent sickness of the Fisher King. The occurrence of this detail may be purely fortuitous, [p.48] but at the same time it is admissible to point out that the Adonis cults do provide us with a parallel in the enforced loss of hair by the women taking part in these rites, while no explanation of this curious feature has so far as I am aware been suggested by critics of the text.[30]

We may also note the fact that the Grail castle is always situated in the close vicinity of water, either on or near the sea, or on the banks of an important river. In two cases the final home of the Grail is in a monastery situated upon an island. The presence of water, either sea, or

---

30. Cf. Perlesvaus, Branch II. Chap. I.

IV. Tammuz and Adonis

river, is an important feature in the Adonis cult, the effigy of the dead god being, not buried in the earth, but thrown into the water.[31]

It will thus be seen that, in suggesting a form of Nature worship, analogous to this well-known cult, as the possible ultimate source from which the incidents and *mise-en-scène* of the Grail stories were derived, we are relying not upon an isolated parallel, but upon a group of parallels, which alike in incident and intention offer, not merely a resemblance to, but also an explanation of, the perplexing problems of the Grail literature. We must now consider the question whether incidents so remote in time may fairly and justly be utilized in this manner. [p49]

---

31. Throwing into, or drenching with, water is a well known part of the 'Fertility' ritual; it is a case of sympathetic magic, acting as a rain charm.

V. Medieval and Modern Forms of Nature Ritual

Is it possible to establish chain of descent connecting early Aryan and Babylonian Ritual with Classic, Medieval and Modern forms of Nature worship? Survival of Adonis cult established. Evidence of Mannhardt and Frazer. Existing Continental customs recognized as survivals of ancient beliefs. Instances. 'Directly related' to Attis-Adonis cult. Von Schroeder establishes parallel between existing Fertility procession and Rig-Veda *poem. Identification of Life Principle with King. Prosperity of land dependent on king as representative of god. Celts. Greeks. Modern instances, the Shilluk Kings. Parallel between Shilluk King, Grail King and Vegetation Deity. Sone de Nansai and the Lament for Tammuz. Identity of situation. Plea for unprejudiced criticism. Impossibility of such parallels being fortuitous; the result of deliberate intention, not an accident of literary invention. If identity of central character be admitted his relation to Waste Land becomes fundamental factor in criticizing versions. Another African survival.*

Readers of the foregoing pages may, not improbably, object that, while we have instanced certain curious and isolated parallels from early Aryan literature and tradition, and, what, from the point of view of declared intention, appears to be a kindred group of religious belief and practice in pre-Historic and Classical times, the two, so far, show no direct signs of affiliation, while both may be held to be far removed, in point of date, alike from one another, and from the romantic literature of the twelfth century.

This objection is sound in itself, but if we can show by modern parallels that the ideas which took form and shape in early Aryan Drama, and Babylonian and Classic Ritual, not only survive to our day, but are found in combination with features corresponding minutely with details recorded in early Aryan literature, we may hold the gulf to be bridged, and the common origin, and close relationship, of the different stages to be an ascertained fact. At the outset, and before examining the evidence collected by scholars, I would remind my readers that the modern Greeks have retained, in many instances under changed names, no inconsiderable portion of their ancient mythological beliefs, among

V. Medieval and Modern Forms of Nature Ritual

them the 'Adonis' celebrations; the 'Gardens of Adonis' blossom and fade to-day, as they did many centuries ago, and I have myself spoken with a scholar who has [p50] seen 'women, at the door of their houses, weeping for Adonis.'[1]

For evidence of the widespread character of Medieval and Modern survivals we have only to consult the epoch-making works of Mannhardt, *Wald und Feld-Kulte,* and Frazer, *The Golden Bough;*[2] in the pages of these volumes we shall find more than sufficient for our purpose. From the wealth of illustration with which these works abound I have selected merely such instances as seem to apply more directly to the subject of our investigation.[3]

Thus, in many places, it is still the custom to carry a figure representing the Vegetation Spirit on a bier, attended by mourning women, and either bury the figure, throw it into water (as a rain charm), or, after a mock death, carry the revivified Deity, with rejoicing, back to the town. Thus in the Lechrain a man in black women's clothes is borne on a bier, followed by men dressed as professional women mourners making lamentation, thrown on the village dung-heap, drenched with water, and buried in straw.[4]

In Russia the Vegetation or Year Spirit is known as Yarilo,[5] and is represented by a doll with phallic attributes, which is enclosed in a coffin, and carried through the streets to the accompaniment of lamentation by women whose emotions have been excited by drink. Mannhardt gives the lament as follows: "Wessen war Er schuldig? Er war so gut! Er wird nicht mehr aufstehen! O! Wie sollen wir uns von Dir trennen? Was ist das Leben wenn [p51] Du nicht mehr da bist? Erhebe Dich, wenn auch nur auf ein Stündchen! Aber Er steht nicht auf, Er steht nicht auf!"[6]

In other forms of the ritual, we find distinct traces of the resuscitation of the Vegetation Deity, occasionally accompanied by evidence of rejuvenation. Thus, in Lausitz, on Laetare Sunday (the 4th Sunday in

---

1. *Ancient Greek Religion, and Modern Greek Folk-Lore,* J. C. Lawson, gives some most interesting evidence as to modern survivals of mythological beliefs.
2. *Wald und Feld-Kulte,* 2nd edition, 2 vols., Berlin, 1904. Cf. Vol. II. p. 286. *The Golden Bough,* 3rd edition, 5 vols.
3. I cite from Mannhardt, as the two works overlap in the particular line of research we are following: the same instances are given in both, but the honour of priority belongs to the German scholar.
4. *Op. cit.* Vol. I. p. 411.
5. See G. Calderon, 'Slavonic Elements in Greek religion,' *Classical Review,* 1918, p. 79.
6. *Op. cit.* p. 416.

Lent), women with mourning veils carry a straw figure, dressed in a man's shirt, to the bounds of the next village, where they tear the effigy to pieces, hang the shirt on a young and flourishing tree, "schöne Wald-Baum," which they proceed to cut down, and carry home with every sign of rejoicing. Here evidently the young tree is regarded as a rejuvenation of the person represented in the first instance by the straw figure.[7]

In many parts of Europe to-day the corresponding ceremonies, very generally held at Whitsuntide, include the mock execution of the individual representing the Vegetation Spirit, frequently known as the King of the May. In Bohemia the person playing the *rôle* of the King is, with his attendants, dressed in bark, and decked with garlands of flowers; at the conclusion of the ceremonies the King is allowed a short start, and is then pursued by the armed attendants. If he is not overtaken he holds office for a year, but if overtaken, he suffers a mock decapitation, head-dress, or crown, being struck off, and the pretended corpse is then borne on a bier to the next village.[8]

Mannhardt, discussing this point, remarks that in the mock execution we must recognize "Ein verbreiteter und jedenfalls uralter Gebrauch." He enumerates the various modes of death, shooting, stabbing (in the latter case a bladder filled with blood, and concealed under the clothes, is pierced); in Bohemia, decapitation, occasionally drowning (which primarily represents a rain charm), is the form [p52] adopted.[9] He then goes on to remark that this ceremonial death must have been generally followed by resuscitation, as in Thuringia, where the 'Wild Man,' as the central figure is there named, is brought to life again by the Doctor, while the survival, in the more elaborate Spring processions of this latter character, even where he plays no special *rôle,* points to the fact that his part in the proceedings was originally a more important one.

That Mannhardt was not mistaken is proved by the evidence of the kindred Dances, a subject we shall consider later; there we shall find the Doctor playing his old-time *rôle,* and restoring to life the slain representative of the Vegetation Spirit.[10] The character of the Doctor, or Medicine Man, formed, as I believe, at one time, no unimportant link in the chain which connects these practices with the Grail tradition.

---

7. *Op. cit.* pp. 155 and 312.
8. *Op. cit.* p. 353.
9. *Op. cit.* p. 358.
10. *Op. cit.* p. 358.

V. Medieval and Modern Forms of Nature Ritual

The signification of the resuscitation ceremony is obscured in cases where the same figure undergoes death and revival without any corresponding change of form. This point did not escape Mannhardt's acute critical eye; he remarks that, in cases where, *e.g.*, in Swabia, the 'King' is described as "ein armer alter Mann," who has lived seven years in the woods (the seven winter months), a scene of rejuvenation should follow—"diese scheint meistenteils verloren gegangen; doch vielleicht *scheint* es nur so." He goes on to draw attention to the practice in Reideberg, bei Halle, where, after burying a straw figure, called the Old Man, the villagers dance round the May-Pole, and he suggests that the 'Old Man' represents the defunct Vegetation Spirit, the May Tree, that Spirit resuscitated, and refers in this connection to the "durchaus verwandten Asiatischen Gebrauchen des Attis, und Adonis-Kultus."[11]

[p53] The foregoing evidence offers, I think, sufficient proof of the, now generally admitted, relationship between Classical, Medieval, and Modern forms of Nature ritual.

But what of the relation to early Aryan practice? Can that, also, be proved?

In this connection I would draw attention to Chapter 17 of *Mysterium und Mimus*, entitled, *Ein Volkstümlicher Umzug beim Soma-Fest*. Here Professor von Schroeder discusses the real meaning and significance of a very curious little poem (*Rig-Veda*, 9. 112); the title by which it is generally known, *Alles lauft nach Geld*, does not, at first sight, fit the content of the verse, and the suggestion of scholars who have seen in it a humorous enumeration of different trades and handicrafts does not explain the fact that the Frog and the Horse appear in it.

To Professor von Schroeder belongs the credit of having discovered that the *personnel* of the poem corresponds with extraordinary exactitude to the Figures of the Spring and Summer 'Fertility-exciting' processions, described with such fulness of detail by Mannhardt. Especially is this the case with the Whitsuntide procession at Värdegötzen, in Hanover, where we find the group of phallic and fertility demons, who, on Prof. von Schroeder's hypothesis, figure in the song, in concrete, and actual form.[12] The Vegetation Spirit appears in the song as an Old Man,

---

11. *Op. cit.* p. 359. Cf. the Lausitz custom given *supra*, which Mannhardt seems to have overlooked.

12. In the poem, besides the ordinary figures of the Vegetation Deity, his female counterpart, and the Doctor, common to all such processions, Laubfrosch, combining the two first, and Horse. Cf. Mannhardt, *Mythol. Forsch.* pp. 142-43; *Mysterium und Mimus*, pp. 408 *et seq.*; also, pp. 443-44. Sir W. Ridgeway (*op. cit.* p. 156) refers slightly to this interpretation of a 'harmless little hymn'—doubtless the poem is harmless; until Prof. von Schroeder pointed out its close affinity with the Fertility processions it was also meaningless.

while his female counterpart, an Old Woman, is described as 'filling the hand-mill.' Prof. von Schroeder points out that in some [p54] parts of Russia the 'Baba-jaga' as the Corn Mother is called, is an Old Woman, who flies through the air in a hand-mill. The Doctor, to whom we have referred above, is mentioned twice in the four verses composing the song; he was evidently regarded as an important figure; while the whole is put into the mouth of a 'Singer' evidently the Spokesman of the party, who proclaims their object, "Verschiednes können suchen wir Gute Dinge," *i.e.*, gifts in money and kind, as such folk processions do to-day.

The whole study is of extraordinary interest for Folk-lore students, and so far as our especial investigation is concerned it seems to me to supply the necessary proof of the identity, and persistence, of Aryan folk-custom and tradition.

A very important modification of the root idea, and one which appears to have a direct bearing on the sources of the Grail tradition, was that by which, among certain peoples, the *rôle* of the god, his responsibility for providing the requisite rain upon which the fertility of the land, and the life of the folk, depended, was combined with that of the King.

This was the case among the Celts; McCulloch, in *The Religion of the Celts*, discussing the question of the early Irish *geasa* or taboo, explains the *geasa* of the Irish kings as designed to promote the welfare of the tribe, the making of rain and sunshine on which their prosperity depended. "Their observance made the earth fruitful, produced abundance and prosperity, and kept both the king and his land from misfortune. The Kings were divinities on whom depended fruitfulness and plenty, and who must therefore submit to obey their '*geasa*.'"[13]

The same idea seems to have prevailed in early Greece; Mr A. B. Cook, in his studies on *The European Sky-God*, [p55] remarks that the king in early Greece was regarded as the representative of Zeus: his duties could be satisfactorily discharged only by a man who was perfect, and without blemish, *i.e.*, by a man in the prime of life, suffering from no defect of body, or mind; he quotes in illustration the speech of Odysseus (*Od.* 19. 109 ff.). "Even as a king without blemish, who ruleth god-fearing over many mighty men, and maintaineth justice, while the black earth beareth wheat and barley, and the trees

---

13. *Op. cit.* Chap. 17, p. 253.

V. Medieval and Modern Forms of Nature Ritual

are laden with fruit, and the flocks bring forth without fail, and the sea yieldeth fish by reason of his good rule, and the folk prosper beneath him.' The king who is without blemish has a flourishing kingdom, the king who is maimed has a kingdom diseased like himself, thus the Spartans were warned by an oracle to beware of a 'lame reign.'"[14]

A most remarkable modern survival of this idea is recorded by Dr Frazer in the latest edition of *The Golden Bough*,[15] and is so complete and suggestive that I make no apology for transcribing it at some length. The Shilluk, an African tribe, inhabit the banks of the White Nile, their territory extending on the west bank from Kaka in the north, to Lake No in the south, on the east bank from Fashoda to Taufikia, and some 35 miles up the Sohat river. Numbering some 40,000 in all, they are a pastoral people, their wealth consisting in flocks and herds, grain and millet. The King resides at Fashoda, and is regarded with extreme reverence, as being a re-incarnation of Nyakang, the semi-divine hero who settled the tribe in their present territory. Nyakang is the rain-giver, on whom their life and prosperity depend; there are several shrines in which sacred Spears, now kept for sacrificial purposes, are preserved, the originals, which were the property of Nyakang, having disappeared.

[p56] The King, though regarded with reverence, must not be allowed to become old or feeble, lest, with the diminishing vigour of the ruler, the cattle should sicken, and fail to bear increase, the crops should rot in the field and men die in ever growing numbers. One of the signs of failing energy is the King's inability to fulfil the desires of his wives, of whom he has a large number. When this occurs the wives report the fact to the chiefs, who condemn the King to death forthwith, communicating the sentence to him by spreading a white cloth over his face and knees during his mid-day slumber. Formerly the King was starved to death in a hut, in company with a young maiden but (in consequence, it is said, of the great vitality and protracted suffering of one King) this is no longer done; the precise manner of death is difficult to ascertain; Dr Seligmann, who was Sir J. G. Frazer's authority, thinks that he is now strangled in a hut, especially erected for that purpose.

At one time he might be attacked and slain by a rival, either of his own family, or of that of one of the previous Kings, of whom there are

---

14. Cf. *Folk-Lore*, Vol. XV. p. 374.
15. *Op. cit.* Vol. V. *The Dying God*, pp. 17 et seq.

V. Medieval and Modern Forms of Nature Ritual

many, but this has long been superseded by the ceremonial slaying of the monarch who after his death is revered as Nyakang.[16]

This survival is of extraordinary interest; it presents us with a curiously close parallel to the situation which, on the evidence of the texts, we have postulated as forming the basic idea of the Grail tradition—the position of a people whose prosperity, and the fertility of their land, are closely bound up with the life and virility of their King, who is not a mere man, but a Divine re-incarnation. If he 'falls into languishment,' as does the Fisher King in *Perlesvaus*, the land and its inhabitants will suffer correspondingly; not only [p57] will the country suffer from drought, "*Nus près n'i raverdia,*" but the men will die in numbers:

"Dames en perdront lor maris"

we may say; the cattle will cease to bear increase:

"Ne se n'i ot beste faon,"

and the people take drastic steps to bring about a rejuvenation; the old King dies, to be replaced by a young and vigorous successor, even as Brons was replaced by Perceval.

Let us now turn back to the preceding chapter, and compare the position of the people of the Shilluk tribe, and the subjects of the Grail King, with that of the ancient Babylonians, as set forth in their Lamentations for Tammuz.

There we find that the absence of the Life-giving deity was followed by precisely the same disastrous consequences; Vegetation fails—

"The wailing is for the plants; the first lament is they grow not.
The wailing is for the barley; the ears grow not."

The reproductive energies of the animal kingdom are suspended—

"For the habitation of flocks it is; they produce not.
For the perishing wedded ones, for perishing children it is; the dark-headed people create not."

---

16. See Dr Seligmann's study, *The Cult of Nyakang and the Divine Kings of the Shilluk* in the Fourth Report of the Wellcome Research Laboratories, Kkartum, 1911, Vol. B.

V. Medieval and Modern Forms of Nature Ritual

Nor can we evade the full force of the parallel by objecting that we are here dealing with a god, not with a man; we possess the recorded names of 'kings who played the *rôle* of Tammuz,' thus even for that early period the commingling of the two conceptions, god and king, is definitely established.

Now in face of this group of parallels, whose close correspondence, if we consider their separation in point of time (3000 B.C.; 1200 A.D.; and the present day), is nothing short of astonishing, is it not absolutely and utterly unreasonable to admit (as scholars no longer hesitate to [p58] do) the relationship between the first and last, and exclude, as a mere literary invention, the intermediate parallel?

The ground for such a denial may be mere prejudice, a reluctance to renounce a long cherished critical prepossession, but in the face of this new evidence does it not come perilously close to scientific dishonesty, to a disregard for that respect for truth in research the imperative duty of which has been so finely expressed by the late M. Gaston Paris.—"Je professe absolument et sans réserve cette doctrine, que la science n'a d'autre objet que la vérité, et la vérité pour elle-même, sans aucun souci des conséquences, bonnes ou mauvaises, regrettables ou heureuses, que cette vérité pourrait avoir dans la pratique."[17] When we further consider that behind these three main parallels, linking them together, there lies a continuous chain of evidence, expressed alike in classical literature, and surviving Folk practice, I would submit that there is no longer any shadow of a doubt that in the Grail King we have a romantic literary version of that strange mysterious figure whose presence hovers in the shadowy background of the history of our Aryan race; the figure of a divine or semi-divine ruler, at once god and king, upon whose life, and unimpaired vitality, the existence of his land and people directly depends.

And if we once grant this initial fact, and resolve that we will no longer, in the interests of an outworn critical tradition, deny the weight of scientific evidence in determining the real significance of the story, does it not inevitably follow, as a logical sequence, that such versions as fail to connect the misfortunes of the land directly with the disability of the king, but make them dependent upon the failure of the Quester, are, by that very fact, stamped as secondary [p59] versions. That by

---

17. Cf. Address on reception into the Academy when M. Paris succeeded to Pasteur's *fauteuil*.

this one detail, of capital importance, they approve themselves as literary treatments of a traditional theme, the true meaning of which was unknown to the author?

Let us for a moment consider what the opposite view would entail; that a story which was originally the outcome of pure literary invention should in the course of re-modelling have been accidentally brought into close and detailed correspondence with a deeply rooted sequence of popular faith and practice is simply inconceivable, the re-modelling, if re-modelling there were, must have been intentional, the men whose handiwork it was were in possession of the requisite knowledge.

But how did they possess that knowledge, and why should they undertake such a task? Surely not from the point of view of antiquarian interest, as might be done to-day; they were no twelfth century Frazers and Mannhardts; the subject must have had for them a more living, a more intimate, interest. And if, in face of the evidence we now possess, we feel bound to admit the existence of such knowledge, is it not more reasonable to suppose that the men who first told the story were the men who *knew*, and that the confusion was due to those who, with more literary skill, but less first-hand information, re-modelled the original theme?

In view of the present facts I would submit that the problem posed in our first chapter may be held to be solved; that we accept as a *fait acquis* the conclusion that the woes of the land are directly dependent upon the sickness, or maiming, of the King, and in no wise caused by the failure of the Quester. The 'Wasting of the land' must be held to have been antecedent to that failure, and the *Gawain* versions in which we find this condition fulfilled are, therefore, prior in origin to the *Perceval*, in which the 'Wasting' is brought about by the action of the hero; in some versions, indeed, has altogether disappeared from the story.

[p60] Thus the position assigned in the versions to this feature of the Waste Land becomes one of capital importance as a critical factor. This is a point which has hitherto escaped the attention of scholars; the misfortunes of the land have been treated rather as an accident, than as an essential, of the Grail story, entirely subordinate in interest to the *dramatis personae* of the tale, or the objects, Lance and Grail, round which the action revolves. As a matter of fact I believe that the 'Waste Land' is really the very heart of our problem; a rightful appreciation of its position and significance will place us in possession of the clue which will lead us safely through the most bewildering mazes of the fully developed tale.

V. Medieval and Modern Forms of Nature Ritual

Since the above pages were written Dr Frazer has notified the discovery of a second African parallel, equally complete, and striking. In *Folk-Lore* (Vol. XXVI.) he prints, under the title *A Priest-King in Nigeria*, a communication received from Mr P. A. Talbot, District Commissioner in S. Nigeria. The writer states that the dominant Ju-Ju of Elele, a town in the N.W. of the Degema district, is a Priest-King, elected for a term of seven years. "The whole prosperity of the town, especially the fruitfulness of farm, byre, and marriage-bed, was linked with his life. Should he fall sick it entailed famine and grave disaster upon the inhabitants." So soon as a successor is appointed the former holder of the dignity is reported to 'die for himself.' Previous to the introduction of ordered government it is admitted that at any time during his seven years' term of office the Priest might be put to death by any man sufficiently strong and resourceful, consequently it is only on the rarest occasions (in fact only one such is recorded) that the Ju-Ju ventures to leave his compound. At the same time the riches derived [p61] from the offerings of the people are so considerable that there is never a lack of candidates for the office.

From this and the evidence cited above it would appear that the institution was widely spread in Africa, and at the same time it affords a striking proof in support of the essential soundness of Dr Frazer's interpretation of the Priest of Nemi, an interpretation which has been violently attacked in certain quarters, very largely on the ground that no one would be found willing to accept an office involving such direct danger to life. The above evidence shows clearly that not only does such an office exist, but that it is by no means an unpopular post. [p62]

VI. The Symbols

Summary of results of previous enquiry. The Medieval Stage. *Grail romances probably contain record of secret ritual of a Fertility cult. The Symbols of the cult—Cup, Lance, Sword, Stone, or Dish. Plea for treating Symbols as a related group not as isolated units. Failure to do so probably cause of unsatisfactory result of long research. Essential to recognize Grail story as an original whole and to treat it in its* ensemble *aspect. We must differentiate between origin and accretion. Instances.* The Legend of Longinus. *Lance and Cup not associated in Christian Art. Evidence. The* Spear *of Eastern Liturgies only a* Knife. The Bleeding Lance. *Treasures of the Tuatha de Danann. Correspond as a group with Grail Symbols. Difficulty of equating Cauldron-Grail. Probably belong to a different line of tradition. Instances given. Real significance of Lance and Cup. Well known as Life Symbols. The Samurai. Four Symbols also preserved as Suits of the Tarot. Origin of Tarot discussed. Probably reached Europe from the East. Use of the Symbols in Magic. Probable explanation of these various appearances to be found in fact that associated group were at one time symbols of a Fertility cult. Further evidence to be examined.*

In the previous chapters we have discussed the Grail Legend from a general, rather than a specific, point of view; *i.e.,* we have endeavoured to ascertain what was the real character of the task imposed upon the hero, and what the nature and value of his achievement.

We have been led to the conclusion that that achievement was, in the first instance, of an altruistic character—it was no question of advantages, temporal or spiritual, which should accrue to the Quester himself, but rather of definite benefits to be won for others, the freeing of a ruler and his land from the dire results of a punishment which, falling upon the King, was fraught with the most disastrous consequences for his kingdom.

We have found, further, that this close relation between the ruler and his land, which resulted in the ill of one becoming the calamity of all, is no mere literary invention, proceeding from the fertile imagination of a twelfth century court poet, but a deeply rooted popular belief, of practically immemorial antiquity and inexhaustible vitality; we can trace

VI. The Symbols

it back thousands of years before the Christian era, we find it fraught with decisions of life and death to-day.

Further, we find in that belief a tendency to express itself in certain ceremonial practices, which retain in a greater or less degree the character of the ritual observances of which they are the survival. Mr E. K. Chambers, in *The Mediaeval Stage,* remarks: "If the comparative study of Religion proves anything it is, that the traditional beliefs [p63] and customs of the mediaeval or modern peasant are in nine cases out of ten but the *detritus* of heathen mythology and heathen worship, enduring with but little external change in the shadow of a hostile faith. This is notably true of the village festivals and their *ludi.* Their full significance only appears when they are regarded as fragments of forgotten cults, the naïve cults addressed by a primitive folk to the beneficent deities of field and wood and river, or the shadowy populace of its own dreams."[1] We may, I think, take it that we have established at least the possibility that in the Grail romances we possess, in literary form, an example of the *detritus* above referred to, the fragmentary record of the secret ritual of a Fertility cult.

Having reached this hypothetical conclusion, our next step must be to examine the Symbols of this cult, the group of mysterious objects which forms the central point of the action, a true understanding of the nature of these objects being as essential for our success as interpreters of the story as it was for the success of the Quester in days of old. We must ask whether these objects, the Grail itself, whether Cup or Dish; the Lance; the Sword; the Stone—one and all invested with a certain atmosphere of awe, credited with strange virtues, with sanctity itself, will harmonize with the proposed solution, will range themselves fitly and fairly within the framework of this hypothetical ritual.

That they should do so is a matter of capital importance; were it otherwise the theory advanced might well, as some of my critics have maintained, 'never get beyond the region of ingenious speculation,' but it is precisely upon the fact that this theory of origin, and so far as criticism has gone, this theory alone, does permit of a natural and unforced interpretation of these related symbols that I rely as one of the most convincing proofs of the correctness of my hypothesis.

[p64] Before commencing the investigation there is one point which I would desire to emphasize, *viz.,* the imperative necessity for treating

---

1. *Op. cit.* Vol. I. p. 94.

VI. The Symbols

the Symbols or Talismans, call them what we will, on the same principle as we have treated the incidents of the story, *i.e.*, as a connected whole. That they be not separated the one *from* the other, and made the subject of independent treatment, but that they be regarded in their relation the one *to* the other, and that no theory of origin be held admissible which does not allow for that relation as a primitive and indispensable factor. It may be the modern tendency to specialize which is apt to blind scholars to the essential importance of regarding their object of study as a whole, that fosters in them a habit of focussing their attention upon that one point or incident of the story which lends itself to treatment in their special line of study, and which induces them to minimize, or ignore, those elements which lie outside their particular range. But, whatever the cause, it is indubitable that this method of 'criticism by isolation' has been, and is, one of the main factors which have operated in retarding the solution of the Grail problem.

So long as critics of the story will insist on pulling it into little pieces, selecting one detail here, another there, for study and elucidation, so long will the *ensemble* result be chaotic and unsatisfactory. We shall continue to have a number of monographs, more or less scholarly in treatment—one dealing with the Grail as a Food-providing talisman, and that alone; another with the Grail as a vehicle of spiritual sustenance. One that treats of the Lance as a Pagan weapon, and nothing more; another that regards it as a Christian relic, and nothing less. At one moment the object of the study will be the Fisher King, without any relation to the symbols he guards, or the land he rules; at the next it will be the relation of the Quester to the Fisher [p65] King, without any explanation of the tasks assigned to him by the story. The result obtained is always quite satisfactory to the writer, often plausible, sometimes in a measure sound, but it would defy the skill of the most synthetic genius to co-ordinate the results thus obtained, and combine them in one harmonious whole. They are like pieces of a puzzle, each of which has been symmetrically cut and trimmed, till they lie side by side, un-fitting, and un-related.

And we have been pursuing this method for over fifty years, and are still, apparently, content to go on, each devoting attention to the symmetrical perfection of his own little section of the puzzle, quite indifferent to the fact that our neighbour is in possession of an equally neatly trimmed fragment, which entirely refuses to fit in with our own!

VI. The Symbols

Is it not time that we should frankly admit the unsatisfactory results of these years of labour, and honestly face the fact that while we now have at our disposal an immense mass of interesting and suggestive material often of high value, we have failed, so far, to formulate a conclusion which, by embracing and satisfying the manifold conditions of the problem, will command general acceptance? And if this failure be admitted, may not its cause be sought in the faulty method which has failed to recognize in the Grail story an original whole, in which the parts—the action, the actors, the Symbols, the result to be obtained, incident, and intention—stood from the very first in intimate relation the one to the other? That while in process of utilization as a literary theme these various parts have suffered modification and accretion from this, or that, side, the problem of the *ultimate* source remains thereby unaffected?

Such a reversal of method as I suggest will, I submit, not only provide us with a critical solution capable of general acceptance, but it will also enable us to utilize, and appreciate at their due value, the result of researches which [p66] at the present moment appear to be mutually destructive the one of the other. Thus, while the purely Folk-lore interpretation of the Grail and Lance excludes the Christian origin, and the theory of the exclusively Christian origin negatives the Folk-lore, the pre-existence of these symbols in a popular ritual setting would admit, indeed would invite, later accretion alike from folk belief and ecclesiastical legend.

We are the gainers by any light that can possibly be thrown upon the process of development of the story, but studies of the separate symbols while they may, and do, afford valuable *data* for determining the character and period of certain accretions, should not be regarded as supplying proof of the origin of the related group.

Reference to some recent studies in the Legend will make my meaning clear. A reviewer of my small *Quest of the Holy Grail* volume remarked that I appeared to be ignorant of Miss Peebles's study *The Legend of Longinus* "which materially strengthens the evidence for the Christian origin."[2] Now this is precisely what, in my view, the study in question, which I knew and possessed, does not do. As evidence for the fact that the Grail legend has taken over certain features derived from the popular 'Longinus' story (which, incidentally, no one disputed), the

---

2. *The Legend of Longinus*, R. J. Peebles (Bryn Mawr College monographs, Vol. IX.).

VI. The Symbols

essay is, I hold, sound, and valuable; as affording material for determining the source of the Grail story, it is, on the other hand, entirely without value.

On the principle laid down above no theory which purports to be explanatory of the source of one symbol can be held satisfactory in a case where that symbol does not stand alone. We cannot accept for the Grail story a theory of origin which concerns itself with the Lance, as independent [p67] of the Grail. In the study referred to the author has been at immense pains to examine the different versions of the 'Longinus' legend, and to trace its development in literature; in no single instance do we find Longinus and his Lance associated with a Cup or Vase, receptacle of the Sacred Blood.

The plain fact is that in Christian art and tradition Lance and Cup are not associated symbols. The Lance or Spear, as an instrument of the Passion, is found in conjunction with the Cross, Nails, Sponge, and Crown of Thorns, (anyone familiar with the wayside Crosses of Catholic Europe will recognize this), not with the Chalice of the Mass.[3] This latter is associated with the Host, or *Agnus Dei*. Still less is the Spear to be found in connection with the Grail in its Food-providing form of a Dish.

No doubt to this, critics who share the views of Golther and Burdach will object, "but what of the Byzantine Mass? Do we not there find a Spear connected with the Chalice?"[4]

I very much doubt whether we do—the so-called 'Holy Spear' of the Byzantine, and present Greek, liturgy is simply a small silver spear-shaped knife, nor can I discover that it was ever anything else. I have made careful enquiries of liturgical scholars, and consulted editions of Oriental liturgies, but I can find no evidence that the knife (the use of which is to divide the Loaf which, in the Oriental rite, corresponds to the Wafer of the Occidental, in a manner symbolically corresponding to the Wounds actually inflicted on the Divine Victim) was ever other than what it is to-day. It seems obvious, from the method of employment, that an [p68] actual Spear could hardly have been used, it would have been an impossibly unwieldy instrument for the purpose.

---

3. I discussed this point with Miss Lucy Broadwood, Secretary of the Folk-Song Society, who has made sketches of these Crosses, and she entirely agrees with me. In my *Quest of the Holy Grail*, pp. 54 *et seq.*, I have pointed out the absolute dearth of ecclesiastical tradition with regard to the story of Joseph and the Grail.

4. Cf. *Littaturzeitung*, XXIV. (1903), p. 2821.

VI. The Symbols

Nor is the 'procession' in which the elements are carried from the Chapel of the Prothēsis to the Sanctuary of a public character comparable with that of the Grail castle; the actual ceremony of the Greek Mass takes place, of course, behind a veil. A point of considerable interest, however, is, what caused this difference in the Byzantine liturgy? What were the influences which led to the introduction of a feature unknown to the Western rite? If, as the result of the evidence set forth in these pages, the ultimate origin of the Grail story be finally accepted as deriving from a prehistoric ritual possessing elements of extraordinary persistence and vitality, then the *mise-en-scène* of that story is older than the Byzantine ritual. Students of the subject are well aware that the tradition of ancient pre-Christian rites and ceremonies lingered on in the East long after they had been banished by the more practical genius of the West. It may well prove that so far from the Grail story being a reminiscence of the Byzantine rite, that rite itself has been affected by a ritual of which the Grail legend preserves a fragmentary record.

In my view a Christian origin for Lance and Cup, as associated symbols, has not been made out; still less can it be postulated for Lance and Cup as members of an extended group, including Dish, Sword, and Stone.

On this point Professor Brown's attempt to find in Irish tradition the origin of the Grail symbols is distinctly more satisfactory.[5]

I cannot accept as decisive the solution proposed, which seems to me to be open to much the same criticism as that which would find in the Lance the Lance of Longinus—both are occupied with details, rather than with *ensemble;* [p69] both would find their justification as offering evidence of accretion, rather than of origin; neither can provide us with the required *mise-en-scène*.

But Professor Brown's theory is the more sound in that he is really dealing with a group of associated symbols; in his view Lance and Grail alike belong to the treasures of the Tuatha de Danann (that legendary race of Irish ancestors, who were at once gods and kings), and therefore *ab initio* belong together. But while I should, on the whole, accept the affiliation of the two groups, and believe that the treasures of the Tuatha de Danann really correspond to the symbols displayed in the hall of the Grail castle, I cannot consider that the one is the origin of the other. There is one very fundamental difference, the importance

---

5. Cf. *The Bleeding Lance,* A. C. L. Brown.

VI. The Symbols

of which I cannot ignore, but which, I believe, has hitherto escaped Professor Brown's attention.

The object corresponding to the Grail itself is the cauldron of the Dagda, "No company ever went from it unthankful" (or 'unsatisfied').[6]

Now this can in no sense be considered as a Cup, or Vase, nor is it the true parallel to a Dish. The connection with the Grail is to be found solely and exclusively in the food-providing properties ascribed to both. But even here the position is radically different; the impression we derive from the Irish text and its analogous parallels is that of size (it is also called a 'tub'), and inexhaustible content, it is a cauldron of plenty.[7] Now, neither of these qualities can be postulated of the Grail; whatever its form, Cup or Dish, it can easily be borne (in uplifted hands, *entre ses mains hautement porte*) by a maiden, which certainly could not be postulated of a cauldron! Nor is there any proof [p70] that the Vessel itself contained the food with which the folk of the Grail castle were regaled; the texts rather point to the conclusion that the appearance of the Grail synchronized with a mysterious supply of food of a choice and varied character. There is never any hint that the folk feed *from the Grail;* the only suggestion of such feeding is in the 'Oiste,' by which the father of the Fisher King (or the King himself) is nourished.

In certain texts the separation of the two is clearly brought out; in *Joseph of Arimathea*, for instance, the Fish caught by Brons is to be placed at one end of the table, the Grail at the other. In Gawain's adventure at the Grail castle, in the prose *Lancelot*, as the Grail is carried through the hall "forthwith were the tables replenished with the choicest meats in the world," but the table before Gawain remains void and bare.[8] I submit that while the Grail is in certain phases a food-supplying talisman it is not one of the same character as the cauldrons of plenty; also while the food supply of these latter has the marked characteristic of *quantity*, that of the Grail is remarkable rather for *quality*, its choice character is always insisted upon.

The perusal of Professor Brown's subsequent study, *Notes on Celtic Cauldrons of Plenty and The Land-Beneath-the-Waves*, has confirmed me in my view that these special objects belong to another line of tradition altogether; that which deals with an inexhaustible submarine source of life, examples of which will be found in the 'Sampo' of the Finnish

---

6. Cf. Brown, *op. cit.* p. 35; also A. Nutt, *Studies in the Legend of the Holy Grail*, p. 184.
7. Cf. Brown, *Notes on Celtic Cauldrons of Plenty*, p. 237.
8. Cf. *Queste*, Malory, Book XIII. Chap. 7, where the effect is the same.

VI. The Symbols

Kalewala, and the ever-grinding mills of popular folk-tale.[9] The fundamental idea here seems to be that of the origin of all Life from Water, a very ancient idea, but one which, though akin to the Grail tradition, is yet quite [p71] distinct therefrom. The study of this special theme would, I believe, produce valuable results.[10]

On the whole, I am of the opinion that the treasures of the Tuatha de Danann and the symbols of the Grail castle go back to a common original, but that they have developed on different lines; in the process of this development one 'Life' symbol has been exchanged for another.[11]

But Lance and Cup (or Vase) were in truth connected together in a symbolic relation long ages before the institution of Christianity, or the birth of Celtic tradition. They are sex symbols of immemorial antiquity and world-wide diffusion, the Lance, or Spear, representing the Male, the Cup, or Vase, the Female, reproductive energy.[12]

Found in juxtaposition, the Spear upright in the Vase, as in the *Bleheris* and *Balin* (both, be it noted, Gawain) forms, their signification is admitted by all familiar with 'Life' symbolism, and they are absolutely in place as forming part of a ritual dealing with the processes of life and reproductive vitality.[13]

[p72] A most remarkable and significant use of these symbols is found in the ceremonies of the Samurai, the noble warrior caste of Japan. The aspirant was (I am told still is) admitted into the caste at the age of fourteen, when he was given over to the care of a guardian at least fifteen years his senior, to whom he took an oath of obedience, which was sworn upon the Spear. He remained celibate during the period covered by the oath. When the Samurai was held to have attained the degree of responsibility which would fit him for the full duties of a

---

9. Cf. *Germanische Elben und Götter beim Estenvolke,* L. von Schroeder (Wien, 1906).

10. I suggested this point in correspondence with Dr Brugger, who agreed with me that it was worth working out.

11. Before leaving the discussion of Professor Brown's theory, I would draw attention to a serious error made by the author of *The Legend of Longinus.* On p. 191, she blames Professor Brown for postulating the destructive qualities of the Lance, on the strength of 'an unsupported passage' in the 'Mons' MS., whereas the Montpellier text says that the Lance shall bring peace. Unfortunately, it is this latter version which is unsupported, all the MSS., without even excepting B.N. 1429, which as a rule agrees with Montpellier, give the 'destructive' version.

12. Cf. Dulaure, *Des Divinités Génératrices,* p. 77. Also additional chapter to last edition by Van Gennep, p. 333; L. von Schroeder, *Mysterium und Mimus,* pp. 279–80, for symbolic use of the Spear. McCulloch, *Religion of the Celts,* p. 302, suggests that it is not impossible that the cauldron = Hindu *yoni,* which of course would bring it into line with the above suggested meaning of the Grail. I think however that the real significance of the cauldron is that previously indicated.

13. It is interesting to note that this relative position of Lance and Grail lingers on in late and fully Christianized versions; cf. Sommer, *The Quest of the Holy Grail, Romania,* XXXVI. p. 575.

VI. The Symbols

citizen, a second solemn ceremony was held, at which he was released from his previous vows, and presented with the Cup; he was henceforth free to marry, but intercourse with women previous to this ceremony was at one time punishable with death.[14]

That Lance and Cup are, *outside* the Grail story, 'Life' symbols, and have been such from time immemorial, is a fact; why, then should they not retain that character inside the framework of that story? An acceptance of this interpretation will not only be in harmony with the general *mise-en-scène*, but it will also explain finally and satisfactorily, (*a*) the dominant position frequently assigned to the Lance; (*b*) the fact that, while the Lance is borne in procession by a youth, the Grail is carried by a maiden—the sex of the bearer corresponds with the symbol borne.[15]

But Lance and Cup, though the most prominent of the Symbols, do not always appear alone, but are associated [p73] with other objects, the significance of which is not always apparent. Thus the Dish, which is sometimes the form assumed by the Grail itself, at other times appears as a *tailléor,* or carving platter of silver, carried in the same procession as the Grail; or there may be two small *tailléors;* finally, a Sword appears in varying *rôles* in the story.

I have already referred to the fact, first pointed out by the late Mr Alfred Nutt,[16] that the four treasures of the Tuatha de Danann correspond generally with the group of symbols found in the Grail romances; this correspondence becomes the more interesting in view of the fact that these mysterious Beings are now recognized as alike Demons of Fertility and Lords of Life. As Mr Nutt subsequently pointed out, the 'Treasures' may well be, Sword and Cauldron certainly are, 'Life' symbols.

Of direct connection between these Celtic objects and the Grail story there is no trace; as remarked above, we have no Irish Folk or Hero tale at all corresponding to the Legend; the relation must, therefore, go back beyond the date of formation of these tales, *i.e.,* it must be considered as one of origin rather than of dependence.

---

14. My informant on this point was a scholar, resident in Japan, who gave me the facts within his personal knowledge. I referred the question to Prof. Basil Hall Chamberlain, who wrote in answer that he had not himself met with the practice but that the Samurai ceremonies differed in different provinces, and my informant might well be correct.

15. This explanation has at least the merit of simplicity as compared with that proposed by the author of *The Legend of Longinus,* pp. 209 *et seq.,* which would connect the feature with an obscure heretical practice of the early Irish church. It would also meet Professor Brown's very reasonable objections, *The Bleeding Lance,* p. 8; cf. also remarks by Baist quoted in the foot-note above.

16. Cf. my *Legend of Sir Perceval,* Vol. II. pp. 314-315, note.

VI. The Symbols

But we have further evidence that these four objects do, in fact, form a special group entirely independent of any appearance in Folk-lore or Romance. They exist to-day as the four suits of the Tarot.

Students of the Grail texts, whose attention is mainly occupied with Medieval Literature, may not be familiar with the word Tarot, or aware of its meaning. It is the name given to a pack of cards, seventy-eight in number, of which twenty-two are designated as the 'Keys.'

These cards are divided into four suits, which correspond with those of the ordinary cards; they are:

Cup (Chalice, or Goblet)—Hearts.
[p74] Lance (Wand, or Sceptre)—Diamonds.
Sword—Spades.
Dish (Circles, or Pentangles, the form varies)—Clubs.

To-day the Tarot has fallen somewhat into disrepute, being principally used for purposes of divination, but its origin, and precise relation to our present playing-cards, are questions of considerable antiquarian interest. Were these cards the direct parents of our modern pack, or are they entirely distinct therefrom?[17]

Some writers are disposed to assign a very high antiquity to the Tarot. Traditionally, it is said to have been brought from Egypt; there is no doubt that parallel designs and combinations are to be found in the surviving decorations of Egyptian temples, notably in the astronomic designs on the ceiling of one of the halls of the palace of Medinet Abou, which is supported on twenty-two columns (a number corresponding to the 'keys' of the Tarot), and also repeated in a calendar sculptured on the southern façade of the same building, under a sovereign of the XXIII dynasty. This calendar is supposed to have been connected with the periodic rise and fall of the waters of the Nile.[18]

The Tarot has also been connected with an ancient Chinese monument, traditionally erected in commemoration of the drying up of the waters of the Deluge by Yao. The face of this monument is divided up into small sections corresponding in size and number with the cards

---

17. Mr A. E. Waite, who has published a book on the subject, informs me that the 17 cards preserved in the Bibliothèque du Roi (Bibl. Nationale?) as specimens of the work of the painter Charles Gringonneur, are really Tarots.
18. Falconnier, in a brochure on *Les XXII Lames Hermétiques du Tarot*, gives reproductions of these Egyptian paintings.

VI. The Symbols

of the Tarot, and bearing characters which have, so far, not been deciphered.

What is certain is that these cards are used to-day by the Gipsies for purposes of divination, and the opinion of those [p75] who have studied the subject is that there is some real ground for the popular tradition that they were introduced into Europe by this mysterious people.

In a very interesting article on the subject in *The Journal of the Gipsy-Lore Society*,[19] Mr De la Hoste Ranking examines closely into the figures depicted on the various cards, and the names attached to the suits by the Gipsies. He comes to the conclusion that many of the words are of Sanskrit, or Hindustani, origin, and sums up the result of the internal evidence as follows: "The Tarot was introduced by a race speaking an Indian dialect. The figure known as 'The Pope' shows the influence of the Orthodox Eastern Faith; he is bearded, and carries the Triple Cross. The card called 'The King' represents a figure with the head-dress of a Russian Grand-Duke, and a shield bearing the Polish eagle. Thus the people who used the Tarot must have been familiar with a country where the Orthodox Faith prevailed, and which was ruled by princes of the status of Grand-Dukes. The general result seems to point to a genuine basis for the belief that the Tarot was introduced into Europe from the East."

As regards the group of symbols in general, Mr W. B. Yeats, whose practical acquaintance with Medieval and Modern Magic is well known, writes: "(1) Cup, Lance, Dish, Sword, in slightly varying forms, have never lost their mystic significance, and are to-day a part of magical operations. (2) The memory kept by the four suits of the Tarot, Cup, Lance, Sword, Pentangle (Dish), is an esoterical notation for fortune-telling purposes."[20]

[p76] But if the connection with the Egyptian and Chinese monuments, referred to above, is genuine, the original use of the 'Tarot' would seem to have been, not to foretell the Future in general, but to predict the rise and fall of the waters which brought fertility to the land.

Such use would bring the 'Suits' into line with the analogous symbols of the Grail castle and the treasures of the Tuatha de Danann, both of which we have seen to be connected with the embodiment of the reproductive forces of Nature.

---

19. *Journal of the Gipsy-Lore Society*, Vol. II. New Series, pp. 14–37.
20. From a private letter. The ultimate object of Magic in all ages was, and is, to obtain control of the sources of Life. Hence, whatever was the use of these objects (of which I know nothing), their appearance in this connection is significant.

VI. The Symbols

If it is difficult to establish a direct connection between these two latter, it is practically impossible to argue any connection between either group and the 'Tarot'; no one has as yet ventured to suggest the popularity of the works of Chrétien de Troyes among the Gipsies! Yet the correspondence can hardly be fortuitous. I would suggest that, while Lance and Cup, in their associated form, are primarily symbols of Human Life energy, in conjunction with others they formed a group of 'Fertility' symbols, connected with a very ancient ritual, of which fragmentary survivals alone have been preserved to us.

This view will, I believe, receive support from the evidence of the ceremonial Dances which formed so important a part of 'Fertility' ritual, and which survive in so many places to this day. If we find these symbols reappearing as a part of these dances, their real significance can hardly be disputed. [p77]

VII. The Sword Dance

Relation of Sword Dance, Morris Dance, and Mumming Play. Their Ceremonial origin now admitted by scholars. Connected with seasonal Festivals and Fertility Ritual. Earliest Sword Dancers, the Maruts. Von Schroeder, Mysterium und Mimus. *Discussion of their nature and functions. The Kouretes. Character of their dance. Miss J. E. Harrison,* Themis. *The Korybantes. Dance probably sacrificial in origin. The Salii. Dramatic element in their dance. Mars, as Fertility god. Mamurius Veturius. Anna Perenna. Character of dance seasonal. Modern British survivals. The Sword Dance. Mostly preserved in North. Variants. Mr E. K. Chambers,* The Medieval Stage. *The Mumming Plays. Description. Characters. Recognized as representing Death and Revival of Vegetation Deity. Dr Jevons,* Masks and the Origin of the Greek Drama. *Morris Dances. No dramatic element. Costume of character significant. Possible survival of theriomorphic origin. Elaborate character of figures in each group. Symbols employed. The Pentangle. The Chalice. Present form shows dislocation. Probability that three groups were once a combined whole and Symbols united. Evidence strengthens view advanced in last Chapter. Symbols originally a group connected with lost form of Fertility Ritual. Possible origin of Grail Knights to be found in Sword Dancers.*

The subject we are now about to consider is one which of late years has attracted considerable attention, and much acute criticism has been expended on the question of its origin and significance. Valuable material has been collected, but the studies, so far, have been individual, and independent, the much needed *travail d'ensemble* has not yet appeared.

One definite result has, however, been obtained; it is now generally admitted that the so-called Sword Dances, with the closely related Morris Dances, and Mumming Plays, are not mere survivals of martial exercises, an inherited tradition from our warrior ancestors, but were solemn, ceremonial (in some cases there is reason to believe, Initiatory) dances, performed at stated seasons of the year, and directly and intimately connected with the ritual of which we have treated in previous chapters, a ritual designed to preserve and promote the regular and ordered sequence of the processes of Nature. And here, again, our enquiry

VII. The Sword Dance

must begin with the very earliest records of our race, with the traditions of our Aryan forefathers.

The earliest recorded Sword Dancers are undoubtedly the Maruts, those swift-footed youths in gleaming armour who are the faithful attendants on the great god, Indra. Professor von Schroeder, in *Mysterium und Mimus*, describes them thus:[1] they are a group of youths of equal age and [p78] identical parentage, they are always depicted as attired in the same manner, "Sie sind reich und prächtig geschmückt, mit Goldschmuck auf der Brust, mit Spangen an den Händen, Hirschfelle tragen sie auf den Schultern. Vor allem aber sind sie kriegerisch gerüstet, funkelnde Speere tragen sie in den Händen, oder auch goldene Äxte. Goldene Harnische oder Mäntel umhüllen sie, goldene Helme schimmern auf ihren Häuptern. Nie erscheinen sie ohne Wehr und Waffen. Es scheint dass diese ganz und gar zu ihren Wesen gehören."

The writer goes on to remark that when such a band of armed youths, all of the same age, always closely associated with each other, are represented as Dancers, and always as Dancers—"dann haben wir unabweislich das Bild eines Waffentanzes vor unseren Augen"—and Professor von Schroeder is undoubtedly right.

Constantly throughout the *Rig-Veda* the Maruts are referred to as Dancers, "gold-bedecked Dancers," "with songs of praise they danced round the spring," "When ye Maruts spear-armed dance, they (*i.e.*, the Heavens) stream together like waves of water."[2]

And a special moment for the dance of these glorious youths "ever young brothers of whom none is elder, none younger"[3] is that of the ceremonial sacrifice, "sie tanzen auf ihren himmlischen Bahnen, sie springen und tanzen auch bei den Opferfesten der Menschen."[4]

The Maruts, as said above, were conceived of as the companions of Indra, and helpers in his fight against his monstrous adversaries; thus they were included in the sacrifices offered in honour of that Deity.

One of the most striking of the ritual Dramas reconstructed by Professor von Schroeder is that which represents [p79] Indra as indignantly rejecting the claim of the Maruts to share in such a sacrifice; they had failed to support him in his conflict with the dragon, Vritra, when by

---

1. *Mysterium und Mimus*, p. 50. This work contains a most valuable and interesting study of the Maruts, and the kindred groups of Sword Dancers.
2. *Op. cit.* pp. 47 *et seq.*
3. *Rig-Veda*, Vol. III. p. 337.
4. *Mysterium und Mimus*, p. 48.

his might he loosed the waters, 'neither to-day, nor to-morrow' will he accept a sacrifice of which they share the honour; it requires all the tact of the Offerer, Agastya, and of the leader of the Maruts to soothe the offended Deity.[5]

Here I would draw attention to the significant fact that the feat celebrated is that to which I have previously referred as the most famous of all the deeds attributed to Indra, the 'Freeing of the Waters,' and here the Maruts are associated with the god.

But they were also the objects of independent worship. They were specially honoured at the Câturmâsya, the feasts which heralded the commencement of the three seasons of four months each into which the Indian year was divided, a division corresponding respectively to the hot, the cool, and the wet, season. The advantages to be derived from the worship of the Maruts may be deduced from the following extracts from the *Rig-Veda*, which devotes more than thirty hymns to their praise. "The adorable Maruts, armed with bright lances, and cuirassed with golden breastplates, enjoy vigorous existence; may the cars of the quick-moving Maruts arrive for our good." "Bringers of rain and fertility, shedding water, augmenting food." "Givers of abundant food." "Your milchkine are never dry." "We invoke the food-laden chariots of the Maruts."[6] Nothing can be clearer than this; the Maruts are 'daimons' of fertility, the worship of whom will secure the necessary supply of the fruits of the earth.

The close association of the Maruts with Indra, the great Nature god, has led some scholars to regard them as personifications [p80] of a special manifestation of Nature, as Wind-gods. Professor von Schroeder points out that their father was the god Rudra, later known as Çiva, the god of departed souls, and of fruitfulness, *i.e.*, a Chthonian deity, and suggests that the Maruts represent the "in Wind und Sturm dahinjagende Seelenschar."[7] He points out that the belief in a troop of departed souls is an integral part of Aryan tradition, and classifies such belief under four main headings.

1. Under the form of a spectral Hunt, the Wild Huntsman well known in European Folk-lore. He equates this with Dionysus Zagreus, and the Hunt of Artemis-Hekate.

---

5. *Op. cit., Indra, die Maruts, und Agastya*, pp. 91 et seq.
6. *Rig-Veda*, Vol. III. pp. 331, 334, 335, 337.
7. *Mysterium un Mimus*, p. 121.

VII. The Sword Dance

2. That of a spectral Army, the souls of warriors slain in fight. The Northern *Einherier* belong to this class, and the many traditions of spectral combats, and ghostly battles, heard, but not seen.

3. The conception of a host of women in a condition of ecstatic exaltation bordering on madness, who appear girdled with snakes, or hissing like snakes, tear living animals to pieces, and devour the flesh. The classic examples here are the Greek Maenads, and the Indian Senâs, who accompany Rudra.

4. The conception of a train of theriomorphic, phallic, demons of fertility, with their companion group of fair women. Such are the Satyrs and Nymphs of Greek, the Gandharvas and Apsaras of Indian, Mythology.

To these four main groups may be added the belief among Germanic peoples, also among the Letts, in a troop of Child Souls.

These four groups, in more or less modified forms, appear closely connected with the dominant Spirit of Vegetation, by whatever name that spirit may be known.

According to von Schroeder there was, among the Aryan peoples generally, a tendency to regard the dead as assuming [p81] the character of daimons of fertility. This view the learned Professor considers to be at the root of the annual celebrations in honour of the Departed, the 'Feast of Souls,' which characterized the commencement of the winter season, and is retained in the Catholic conception of November as the month of the Dead.[8]

In any case we may safely conclude that the Maruts, represented as armed youths, were worshipped as deities of fruitfulness; that their dances were of a ceremonial character; and that they were, by nature and origin, closely connected with spirits of fertility of a lower order, such as the Gandharvas. It also appears probable that, if the Dramas of which traces have been preserved in the *Rig-Veda*, were, as scholars are now of opinion, once actually represented, the mythological conception of the Maruts must have found its embodiment in youths, most probably of the priestly caste, who played their *rôle*, and actually danced the ceremonial Sword Dance. As von Schroeder says, "Kein Zweifel dass sie dabei von menschlichen, resp. priesterlichen Personen dargestellt wurden."[9]

---

8. *Vollendung des Arische Mysterium*, p. 13. The introductory section of this book, containing a study of early Aryan belief, and numerous references to modern survivals, is both interesting and valuable. The latter part, a panegyric on the Wagnerian drama, is of little importance.

9. *Mysterium und Mimus*, p. 131.

VII. The Sword Dance

When we turn from the early Aryan to the classic Greek period we find in the Kouretes, and in a minor degree in the Korybantes, a parallel so extraordinarily complete, alike in action and significance, that an essential identity of origin appears to be beyond doubt.

The Kouretes were, as their name indicates, a band of armed youths, of semi-divine origin, "Kureten sind von Haus aus halb-göttlich dämonische Wesen nicht nur menschliche Priester, oder deren mythische Vertreter."[10] Again, [p82] they are to be considered as "elementare Urwesen," and as such of "Göttliche Abkunft."[11] Preller regards them as "Dämonen des Gebirgs,"[12] while a passage from Hesiod, quoted by Strabo, equates them with nymphs and satyrs, *i.e.*, fertility demons.[13]

When we remember that the Gandharvas are the Indian equivalent of the Satyrs the close parallel between the Maruts and the Kouretes, both alike bands of armed youths, of elementary origin, and connected with beings of a lower grade, is striking.

The home of the Kouretes was in Crete, where they were closely associated with the worship of the goddess Rhea. The traditional story held that, in order to preserve the infant Zeus from destruction by his father Kronos, they danced their famous Sword Dance round the babe, overpowering his cries by the clash of their weapons.

Their dance was by some writers identified with the Pyrrhic dance, first performed by Athene, in honour of her victory over the Giants, and taught by her to the Kouretes. It had however, as we shall see, a very distinct aim and purpose, and one in no way connected with warlike ends.

In Miss J. E. Harrison's deeply interesting volume, *Themis*,[14] she gives the translation of a fragmentary *Hymn of the Kouretes*, discovered among the ruins of a temple in Crete, a text which places beyond all doubt the fact that, however mythical in origin, the Kouretes, certainly, had actual human representatives, and that while in the case of the Maruts there may be a question as to whether their dance actually took place, or not, so far as the Kouretes are concerned there can be no such doubt.

[p83] The following is the text as preserved to us; the slabs on which it is inscribed are broken, and there are consequent lacunae.

---

10. Cf. Röscher's *Lexikon*, under heading *Kureten*.
11. *Op. cit.*
12. Cf. Preller, *Graechishe Mythologie*, p. 134.
13. Quoted by Preller, p. 654.
14. *Themis*, A Study in Greek Social Origins (Cambridge, 1912), pp. 6 *et seq.*

VII. The Sword Dance

"Io, Kouros most great, I give thee hail, Kronian, lord of all that is wet and gleaming, thou art come at the head of thy Daimones. To Dikte for the year, Oh march, and rejoice in the dance and song,

"That we make to thee with harps and pipes mingled together, and sing as we come to a stand at thy well-fenced altar.

"Io, &c.

"For here the shielded Nurturers took thee, a child immortal, from Rhea, and with noise of beating feet hid thee away.

"Io, &c.

"And the Horai began to be fruitful year by year, and Dikè to possess mankind and all wild living things were held about by wealth-loving Peace.

"Io, &c.

"And the Horai began to be fruitful year by year, and Dikè to possess mankind and all wild living things were held about by wealth-loving Peace.

"Io, &c.

"To us also leap for full jars, and leap for fleecy flocks, and leap for fields of fruit, and for hives to bring increase.

"Io, &c.

"Leap for our cities, and leap for our sea-borne ships, and leap for our young citizens, and for goodly Themis."

This hymn is most extraordinarily interesting; it places beyond all doubt what was the root intention of this ceremonial dance; it was designed to stimulate the reproductive energies of Nature, to bring into being fruitful fields, and vineyards, plenteous increase in the flocks and herds, and to people the cities with youthful citizens; and the god is entreated not merely to accept the worship offered, but himself to join in the action which shall produce such fair results, to leap for full jars, and fleecy flocks, and for youthful citizens.

[p84] The importance of movement, notably of what we may call group movement, as a stimulant to natural energies, is thoroughly recognized among primitive peoples; with them Dance holds a position equivalent to that which, in more advanced communities, is assigned to Prayer. Professor von Schroeder comments on this, "Es ist merkwürdig genug zu sehen wie das Tanzen nach dem Glauben primitiver Völker eine ähnliche Kraft und Bedeutung zu haben scheint wie man sie auf

VII. The Sword Dance

höheren Kulturstufen dem inbrünstigen Gebete zuschreibt."[15] He cites the case of the Tarahumara Indians of Central America; while the family as a whole are labouring in the fields it is the office of one man to dance uninterruptedly on the dance place of the house; if he fails in his office the labour of the others will be unsuccessful. The one sin of which a Tarahumara Indian is conscious is that of not having danced enough. Miss Harrison, in commenting on the dance of the Kouretes, remarks that among certain savage tribes when a man is too old to dance he hands on his dance to another. He then ceases to exist socially; when he dies his funeral is celebrated with scanty rites; having 'lost his dance' he has ceased to count as a social unit.[16]

With regard to the connection of the Kouretes with the infant Zeus, Miss Harrison makes the interesting suggestion that we have here a trace of an Initiation Dance, analogous to those discussed by M. Van Gennep in his *Rites du Passage*, that the original form was Tĭtăns, 'White-clay men,' which later became Titāns, 'Giants,' and she draws attention to the fact that daubing the skin with white clay is a frequent practice in these primitive rituals. To this I would add that it is a noteworthy fact that in our modern survivals of these dances the performers are, as a rule, dressed in white.

[p85] The above suggestion is of extreme significance, as it brings out the possibility that these celebrations were not only concerned with the prosperity of the community, as a whole, but may also have borne a special, and individual, aspect, and that the idea of Initiation into the group is closely connected with the ceremonial exercise of group functions.

To sum up, there is direct proof that the classic Greeks, in common with their Aryan forefathers, held the conception of a group of Beings, of mythic origin, represented under the form of armed youths, who were noted dancers, and whose activities were closely connected with the processes of Nature. They recognized a relation between these beings, and others of a less highly developed aspect, phallic demons, often of theriomorphic form. Thus the dance of the Kouretes should be considered as a ceremonial ritual action, rather than as a warlike exercise; it was designed to promote the fruitfulness of the earth, not to display the skill of the dancers in the handling of weapons. When we turn to an analogous group, that of the Korybantes, we find that, while presenting

---

15. *Mysterium un Mimus*, p. 23.
16. *Themis*, p. 24.

VII. The Sword Dance

a general parallel to the Kouretes (with whom they are often coupled in mythologies), they also possess certain distinct characteristics, which form a connecting link with other, and later, groups.

The Korybantes were of Phrygian origin, attached to the worship of the goddess Kybele, and Attis, the well-known Phrygian counterpart to the Phoenician Adonis, and originally the most important embodiment of the Vegetation Spirit. Röscher considers them to be of identical origin with the Kouretes, *i.e.*, as elementary 'daimons,' but the Korybantes of Classic art and tradition are undoubtedly human beings. Priests of Kybele, they appear in surviving bas-reliefs in company with that goddess, and with Attis.

The dance of the Korybantes is distinguished from that [p86] of the Kouretes by its less restrained, and more orgiastic character; it was a wild and whirling dance resembling that of the modern Dervishes, accompanied by self-mutilation and an unrhythmic clashing of weapons, designed, some writers think, to overpower the cries of the victims.

If this suggestion be correct it would seem to indicate that, if the Dance of the Kouretes was originally an Initiation Dance, that of the Korybantes was Sacrificial in character. We shall see later that certain features in the surviving forms of the Sword Dance also point in this direction.

The interest of the Korybantes for our investigation lies in the fact that here again we have the Sword Dance in close and intimate connection with the worship of the Vegetation Spirit, and there can be no doubt that here, as elsewhere, it was held to possess a stimulating virtue.

A noticeable point in the modern survivals of these Dances is that the Dance proper is combined with a more or less coherent dramatic action. The Sword Dance originally did not stand alone, but formed part of a Drama, to the action of which it may be held to have given a cumulative force.

On this point I would refer the reader to Professor von Schroeder's book, where this aspect of the Dance is fully discussed.[17]

We have already spoken of the Maruts, and their dramatic connection with Indra; the Greek Dancers offer us no direct parallel, though the connection of the Kouretes with the infant Zeus may quite possibly indicate the existence in the original form of the Dance, of a more distinctly dramatic element.

---

17. Cf. *Mysterium und Mimus*, section *Indra, die Maruts, und Agastya* specially pp. 151 *et seq*.

VII. The Sword Dance

We have, however, in the Roman Salii a connecting link which proves beyond all doubt that our modern dances, and analogous representations, are in fact genuine survivals of [p87] primitive ceremonies, and in no way a mere fortuitous combination of originally independent elements.

The Salii formed a college of priests, twelve in number, dedicated to the service of Mars, who, it is important to remember, was originally a god of growth and vegetation, a Spring Deity, who bestowed his name on the vernal month of March; only by degrees did the activities of the god become specially connected with the domain of War.[18]

There seem to have been two groups of Salii, one having their college on the Palatine, the other on the Quirinal; the first were the more important. The Quirinal group shared in the celebrations of the latter part of the month only.

The first of March was the traditional birthday of Mars, and from that date, during the whole of the month, the Salii offered sacrifices and performed dances in his honour. They wore pointed caps, or helmets, on their head, were girt with swords, and carried on the left arm shields, copied from the 'ancilia' or traditional shield of Mars, fabled to have fallen from heaven. In their right hand they bore a small lance.

Dionysus of Halicarnassus, in a passage describing the Salii, says, "they carried in their right hand a spear, or staff, or something of that sort." Miss Harrison, quoting this passage, gives a reproduction of a bas-relief representing the Salii carrying what she says "are clearly drumsticks." (As a matter of fact they very closely resemble the 'Wands' which in the Tarot cards sometimes represent the 'Lance' suit.)

Miss Harrison suggests that the original shields were made of skins, stretched upon a frame, and beaten by these 'drumsticks.' This may quite well have been the case, and it would bear out my contention that the original contact [p88] of weapon and shield was designed rather as a rhythmic accompaniment to the Dance, than as a display of skill in handling sword and lance, *i.e.*, that these dances were not primarily warlike exercises.

At the conclusion of their songs the Salii invoked Mamurius Veturius, the smith who was fabled to have executed the copies of the original shield, while on the 14th of March, a man, dressed in skins, and

---

18. Cf. von Schroeder, *op. cit.* pp. 141 *et seq.* for a very full account of the ceremonies; also, *Themis*, p. 194; Mannhardt, *Wald und Feld-Kulte*, and Röscher's *Lexikon*, under heading *Mars*, for various reasons.

VII. The Sword Dance

supposed to represent the aforesaid smith, was led through the streets, beaten by the Salii with rods, and thrust out of the city.

The following day, the 15th, was the feast of Anna Perenna, fabled to be an old woman, to whom Mars had confided the tale of his love for Nerio, and who, disguising herself as the maiden, had gone through the ceremony of marriage with the god. This feast was held outside the gates. On the 23rd the combined feast of Mars and Nerio was held with great rejoicing throughout the city. Modern scholars have unanimously recognized in Mamurius Veturius and Anna Perenna the representatives of the Old Year, the Vegetation Spirit, and his female counterpart, who, grown old, must yield place to the young god and his correspondingly youthful bride. Reference to Chapter 5, where the medieval and modern forms of this Nature ritual are discussed, and instances of the carrying out of Winter, and ceremonial bringing in of Spring, are given, will suffice to show how vital and enduring an element in Folk-lore is this idea of driving out the Old Year, while celebrating the birth of the New. Here then, again, we have a ritual Sword Dance closely associated with the practice of a Nature cult; there can, I think, be no doubt that *ab initio* the two were connected with each other.

But the dance of the Salii with its dramatic Folk-play features forms an interesting link between the classic Dance of the Kouretes, and the modern English survivals, in which [p89] the dramatic element is strongly marked. These English forms may be divided into three related groups, the Sword Dance, the Morris Dance, and the Mumming Play. Of these the Morris Dance stands somewhat apart; of identical origin, it has discarded the dramatic element, and now survives simply as a Dance, whereas the Sword Dance is always dramatic in form, and the Mumming Play, acted by characters appearing also in the Sword Dance, invariably contains a more or less elaborate fight.[19]

The Sword Dance proper appears to have been preserved mostly in the North of England, and in Scotland. Mr Cecil Sharp has found four distinct varieties in Yorkshire alone. At one time there existed a special variant known as the *Giants' Dance,* in which the leading characters were known by the names of Wotan, and Frau Frigg; one figure of this dance consisted in making a ring of swords round the neck of a lad, without wounding him.

---

19. *Folk-Lore,* Vols. VII., X., and XVI. contain interesting and fully illustrated accounts of some of these dances and plays.

VII. The Sword Dance

Mr E. K. Chambers has commented on this as the survival of a sacrificial origin.[20] The remarks of this writer on the Sword Dance in its dramatic aspect are so much to the point that I quote them here. "The Sword Dance makes its appearance, not like heroic poetry in general, as part of the minstrel repertory, but as a purely popular thing at the agricultural festivals. To these festivals we may therefore suppose it to have originally belonged." Mr Chambers goes on to remark that the dance of the Salii discussed above, was clearly agricultural, "and belongs to Mars not as War god, but in his more primitive quality of a fertilization Spirit."

In an Appendix to his most valuable book the same writer gives a full description, with text, of the most famous [p90] surviving form of the Sword Dance, that of Papa Stour (old Norwegian *Pâpey in Stôra*), one of the Shetland Islands.

The dance was performed at Christmas (Yule-tide). The dancers, seven in number, represented the seven champions of Christendom; the leader, Saint George, after an introductory speech, performed a solo dance, to the music of an accompanying minstrel. He then presented his comrades, one by one, each in turn going through the same performance. Finally the seven together performed an elaborate dance. The complete text of the speeches is given in the Appendix referred to.[21]

The close connection between the English Sword Dance, and the Mumming Play, is indicated by the fact that the chief character in these plays is, generally speaking, Saint George. (The title has in some cases become corrupted into *King* George.) In Professor von Schroeder's opinion this is due to Saint George's legendary *rôle* as Dragon slayer, and he sees in the importance assigned to this hero an argument in favour of his theory that the "Slaying of the Dragon" was the earliest Aryan Folk-Drama.

In *Folk-Lore,* Vol. X., a fully illustrated description of the Mumming Play, as performed at Newbold, a village near Rugby, is given.[22] Here the characters are Father Christmas, Saint George, a Turkish Knight, Doctor, Moll Finney (mother of the Knight), Humpty Jack, Beelzebub, and 'Big-Head-and-Little-Wit.' These last three have no share in

---

20. *The Mediaeval Stage,* Vol. III. p. 202. It would be interesting to know the precise form of this ring; was it the Pentangle?
21. Cf. also *Mysterium und Mimus,* pp. 110, 111, for a general description of the dance, minus the text of the speeches.
22. Pp. 186-194.

VII. The Sword Dance

the action proper, but appear in a kind of Epilogue, accompanying a collection made by Beelzebub.

The Play is always performed at Christmas time, consequently Father Christmas appears as stage-manager, and introduces the characters. The action consists in a general challenge issued by Saint George, and accepted by the [p91] Turkish Knight. A combat follows, in which the Turk is slain. His mother rushes in, weeps over the body, and demands the services of a Doctor, who appears accordingly, vaunts his skill in lines interspersed with unintelligible gibberish, and restores the Turk to life. In the version which used to be played throughout Scotland at Hogmanay (New-Year-tide), the characters are Bol Bendo, the King of France, the King of Spain, Doctor Beelzebub, Golishan, and Sir Alexander.[23] The fight is between Bol Bendo (who represents the Saint George of the English version), and Golishan. The latter is killed, and, on the demand of Sir Alexander (who acts as stage-manager), revived by the doctor, this character, as in the English version, interlarding the recital of his feats of healing skill with unintelligible phrases.[24] There is a general consensus of opinion among Folk-lore authorities that in this rough drama, which we find played in slightly modified form all over Europe (in Scandinavia it is the Julbock, a man dressed in skins, who, after a dramatic dance, is killed and revived[25]), we have a symbolic representation of the death and re-birth of the year; a counterpart to those ceremonies of driving out Winter, and bringing in Spring, which we have already described.

This chapter had already been written when an important article, by Dr Jevons, entitled *Masks and the Origin of the Greek Drama* appeared in *Folk-Lore* (Vol. XXVII.) The author, having discussed the different forms [p92] of Greek Drama, and the variety of masks employed, decides that "Greek Comedy originated in Harvest Festivals, in some ceremony in which the Harvesters went about in procession wearing masks." This ceremony he connects directly with the English Mumming Plays, suggesting that "the characters represented on this occasion were the Vegetation Spirit, and those who were concerned

---

23. Cf. *Folk-Lore*, Vol. XVI. pp. 212 et seq.

24. I would draw attention to the curious name of the adversary, Golishan; it is noteworthy that in one Arthurian romance Gawain has for adversary Golagros, in another Percival fights against Golerotheram. Are these all reminiscences of the giant Goliath, who became the synonym for a dangerous, preferably heathen, adversary, even as Mahomet became the synonym for an idol?

25. Cf. Mannhardt, *Wald und Feld-Kulte*, Vol. II. pp. 191 et seq. for a very full account of the Julbock (Yule Buck).

VII. The Sword Dance

in bringing about his revivification—in fine, Greek Comedy and the Mumming Play both sprang from the rite of revivification." At a later stage of our enquiry we shall have occasion to return to this point, and realize its great importance for our theory.

The Morris Dances differ somewhat from the Sword, and Mumming Dances. The performances as a rule take place in the Spring, or early Summer, chiefly May, and Whitsuntide. The dances retain little or no trace of dramatic action but are dances pure and simple. The performers, generally six in number, are attired in white elaborately-pleated shirts, decked with ribbons, white mole-skin trousers, with bells at the knee, and beaver hats adorned with ribbons and flowers. The leader carries a sword, on the point of which is generally impaled a cake; during the dancing slices of this cake are distributed to the lookers on, who are supposed to make a contribution to the 'Treasury,' a money-box carried by an individual called the Squire, or Clown, dressed in motley, and bearing in the other hand a stick with a bladder at one end, and a cow's tail at the other.

In some forms of the dance there is a 'Lord' and a 'Lady,' who carry 'Maces' of office; these maces are short staves, with a transverse piece at the top, and a hoop over it. The whole is decorated with ribbons and flowers, and bears a curious resemblance to the *Crux Ansata*.[26] In certain [p93] figures of the dance the performers carry handkerchiefs, in others, wands, painted with the colours of the village to which they belong; the dances are always more or less elaborate in form.

The costume of the 'Clown' (an animal's skin, or cap of skin with tail pendant) and the special character assumed by the Maytide celebrations in certain parts of England, *e.g.*, Cornwall and Staffordshire,[27] would seem to indicate that, while the English Morris Dance has dropped the dramatic action, the dancers not being designated by name, and playing no special *rôle*, it has, on the other hand, retained the theriomorphic features so closely associated with Aryan ritual, which the Sword Dance, and Mumming Play, on their side, have lost.[28]

A special note of these English survivals, and one to which I would now draw attention, is the very elaborate character of the figures, and

---

26. Cf. *Folk-Lore*, Vol. VIII. 'Some Oxfordshire Seasonal Festivals,' where full illustrations of the Bampton Morris Dancers and their equipment will be found.
27. Cf. *The Padstow Hobby-Horse, F.-L.* Vol. XVI. p. 56; *The Staffordshire Horn-Dance, Ib.* Vol. VII. p. 382, and VIII. p. 70.
28. Cf. *supra*, pp. 53, 80, 85.

VII. The Sword Dance

the existence of a distinct symbolic element. I am informed that the Sword dancers of to-day always, at the conclusion of a series of elaborate sword-lacing figures, form the Pentangle; as they hold up the sign they cry, triumphantly, "*A Nut! A Nut!*" The word *Nut* = *Knot* (as in the game of '*Nuts, i.e.,* breast-knots, nosegays, *in May*'). They do this often even when performing a later form of the Mumming Play.

I have already drawn attention to the fact that in *Gawain and the Green Knight* the hero's badge is the Pentangle (or Pentacle), there explained as called by the English 'the Endless Knot.'[29] In the previous chapter I have noted that the Pentangle frequently in the Tarot suits replaces the Dish; in Mr Yeats's remarks, cited above, the two are held to be [p94] interchangeable, one or the other always forms one of the group of symbols.

In one form of the Morris Dance, that performed in Berkshire, the leader, or 'Squire' of the Morris carries a Chalice! At the same time he bears a Sword, and a bull's head at the end of a long pole. This figure is illustrated in Miss Mary Neal's *Esperance Morris Book*.[30]

Thus our English survivals of these early Vegetation ceremonies preserve, in a more or less detached form, the four symbols discussed in the preceding chapter, Grail, Sword, Lance, and Pentangle, or Dish. It seems to me that, in view of the evidence thus offered, it is not a very hazardous, or far-fetched hypothesis to suggest that these symbols, the exact value of which, as a group, we cannot clearly determine, but of which we know the two most prominent, Cup and Lance, to be sex symbols, were originally 'Fertility' emblems, and as such employed in a ritual designed to promote, or restore, the activity of the reproductive energies of Nature.

As I have pointed out above an obvious dislocation has taken place in our English survivals. Sword Dance, Mumming Play, and Morris Dance, no longer form part of one ceremony, but have become separated, and connected, on the one hand with the Winter, on the other with the early Summer, Nature celebrations; it is thus not surprising that the symbols should also have become detached. The fact that the three groups manifestly form part of an original whole is an argument

---

29. Cf. *Legend of Sir Perceval*, Vol. II. p. 264.
30. See *English Folk-Song and Dance* by Frank Kidson and Mary Neal, Cambridge, 1915, plate facing p. 104. A curious point in connection with the illustration is that the Chalice is surmounted by a Heart, and in the Tarot suits *Cups* are the equivalent of our *Hearts*. The combination has now become identified with the cult of the Sacred Heart, but is undoubtedly much older.

VII. The Sword Dance

in favour of the view that at one moment all the symbols were used together, and the Grail chalice [p95] carried in a ceremony in which Sword, Lance, and Pentangle, were also displayed.

But there is another point I would suggest. Is it not possible that, in these armed youths, who were in some cases, notably in that of the Salii, at once warriors and priests, we have the real origin of the Grail Knights? We know now, absolutely, and indubitably, that these Sword Dances formed an important part of the Vegetation ritual; is it not easily within the bounds of possibility that, as the general ceremonial became elevated, first to the rank of a Mystery Cult, and then used as a vehicle for symbolic Christian teaching, the figures of the attendant warrior-priests underwent a corresponding change? From Salii to Templars is not after all so 'far a cry' as from the glittering golden-armed Maruts, and the youthful leaping Kouretes, to the grotesque tatterdemalion personages of the Christmas Mumming Play. We have learnt to acknowledge the common origin of these two latter groups; may we not reasonably contemplate a possible relation existing between the two first named? [p96]

VIII. The Medicine Man

The rôle of the Medicine Man, or Doctor in Fertility Ritual. Its importance and antiquity. The Rig-Veda *poem. Classical evidence, Mr F. Cornford. Traces of Medicine Man in the Grail romances. Gawain as Healer. Persistent tradition. Possible survival from pre-literary form. Evidence of the* Triads. *Peredur as Healer. Evolution of theme.* Le Dist de l'Erberie.

In previous chapters I have referred to the part played by the Doctor in a large number of the surviving 'Fertility' ceremonies, and to the fact, noted by other writers, that even where an active share is no longer assigned to the character, he still appears among the *dramatis personae* of these Folk-plays and processions.[1] We will now examine more closely the *rôle* allotted to this mysterious personage; we shall find it to be of extreme antiquity and remarkable significance.

In the interesting and important work by Professor von Schroeder, to which I have already often referred, we find the translation of a curious poem (*Rig-Veda*, 10. 97), a monologue placed in the mouth of a Doctor, or Medicine Man, who vaunts the virtue of his herbs, and their power to cure human ills.[2] From the references made to a special sick man von Schroeder infers that this poem, like others in the collection, was intended to be acted, as well as recited, and that the personage to be healed, evidently present on the scene, was probably represented by a dummy, as no speeches are allotted to the character.

The entire poem consists of 23 verses of four lines each, and is divided by the translator into three distinct sections; the first is devoted to the praise of herbs in general, their power to cure the sick man before them, and at the same [p97] time to bring riches to the Healer—the opening verses run:

"Die Kräuter alt, entsprossen einst

---

1. Cf. *supra*, Chap. 5, pp. 52, 54; Chap. 7, pp. 90, 91.
2. *Mysterium und Mimus*, p. 369, *Der Mimus des Medizinmannes*.

VIII. The Medicine Man

Drei Alter vor den Göttern noch,
Die braunen will Ich preisen jetzt!
Hundert und sieben Arten sinds.

"Ja, hundert Arten, Mütterlein,
Und tausend Zweige habt ihr auch,
Ihr, die ihr hundert Kräfte habt,
Macht diesen Menschen mir gesund.

"Ihr Kräuter hört, ihr Mütterchen,
Ihr göttlichen, das sag ich euch:
Ross, Rind und Kleid gewänn' ich gern
Und auch dein Leben, lieber Mann!
. . . .
Fürwahr ihr bringt mir Rinder ein,
Wenn ihr ihn rettet diesen Mann."

He then praises the power of all herbs:

"Vom Himmel kam der Kräuter Schar
Geflogen, und da sprechen sie;
Wen wir noch lebend treffen an
Der Mann soll frei von Schaden sein."

Finally the speaker singles out one herb as superior to all others:

"Die Kräuter viel in Soma's Reich
Die hundertfach verständigen,
Von denen bist das beste du
Erfüllst den Wunsch, und heilst das Herz."

He conjures all other herbs to lend their virtue to this special remedy:

"Ihr Kräuter all' in Soma's Reich
Verbreitet auf der Erde hin,
Ihr, von Brihaspati erzeugt,
Gebt diesem Kraute eure Kraft!

[p98] "Nicht nehme Schaden, der euch gräbt,

VIII. The Medicine Man

Noch der, für Welchen Ich euch grub!
Bei uns soll Alles, Mensch, und Vieh,
Gesund und ohne Schaden sein.

"Ihr, die ihr höret dies mein Wort,
Ihr, die ihr in der Ferne seid,
Ihr Pflanzen all,' vereignet euch,
Gebt diesem Kraute eure Kraft!"

And the herbs, taking counsel together with Soma their king, answer:

"Für Wen uns ein Brahmane braucht
Den, König, wollen retten wir,"

a line which throws a light upon the personality of the speaker; he is obviously a Brahmin, and the Medicine Man here, as elsewhere, unites the functions of Priest and Healer.

Professor von Schroeder suggests that this Dramatic Monologue formed part of the ceremonies of a Soma feast, that it is the Soma plant from which the heavenly drink is brewed which is to be understood as the first of all herbs and the curer of all ills, and the reference to Soma as King of the herbs seems to bear out this suggestion.

In a previous chapter[3] I have referred to a curious little poem, also found in the *Rig-Veda,* and translated by von Schroeder under the title *A Folk-Procession at a Soma-Feast,* the *dramatis personae* of the poem offering, as I pointed out, a most striking and significant parallel to certain surviving Fertility processions, notably that of Värdegötzen in Hanover. In this little song which von Schroeder places in the mouth of the leader of the band of maskers, the Doctor is twice referred to; in the opening lines we have the Brahmin, the Doctor, the Carpenter, the Smith, given as men plying different trades, and each and all in search of gain; in the final verse the speaker announces, "I am a Poet (or [p99] Singer), my father a Doctor." Thus of the various trades and personages enumerated the Doctor alone appears twice over, an indication of the importance attached to this character.

---

3. Cf. Chap. 5, pp. 53, 54.

VIII. The Medicine Man

Unfortunately, in view of the fragmentary condition of the survivals of early Aryan literature, and the lack of explanatory material at our disposal, it is impossible to decide what was the precise *rôle* assigned to the 'Medicine Man'; judging from the general character of the surviving dramatic fragments and the close parallel which exists between these fragments and the Medieval and Modern Fertility ceremonies, it seems extremely probable that his original *rôle* was identical with that assigned to his modern counterpart, *i.e.*, that of restoring to life or health the slain, or suffering, representative of the Vegetation Spirit.

This presumption gains additional support from the fact that it is in this character that the Doctor appears in Greek Classical Drama. Von Schroeder refers to the fact that the Doctor was a stock figure in the Greek 'Mimus'[4] and in Mr Cornford's interesting volume entitled *The Origin of Attic Comedy*, the author reckons the Doctor among the stock Masks of the early Greek Theatre, and assigns to this character the precise *rôle* which later survivals have led us to attribute to him.

The significance of Mr Cornford's work lies in the fact that, while he accepts Sir Gilbert Murray's deeply interesting and suggestive theory that the origins of Greek Tragedy are to be sought in "the Agon of the Fertility Spirit, his Pathos, and Theophany," he contends that a similar origin may be postulated for Attic Comedy—that the stock Masks (characters) agree with a theory of derivation of such Comedy from a ritual performance celebrating the renewal of the seasons.[5] "They were at first serious, and even awful, figures in a Religious Mystery, the God who [p100] every year is born, and dies, and rises again; his Mother and his Bride; the Antagonist who kills him; the Medicine Man who restores him to life."[6]

I would submit that the presence of such a character in the original ritual drama of Revival which, on my theory, underlies the romantic form of the Grail legend, may, in view of the above evidence, and of

---

4. *Op. cit.* p. 371.
5. *Op. cit.* pp. 78 *et seq.*
6. I would draw attention to the fact that while scholars are now coming to the conclusion that Classic Drama, whether Tragedy or Comedy, reposes for its origin upon this ancient ritual, others have pointed out that Modern Drama derives from the ritual Play of the Church, the first recorded medieval drama being the Easter *Quem Quaeritis?* the dramatic celebration of Our Lord's Resurrection. Cf. Chambers, *The Mediaeval Stage*, where this thesis is elaborately developed and illustrated. It is a curious fact that certain texts of this, the 'Classical' Passion Play, contain a scene between the Maries and the 'Unguentarius' from whom they purchase spices for the embalmment of Our Lord. Can this be a survival of the Medicine Man? (Cf. *op. cit.* Vol. II. p. 33.)

VIII. The Medicine Man

that brought forward in the previous chapters, be accepted as at least a probable hypothesis.

But, it may be objected, granting that the Doctor in these Fertility processions and dramas represents a genuine survival of a feature of immemorial antiquity, a survival to be traced alike in Aryan remains, in Greek literature, and in Medieval ceremony, what is the precise bearing upon the special subject of our investigations? There is no Doctor in the Grail legend, although there is certainly abundant scope for his activities!

There may be no Doctor in the Grail legend to-day, but was there never such a character? How if this be the key to explain the curious and persistent attribution of healing skill to so apparently unsuitable a personage as Sir Gawain? I would draw the attention of my readers to a passage in the *Perceval* of Chrétien de Troyes, where Gawain, finding a wounded knight by the roadside, proceeds to treat him:

"Et Mesire Gauvain savoit
Plus que nuls homs de garir plaie;
Une herbe voit en une haie
Trop bonne pour douleur tolir
De plaie, et il la va cueillir."[7]

[p101] Other MSS. are rather fuller:

"Et Messires Gauvain savoit
Plus que nus hons vivant de plaies,
Unes herbe voit les une haies
Qu'il connoissoit lonc temps avoit
Que son mestre apris li avoit
Enseigniee et bien moustree,
Et il l'avoit bien esgardee
Si l'a molt bien reconneue."[8]

We find reference to Gawain's possession of medical knowledge elsewhere. In the poem entitled *Lancelot et le cerf au pied blanc*, Gawain, finding his friend desperately wounded, carries him to a physician whom he instructs as to the proper treatment.[9]

---

7. Bibl. Nat., fonds Français, 12577, fo. 40.
8. Bibl. Nat., f. F. 1453, fo. 49. *Parzival*, Bk. X. ll. 413-22.
9. *Lanceloet*, Jonckbloet, Vol. II. ll. 22271-23126.

"Ende Walewein wiesde den Ersatere mere
Ene const, die daertoe halp wel sere."[10]

In the parallel adventure related in *Morien* Gawain heals Lancelot without the aid of any physician:[11]

"Doe was Walewein harde blide
Ende bant hem sine wonden ten tide
Met selken crude die daer dochten
Dat si niet bloden mochten."[12]

They ride to an anchorite's cell:

"Si waren doe in dire gedochten
Mochten sie daer comen tier stont
Datten Walewein soude maken gesont."[13]

The Dutch *Lancelot* has numerous references to Gawain's skill in healing. Of course the advocates of the originality of Chrétien de Troyes will object that these references, though found in poems which have no connection with [p102] Chrétien, and which are translations from lost French originals of an undetermined date, are one and all loans from the more famous poem. This, however, can hardly be contended of the Welsh *Triads;* there we find Gwalchmai, the Welsh Gawain, cited as one of the three men "To whom the nature of every object was known,"[14] an accomplishment exceedingly necessary for a 'Medicine Man,' but not at first sight especially needful for the equipment of a knight.[15] This persistent attribution of healing skill is not, so far as my acquaintance with medieval Romance goes, paralleled in the case of any other knight; even Tristan, who is probably the most accomplished of heroes of romance, the most thoroughly trained in all

---

10. *Op. cit.* ll. 22825–26.
11. *Op. cit.* Vol. I. ll. 42540–47262.
12. *Op. cit.* ll. 46671–74.
13. *Op. cit.* ll. 46678–80.
14. Cf. Loth, *Les Mabinogion*, Vol. II. p. 230, and note. The other two are Riwallawn Walth Banhadlen, and Llacheu son of Arthur.
15. The only instance in which I have found medicine directly connected with the knightly order is in the case of the warrior clan of the Samurai, in Japan, where members, physically unfitted for the task of a warrior, were trained as Royal Doctors, the Folk Doctors being recruited from a class below the Samurai. Cf. *Medizin der Natur-Völker*, Bartels, p. 65.

VIII. The Medicine Man

branches of knightly education, is not credited with any such knowledge. No other knight, save Gawain, has the reputation of a Healer, yet Gawain, the Maidens' Knight, the 'fair Father of Nurture' is, at first sight, hardly the personage one might expect to possess such skill. Why he should be so persistently connected with healing was for long a problem to me; recently, however, I have begun to suspect that we have in this apparently motiveless attribution the survival of an early stage of tradition in which not only did Gawain cure the Grail King, but he did so, not by means of a question, or by the welding of a broken sword, but by more obvious and natural means, the administration of a healing herb. Gawain's character of Healer belongs to him in his *rôle* of Grail Winner.

Some years ago, in the course of my reading, I came across a passage in which certain knights of Arthur's court, [p103] riding through a forest, come upon a herb 'which belonged to the Grail.' Unfortunately the reference, at the time I met with it, though it struck me as curious, did not possess any special significance, and either I omitted to make a note of it, or entered it in a book which, with sundry others, went mysteriously astray in the process of moving furniture. In any case, though I have searched diligently I have failed to recover the passage, but I note it here in the hope that one of my readers may be more fortunate.[16]

It is perhaps not without significance that a mention of Peredur (Perceval) in Welsh poetry may also possibly contain a reference to his healing office. I refer to the well-known *Song of the Graves* in the Black Book of Carmarthen where the grave of Mor, son of Peredur Penwetic, is referred to. According to Dr G. Evans the word *penwedic*, or *perfeddyg*, as it may also be read, means *chief Healer*. Peredur, it is needless to say, is the Welsh equivalent of Perceval, Gawain's successor and supplanter in the *rôle* of Grail hero.

I have no desire to press the point unduly, but it is certainly significant that, entirely apart from any such theory of the evolution of the Grail legend as that advanced in these pages, a Welsh scholar should have suggested a rendering of the title of the Grail hero which is in complete harmony with that theory; a rendering also which places him side by side with his compatriot Gwalchmai, even as the completely evolved Grail story connects him with Gawain. In any case there is food for reflection in the fact that the possibility of such an origin once admitted,

---

16. [*Editor's note:* See Malory, book 4, chapter 5.]

VIII. The Medicine Man

the most apparently incongruous, and inharmonious, elements of the story show themselves capable of a natural and unforced explanation.

In face of the evidence above set forth it seems impossible to deny that the Doctor, or Medicine Man, did, from the very earliest ages, play an important part in Dramatic Fertility [p104] Ritual, that he still survives in the modern Folk-play, the rude representative of the early ritual form, and it is at least possible that the attribution of healing skill to so romantic and chivalrous a character as Sir Gawain may depend upon the fact that, at an early, and pre-literary stage of his story, he played the *rôle* traditionally assigned to the Doctor, that of restoring to life and health the dead, or wounded, representative of the Spirit of Vegetation.

If I am right in my reading of this complicated problem the *mise-en-scène* of the Grail story was originally a loan from a ritual actually performed, and familiar to those who first told the tale. This ritual, in its earlier stages comparatively simple and objective in form, under the process of an insistence upon the inner and spiritual significance, took upon itself a more complex and esoteric character, the rite became a Mystery, and with this change the *rôle* of the principal actors became of heightened significance. That of the Healer could no longer be adequately fulfilled by the administration of a medicinal remedy; the relation of Body and Soul became of cardinal importance for the Drama, the Medicine Man gave place to the Redeemer; and his task involved more than the administration of the original Herbal remedy. In fact in the final development of the story the *Pathos* is shared alike by the representative of the Vegetation Spirit, and the Healer, whose task involves a period of stern testing and probation.

If we wish to understand clearly the evolution of the Grail story we must realize that the simple Fertility Drama from which it sprung has undergone a gradual and mysterious change, which has invested it with elements at once 'rich and strange,' and that though Folk-lore may be the key to unlock the outer portal of the Grail castle it will not suffice to give us the entrance to its deeper secrets. [p105]

Appendix to Chapter 8

While having no connection with the main subject of our study, the Grail legend, I should like to draw the attention of students of Medieval literature to the curious parallel between the *Rig-Veda* poem of the *Medicine Man* or *Kräuter-Lied* as it is also called, and Rustebœuf's *Dist de l'Erberie*. Both are monologues, both presuppose the presence of an audience, in each case the speaker is one who vaunts his skill in the use of herbs, in each case he has in view the ultimate gain to himself. Here are the opening lines of the Medieval poem:[17]

"Seignor qui ci estes venu
Petit et grant, jone et chenu,
Il vos est trop bien avenu
Sachiez de voir;
Je ne vos vueil pas deçevoir
Bien le porroz aperçevoir
Ainz que m'en voise.
Asiez vos, ne fetes noise
Si escotez s'il ne vos poise
Je sui uns mires."

He has been long with the lord of Caire, where he won much gold; in Puille, Calabre, Luserne.

"Ai herbes prises
Qui de granz vertuz sont enprises
Sus quelque mal qu'el soient mises
Le maus s'enfuit."

There is no reference in the poem to a cure about to be performed in the presence of the audience, which does not however exclude the possibility of such cure being effected.

[p106] It would be interesting to know under what circumstances such a poem was recited, whether it formed part of a popular representation. The audience in view is of a mixed character, young and old, great and small, and one has a vision of the Quack Doctor at some village fair, on the platform before his booth, declaiming the virtues of his nostrums before an audience representative of all ranks and ages. It is a far cry from such a Medieval scene to the prehistoric days of the *Rig-Veda*, but the *mise-en-scène* is the same; the popular 'seasonal' feast, the Doctor with his healing herbs, which he vaunts in skilful rhyme, the

---

17. Cf. *Œuvres de Rutebœuf*, Kressner, p. 115.

hearers, drawn from all ranks, some credulous, some amused. There seems very little doubt that both poems are specimens, and very good specimens, of a *genre* the popularity and vitality of which are commensurate with the antiquity of its origin.[18] [p107]

---

18. My attention was drawn to the poem by references to it in *The Mediaeval Stage,* Chambers.

IX. The Fisher King

Summary of evidence presented. Need of a 'test' element. To be found in central figure. Mystery of his title. Analysis of variants. Gawain version. Perceval version. Borron alone attempts explanation of title. Parzival. Perlesvaus. Queste. Grand Saint Graal. Comparison with surviving ritual variants. Original form King dead, and restored to life. Old Age and Wounding themes. Legitimate variants. Doubling of character a literary device. Title. Why Fisher King? Examination of Fish Symbolism. Fish a Life symbol. Examples. Indian—Manu, Vishnu, Buddha. Fish in Buddhism. Evidence from China. Orpheus. Babylonian evidence. Tammuz Lord of the Net. Jewish Symbolism. The Messianic Fish-meal. Adopted by Christianity. Evidence of the catacombs. Source of Borron's Fish-meals. Mystery tradition not Celtic Folk-tale. Comparison of version with Finn story. With Messianic tradition. Epitaph of Bishop Aberkios. Voyage of Saint Brandan. Connection of Fish with goddess Astarte. Cumont. Connection of Fish and Dove. Fish as Fertility Symbol. Its use in Marriage ceremonies. Summing up of evidence. Fisher King inexplicable from Christian point of view. Folk-lore solution unsatisfactory. As a Ritual survival completely in place. Centre of action, and proof of soundness of theory.

The gradual process of our investigation has led us to the conclusion that the elements forming the existing Grail legend—the setting of the story, the nature of the task which awaits the hero, the symbols and their significance—one and all, while finding their counterpart in prehistoric record, present remarkable parallels to the extant practice and belief of countries so widely separate as the British Isles, Russia, and Central Africa.

The explanation of so curious a fact, for it is a fact, and not a mere hypothesis, may, it was suggested, most probably be found in the theory that in this fascinating literature we have the, sometimes partially understood, sometimes wholly misinterpreted, record of a ritual, originally presumed to exercise a life-giving potency, which, at one time of universal observance, has, even in its decay, shown itself possessed of elements of the most persistent vitality.

That if the ritual, which according to our theory lies at the root of the Grail story, be indeed the ritual of a Life Cult, it should, *in* and *per*

IX. The Fisher King

se, possess precisely these characteristics, will, I think, be admitted by any fair-minded critic; the point of course is, can we definitely *prove* our theory, *i.e.,* not merely point to striking parallels, but select, from the figures and incidents composing our story, some one element, which, by showing itself capable of explanation on this theory, and on this theory alone, may be held to afford decisive proof of the soundness of our hypothesis?

[p108] It seems to me that there is one such element in the bewildering complex, by which the theory can be thus definitely tested, that is the personality of the central figure and the title by which he is known. If we can prove that the Fisher King, *qua* Fisher King, is an integral part of the ritual, and can be satisfactorily explained alike by its intention, and inherent symbolism, we shall, I think, have taken the final step which will establish our theory upon a sure basis. On the other hand, if the Fisher King, *qua* Fisher King, does not fit into our framework we shall be forced to conclude that, while the *provenance* of certain elements of the Grail literature is practically assured, the *ensemble* has been complicated by the introduction of a terminology, which, whether the outcome of serious intention, or of mere literary caprice, was foreign to the original source, and so far, defies explanation. In this latter case our theory would not necessarily be *manqué,* but would certainly be seriously incomplete.

We have already seen that the personality of the King, the nature of the disability under which he is suffering, and the reflex effect exercised upon his folk and his land, correspond, in a most striking manner, to the intimate relation at one time held to exist between the ruler and his land; a relation mainly dependent upon the identification of the King with the Divine principle of Life and Fertility.

This relation, as we have seen above, exists to-day among certain African tribes.

If we examine more closely into the existing variants of our romances, we shall find that those very variants are not only thoroughly *dans le cadre* of our proposed solution, but also afford a valuable, and hitherto unsuspected, indication of the relative priority of the versions.

In Chapter I, I discussed the task of the hero in general, here I propose to focus attention upon his host, and while [p109] in a measure traversing the same ground, to do so with a view to determining the true character of this enigmatic personage.

IX. The Fisher King

In the *Bleheris* version,[1] the lord of the castle is suffering under no disability whatever; he is described as "tall, and strong of limb, of no great age, but somewhat bald." Besides the King there is a Dead Knight upon a bier, over whose body Vespers for the Dead are solemnly sung. The wasting of the land, partially restored by Gawain's question concerning the Lance, has been caused by the 'Dolorous Stroke,' *i.e.,* the stroke which brought about the death of the Knight, whose identity is here never revealed. Certain versions which interpolate the account of Joseph of Arimathea and the Grail, allude to 'Le riche Pescheur' and his heirs as Joseph's descendants, and, presumably, for it is not directly stated, guardians of the Grail,[2] but the King himself is here never called by that title. From his connection with the Waste Land it seems more probable that it was the Dead Knight who filled that *rôle*.

In the second version of which Gawain is the hero, that of *Diû Crône*,[3] the Host is an old and infirm man. After Gawain has asked the question we learn that he is really dead, and only compelled to retain the semblance of life till the task of the Quester be achieved. Here, again, he is not called the Fisher King.

In the *Perceval* versions, on the contrary, we find the name invariably associated with him, but he is not always directly connected with the misfortunes which have fallen upon his land. Thus, while the Wauchier texts are incomplete, breaking off at the critical moment of asking the [p110] question, Manessier who continues, and ostensibly completes, Wauchier, introduces the Dead Knight, here Goondesert, or Gondefer (which I suspect is the more correct form), brother of the King, whose death by treachery has plunged the land in misery, and been the direct cause of the self-wounding of the King.[4] The healing of the King and the restoration of the land depend upon Perceval's slaying the murderer Partinal. These two versions show a combination of Perceval and Gawain themes, such as their respective dates might lead us to expect.

Robert de Borron is the only writer who gives a clear, and tolerably reasonable, account of why the guardian of the Grail bears the title of Fisher King; in other cases, such as the poems of Chrétien and Wolfram,

---

1. Cf. my *Sir Gawain and the Grail Castle,* pp. 3-30. The best text is that of MS. B.N., fonds Franç. 12576, ff. 87*vo*-91. The above remarks apply also to the *Elucidation,* which is using a version of the Bleheris form.
2. B.N. 12577, fo. 136*vo*.
3. Cf. *Sir Gawain at the Grail Castle,* pp. 33-46.
4. Cf. B.N. 12576, ff. 220-222*vo* and fo. 258.

IX. The Fisher King

the name is connected with his partiality for fishing, an obviously *post hoc* addition.

The story in question is found in Borron's *Joseph of Arimathea*.[5] Here we are told how, during the wanderings of that holy man and his companions in the wilderness, certain of the company fell into sin. By the command of God, Brons, Joseph's brother-in-law, caught a Fish, which, with the Grail, provided a mystic meal of which the unworthy cannot partake; thus the sinners were separated from the righteous. Henceforward Brons was known as 'The Rich Fisher.' It is noteworthy, however, that in the Perceval romance, ascribed to Borron, the title is as a rule, *Roi* Pescheur, not *Riche* Pescheur.[6]

In this romance the King is not suffering from any special malady, but is the victim of extreme old age; [p111] not surprising, as he is Brons himself, who has survived from the dawn of Christianity to the days of King Arthur. We are told that the effect of asking the question will be to restore him to youth;[7] as a matter of fact it appears to bring about his death, as he only lives three days after his restoration.[8]

When we come to Chrétien's poem we find ourselves confronted with a striking alteration in the presentment. There are, not one, but two, disabled kings; one suffering from the effects of a wound, the other in extreme old age. Chrétien's poem being incomplete we do not know what he intended to be the result of the achieved Quest, but we may I think reasonably conclude that the wounded King at least was healed.[9]

The *Parzival* of von Eschenbach follows the same tradition, but is happily complete. Here we find the wounded King was healed, but what becomes of the aged man (here the grandfather, not as in Chrétien the father, of the Fisher King) we are not told.[10]

The *Perlesvaus* is, as I have noted above,[11] very unsatisfactory. The illness of the King is badly motivated, and he dies before the achievement of the Quest. This romance, while retaining certain interesting, and

---

5. Hucher, *Le Saint Graal*, Vol. I. pp. 251 *et seq.*, 315 *et seq.*
6. Cf. Modena MS. pp. 11, 12, 21, etc.; Dr Nitze, *The Fisher-King in the Grail Romances*, p. 373, says Borron uses the term *Rice* Pescheur, as opposed to the *Roi* Pescheur of Chrétien. This remark is only correct as applied to the *Joseph*.
7. Modena MS p. 61 and note.
8. Ibid. p. 63.
9. The evidence of the Parzival and the parallel Grail sections of Sone de Nansai, which appear to repose ultimately on a source common to all three authors, makes this practically certain.
10. This is surely a curious omission, if the second King were as essential a part of the scheme as Dr Nitze supposes.
11. Cf. Chapter 2, p. 15.

undoubtedly primitive features, is, as a whole, too late, and *remaniée* a redaction to be of much use in determining the question of origins.

The same may be said of the *Grand Saint Graal* and *Queste* versions, both of which are too closely connected with [p112] the prose *Lancelot*, and too obviously intended to develope and complete the *données* of that romance to be relied upon as evidence for the original form of the Grail legend.[12] The version of the *Queste* is very confused: there are two kings at the Grail castle, Pelles, and his father; sometimes the one, sometimes the other, bears the title of Roi Pescheur.[13] There is besides, an extremely old, and desperately wounded, king, Mordrains, a contemporary of Joseph, who practically belongs, not to the Grail tradition, but to a Conversion legend embodied in the *Grand Saint Graal*.[14] Finally, in the latest cyclic texts, we have three Kings, all of whom are wounded.[15]

The above will show that the presentment of this central figure is much confused; generally termed Le Roi Pescheur, he is sometimes described as in middle life, and in full possession of his bodily powers. Sometimes while still comparatively young he is incapacitated by the effects of a wound, and is known also by the title of Roi Mehaigné, or Maimed King. Sometimes he is in extreme old age, and in certain closely connected versions the two ideas are combined, and we have a wounded Fisher King, and an aged father, or grandfather. But I would draw attention to the significant fact that in no case is the Fisher King a youthful character; that distinction is reserved for his Healer, and successor.

[p113] Now is it possible to arrive at any conclusion as to the relative value and probable order of these conflicting variants? I think that if we admit that they do, in all probability, represent a more or less coherent survival of the Nature ritual previously discussed, we may, by help of what we know as to the varying forms of that ritual, be enabled to bring some order out of this confusion.

---

12. I cannot agree with Dr Nitze's remark (*op. cit.* p. 374) that "in most versions the Fisher King has a mysterious double." I hold that feature to be a peculiarity of the Chrétien-Wolfram group. It is not found in the Gawain versions, in Wauchier, nor in Manessier. Gerbert is using the *Queste* in the passage relative to Mordrains, and for the reason stated above I hold that neither *Queste* nor *Grand Saint Graal* should be cited when we are dealing, as Dr Nitze is here dealing, with questions of ultimate origin.

13. Cf. my *Legend of Sir Lancelot*, pp. 167 and 168.

14. Cf. Heinzel, *Ueber die Alt-Franz. Gral-Romanen*, pp. 136 and 137.

15. Cf. *Legend of Sir Perceval*, Vol. II. p. 343, *note*. These three kings are found in the curious Merlin MS. B.N., f. Franç. 337, fo. 249 *et seq*.

IX. The Fisher King

If we turn back to Chapters 4, 5, and 7, and consult the evidence there given as to the Adonis cults, the Spring Festivals of European Folk, the Mumming Plays of the British Isles, the main fact that emerges is that in the great majority of these cases the representative of the Spirit of Vegetation is considered as dead, and the object of these ceremonies is to restore him to life. This I hold to be the primary form.

This section had already been written when I came across the important article by Dr Jevons, referred to in a previous chapter.[16] Certain of his remarks are here so much to the point that I cannot refrain from quoting them. Speaking of the Mumming Plays, the writer says: "The one point in which there is no variation is that—the character is killed and brought to life again. The play is a ceremonial performance, or rather it is the development in dramatic form of what was originally a religious or magical rite, representing or realizing the revivification of the character slain. This revivification is the one essential and invariable feature of all the Mummer's plays in England."[17]

In certain cases, *e.g.,* the famous Roman Spring festival of Mamurius Veturius and the Swabian ceremony referred to above,[18] the central figure is an old man. In no case do I find that the representative of Vegetation is merely [p114] wounded, although the nature of the ritual would obviously admit of such a variant.

Thus, taking the extant and recognized forms of the ritual into consideration, we might expect to find that in the earliest, and least contaminated, version of the Grail story the central figure would be dead, and the task of the Quester that of restoring him to life. Viewed from this standpoint the *Gawain* versions (the priority of which is maintainable upon strictly literary grounds, Gawain being the original Arthurian romantic hero) are of extraordinary interest. In the one form we find a Dead Knight, whose fate is distinctly stated to have involved his land in desolation, in the other, an aged man who, while preserving the semblance of life, is in reality dead.

This last version appears to me, in view of our present knowledge, to be of extreme critical value. There can, I think, be little doubt that in the primary form underlying our extant versions the King was dead, and restored to life; at first, I strongly suspect, by the agency of some

---

16. *Vide supra,* pp. 91. 92.
17. *Op. cit.* p. 184.
18. Cf. Chapter 5, p. 52, Chap. 7, p. 88.

mysterious herb, or herbs, a feature retained in certain forms of the Mumming play.

In the next stage, that represented by Borron, he is suffering from extreme old age, and the task of the Quester is to restore him to youth. This version is again supported by extant parallels. In each of these cases it seems most probable that the original ritual (I should wish it to be clearly understood that I hold the Grail story to have been primarily dramatic, and actually performed) involved an act of substitution. The Dead King in the first case being probably represented by a mere effigy, in the second being an old man, his place was, at a given moment of the ritual, taken by the youth who played the *rôle* of the Quester. It is noteworthy that, while both Perceval and Galahad are represented as mere lads, Gawain, whatever his age at the [p115] moment of the Grail quest, was, as we learn from *Diû Crône*, dowered by his fairy Mistress with the gift of eternal youth.[19]

The versions of Chrétien and Wolfram, which present us with a wounded Fisher King, and a father, or grandfather,[20] in extreme old age, are due in my opinion to a literary device, intended to combine two existing variants. That the subject matter was well understood by the original redactor of the common source is proved by the nature of the injury,[21] but I hold that in these versions we have passed from the domain of ritual to that of literature. Still, we have a curious indication that the Wounding variant may have had its place in the former. The suggestion made above as to the probable existence in the primitive ritual of a substitution ceremony, seems to me to provide a possible explanation of the feature found alike in Wolfram, and in the closely allied Grail section of *Sone de Nansai; i.e.,* that the wound of the King was a punishment for sin, he had conceived a passion for a Pagan princess.[22] Now there would be no incongruity in representing the Dead King as reborn in youthful form, the aged King as *revenu dans sa juvence,* but when the central figure was a man in the prime of life some reason had to be found, his strength and vitality being restored, for his supersession by the appointed Healer. This supersession was adequately motivated by the supposed transgression of a fundamental Christian law, entailing as consequence the forfeiture of his crown.

---

19. *Diû Crone*, ll. 17329 *et seq.*
20. In the *Parzival* Titurel is grandfather to Anfortas, Frimutel intervening; critics of the poem are apt to overlook this difference between the German and French versions.
21. Cf. Chapter 2, p. 20.
22. Cf. here my notes on *Sone de Nansai* (Romania, Vol. XLIII. p. 412).

IX. *The Fisher King*

I would thus separate the *doubling* theme, as found in Chrétien and Wolfram, from the *wounded* theme, equally [p116] common to these poets. This latter might possibly be accounted for on the ground of a ritual variant; the first is purely literary, explicable neither on the exoteric, nor the esoteric, aspect of the ceremony. From the exoteric point of view there are not, and there cannot be, two Kings suffering from parallel disability; the ritual knows one Principle of Life, and one alone. Equally from the esoteric standpoint Fisher King, and Maimed King, representing two different aspects of the same personality, may, and probably were, represented as two individuals, but one alone is disabled. Further, as the two are, in very truth, one, they should be equals in age, not of different generations. Thus the *Bleheris* version which gives us a Dead Knight, presumably, from his having been slain in battle, still in vigorous manhood, and a hale King is, ritually, the more correct. The original of Manessier's version must have been similar, but the fact that by the time it was compiled the Fisher King was generally accepted as being also the Maimed King led to the introduction of the very awkward, and poorly motivated, self-wounding incident. It will be noted that in this case the King is not healed either at the moment of the slaying of his brother's murderer (which would be the logical result of the *données* of the tale), nor at the moment of contact with the successful Quester, but at the mere announcement of his approach.[23]

Thus, if we consider the King, apart from his title, we find that alike from his position in the story, his close connection with the fortunes of his land and people, and the varying forms of the disability of which he is the victim, [117] he corresponds with remarkable exactitude to the central figure of a well-recognized Nature ritual, and may therefore justly be claimed to belong *ab origine* to such a hypothetical source.

But what about his title, why should he be called the *Fisher* King?

Here we strike what I hold to be the main crux of the problem, a feature upon which scholars have expended much thought and ingenuity, a feature which the authors of the romances themselves either did not always understand, or were at pains to obscure by the introduction of the obviously *post hoc* "motif" above referred to, *i.e.*, that he was

---

23. In connection with my previous remarks on the subject (p. 112) I would point out that the Queste and Grand Sainte Graal versions repeat the Maimed King *motif* in the most unintelligent manner. The element of old age, inherent in the Evalach-Mordrains incident, is complicated and practically obscured, by an absurdly exaggerated wounding element, here devoid of its original significance.

IX. The Fisher King

called the Fisher King because of his devotion to the pastime of fishing: *à-propos* of which Heinzel sensibly remarks, that the story of the Fisher King "presupposes a legend of this personage only vaguely known and remembered by Chrétien."[24]

Practically the interpretations already attempted fall into two main groups, which we may designate as the Christian-Legendary, and the Celtic-Folk-lore interpretations. For those who hold that the Grail story is essentially, and fundamentally, Christian, finding its root in Eucharistic symbolism, the title is naturally connected with the use of the Fish symbol in early Christianity: the *Icthys* anagram, as applied to Christ, the title 'Fishers of Men,' bestowed upon the Apostles, the Papal ring of the Fisherman—though it must be noted that no manipulation of the Christian symbolism avails satisfactorily to account for the lamentable condition into which the bearer of the title has fallen.[25]

[p118] The advocates of the Folk-lore theory, on the other hand, practically evade this main difficulty, by basing their interpretation upon Borron's story of the catching of the Fish by Brons, equating this character with the Bran of Welsh tradition, and pointing to the existence, in Irish and Welsh legend, of a Salmon of Wisdom, the tasting of whose flesh confers all knowledge. Hertz acutely remarks that the incident, as related by Borron, is not of such importance as to justify the stress laid upon the name, Rich Fisher, by later writers.[26] We may also note in this connection that the Grail romances never employ the form '*Wise* Fisher,' which, if the origin of the name were that proposed above, we might reasonably expect to find. It is obvious that a satisfactory solution of the problem must be sought elsewhere.

In my opinion the key to the puzzle is to be found in the rightful understanding of the *Fish-Fisher* symbolism. Students of the Grail literature have been too prone to treat the question on the Christian basis alone, oblivious of the fact that Christianity did no more than take over,

---

24. Heinzel, *op. cit.* p. 13.
25. For an instance of the extravagances to which a strictly Christian interpretation can lead, cf. Dr Sebastian Evans's theories set forth in his translation of the *Perlesvaus* (*The High History of the Holy Grail*) and in his *The Quest of the Holy Grail*. The author places the origin of the cycle in the first quarter of the thirteenth century, and treats it as an allegory of the position in England during the Interdict pronounced against King John, and the consequent withholding of the Sacraments. His identification of the character with historical originals is most ingenious, an extraordinary example of misapplied learning.
26. For a general discussion of the conflicting views cf. Dr Nitze's study, referred to above. The writer devotes special attention to the works of the late Prof. Heinzel and Mr Alfred Nutt as leading representatives of their respective schools.

IX. The Fisher King

and adapt to its own use, a symbolism already endowed with a deeply rooted prestige and importance.

So far the subject cannot be said to have received adequate treatment; certain of its aspects have been more or less fully discussed in monographs and isolated articles, but we still await a comprehensive study on this most important question.[27]

[p119] So far as the present state of our knowledge goes we can affirm with certainty that the Fish is a Life symbol of immemorial antiquity, and that the title of Fisher has, from the earliest ages, been associated with Deities who were held to be specially connected with the origin and preservation of Life.

In Indian cosmogony Manu finds a little fish in the water in which he would wash his hands; it asks, and receives, his protection, asserting that when grown to full size it will save Manu from the universal deluge. This is Jhasa, the greatest of all fish.[28]

The first Avatar of Vishnu the Creator is a Fish. At the great feast in honour of this god, held on the twelfth day of the first month of the Indian year, Vishnu is represented under the form of a golden Fish, and addressed in the following terms: "Wie Du, O Gott, in Gestalt eines Fisches die in der Unterwelt befindlichen Veden gerettet hast, so rette auch mich."[29] The Fish Avatar was afterwards transferred to Buddha.

In Buddhist religion the symbols of the Fish and Fisher are freely employed. Thus in Buddhist monasteries we find drums and gongs in the shape of a fish, but the true meaning of the symbol, while still regarded as sacred, has been lost, and the explanations, like the explanations of the Grail romances, are often fantastic afterthoughts.

In the Mahāyana scriptures Buddha is referred to as the Fisherman who draws fish from the ocean of Samsara to [p120] the light of Salvation. There are figures and pictures which represent Buddha in the act of fishing, an attitude which, unless interpreted in a symbolic sense, would be utterly at variance with the tenets of the Buddhist religion.[30]

---

27. R. Pischel's *Ueber die Ursprung des Christlichen Fisch-Symbols* is specifically devoted to the possible derivation from Indian sources. Scheftelowitz, *Das Fischsymbolik in Judentem und Christentum* (*Archiv für Religionswissenschaft*, Vol. XIV.), contains a great deal of valuable material. R. Eisler, *Orpheus the Fisher* (*The Quest*, Vols. I and II.), *John, Jonas, Oannes* (ibid. Vol. III.), *The Messianic Fish-meal of the Primitive Church* (ibid. Vol. IV.), are isolated studies, forming part of a comprehensive work on the subject, the publication of which has unfortunately been prevented by the War.

28. *Mahâbhârata*, Bk. III.

29. Cf. Scheftelowitz, *op. cit.* p. 51.

30. Cf. *The Open Court*, June and July, 1911, where reproductions of these figures will be found.

IX. The Fisher King

This also holds good for Chinese Buddhism. The goddess Kwanyin (= Avalokiteśvara), the female Deity of Mercy and Salvation, is depicted either on, or holding, a Fish. In the Han palace of Kun-Ming-Ch'ih there was a Fish carved in jade to which in time of drought sacrifices were offered, the prayers being always answered.

Both in India and China the Fish is employed in funeral rites. In India a crystal bowl with Fish handles was found in a reputed tomb of Buddha. In China the symbol is found on stone slabs enclosing the coffin, on bronze urns, vases, etc. Even as the Babylonians had the Fish, or Fisher, god, Oannes who revealed to them the arts of Writing, Agriculture, etc., and was, as Eisler puts it, 'teacher and lord of all wisdom,' so the Chinese Fu-Hi, who is pictured with the mystic tablets containing the mysteries of Heaven and Earth, is, with his consort and retinue, represented as having a fish's tail.[31]

The writer of the article in *The Open Court* asserts that "the Fish was sacred to those deities who were supposed to lead men back from the shadows of death to life."[32] If this be really the case we can understand the connection of the symbol first with Orpheus, later with Christ, as Eisler remarks: "Orpheus is connected with nearly all the mystery, and a great many of the ordinary chthonic, cults in Greece and Italy. Christianity took its first tentative steps into [p121] the reluctant world of Graeco-Roman Paganism under the benevolent patronage of Orpheus."[33]

There is thus little reason to doubt that, if we regard the Fish as a Divine Life symbol, of immemorial antiquity, we shall not go very far astray.

We may note here that there was a fish known to the Semites by the name of Adonis, although as the title signifies 'Lord,' and is generic rather than specific, too much stress cannot be laid upon it. It is more interesting to know that in Babylonian cosmology Adapa the Wise, the son of Ea, is represented as a Fisher.[34] In the ancient Sumerian laments for Tammuz, previously referred to, that god is frequently addressed as *Divine Lamgar, Lord of the Net,* the nearest equivalent I have so far found to our 'Fisher King.'[35] Whether the phrase is here used in an actual or a symbolic sense the connection of idea is sufficiently striking.

---

31. *Op. cit.* p. 403. Cf. here an illustration in Miss Harrison's *Themis* (p. 262), which shows Cecrops, who played the same rôle with regard to the Greeks, with a serpent's tail.
32. *Ibid.* p. 168. In this connection note the prayer to Vishnu, quoted above.
33. Cf. Eisler, *Orpheus the Fisher* (*The Quest*, Vol. I. p. 126).
34. Cf. W. Staerk, *Ueber den Ursprung der Gral-Legende,* pp. 55, 56.
35. Cf. S. Langdon, *Sumerian and Babylonian Psalms,* pp. 301, 305, 307, 313.

IX. The Fisher King

In the opinion of the most recent writers on the subject the Christian Fish symbolism derives directly from the Jewish, the Jews, on their side having borrowed freely from Syrian belief and practice.[36]

What may be regarded as the central point of Jewish Fish symbolism is the tradition that, at the end of the world, Messias will catch the great Fish Leviathan, and divide its flesh as food among the faithful. As a foreshadowing of this Messianic Feast the Jews were in the habit of eating fish upon the Sabbath. During the Captivity, [p122] under the influence of the worship of the goddess Atargatis, they transferred the ceremony to the Friday, the eve of the Sabbath, a position which it has retained to the present day. Eisler remarks that "in Galicia one can see Israelite families in spite of their being reduced to the extremest misery, procuring on Fridays a single gudgeon, to eat, divided into fragments, at night-fall. In the 16th century Rabbi Solomon Luria protested strongly against this practice. Fish, he declared, should be eaten on the Sabbath itself, not on the Eve."[37]

This Jewish custom appears to have been adopted by the primitive Church, and early Christians, on their side, celebrated a Sacramental Fish-meal. The Catacombs supply us with numerous illustrations, fully described by the two writers referred to. The elements of this mystic meal were Fish, Bread, and Wine, the last being represented in the Messianic tradition: "At the end of the meal God will give to the most worthy, *i.e.*, to King David, the Cup of Blessing—one of fabulous dimensions."[38]

Fish play an important part in Mystery Cults, as being the 'holy' food. Upon a tablet dedicated to the Phrygian *Mater Magna* we find Fish and Cup; and Dölger, speaking of a votive tablet discovered in the Balkans, says, "Hier ist der Fisch immer und immer wieder allzu deutlich als die heilige Speise eines Mysterien-Kultes hervorgehoben."[39]

Now I would submit that here, and not in Celtic Folk-lore, is to be found the source of Borron's Fish-meal. Let us consider the circumstances. Joseph and his followers, in the course of their wanderings, find

---

36. Cf. Eisler, *The Messianic Fish-meal of the Primitive Church* (*The Quest*, Vol. IV.), where the various frescoes are described; also the article by Scheftelowitz, already referred to. While mainly devoted to Jewish beliefs and practices, this study contains much material derived from other sources. So far it is the fullest and most thoroughly *documenté* treatment of the subject I have met with.
37. Cf. Eisler, *op. cit.* and Scheftelowitz, pp. 19. 20.
38. Cf. Eisler, *op. cit.* p. 508.
39. Cf. Scheftelowitz, *op. cit.* pp. 337, 338, and note 4.

IX. The Fisher King

themselves in danger of famine. The position is somewhat curious, as apparently [p123] the leaders have no idea of the condition of their followers till the latter appeal to Brons.[40]

Brons informs Joseph, who prays for aid and counsel from the Grail. A Voice from Heaven bids him send his brother-in-law, Brons, to catch a fish. Meanwhile he, Joseph, is to prepare a table, set the Grail, covered with a cloth, in the centre opposite his own seat, and the fish which Brons shall catch, on the other side. He does this, and the seats are filled—"Si s'i asieent une grant partie et plus i ot de cels qui n'i sistrent mie, que de cels qui sistrent." Those who are seated at the table are conscious of a great "douceur," and "l'accomplissement de lor cuers," the rest feel nothing.

Now compare this with the Irish story of the Salmon of Wisdom.[41]

Finn Mac Cumhail enters the service of his namesake, Finn Eger, who for seven years had remained by the Boyne watching the Salmon of Lynn Feic, which it had been foretold Finn should catch. The younger lad, who conceals his name, catches the fish. He is set to watch it while it roasts but is warned not to eat it. Touching it with his thumb he is burned, and puts his thumb in his mouth to cool it. Immediately he becomes possessed of all knowledge, and thereafter has only to chew his thumb to obtain wisdom. Mr Nutt remarks: "The incident in Borron's poem has been recast in the mould of mediaeval Christian Symbolism, but I think the older myth can still be clearly discerned, and is wholly responsible for the incident as found in the *Conte du Graal*."

But when these words were written we were in ignorance of the Sacramental Fish-meal, common alike to Jewish, Christian, and Mystery Cults, a meal which offers a far closer parallel to Borron's romance than does the Finn story, in [p124] which, beyond the catching of a fish, there is absolutely no point of contact with our romance, neither Joseph nor Brons derives wisdom from the eating thereof; it is not they who detect the sinners, the severance between the good and the evil is brought about automatically. The Finn story has no common meal, and no idea of spiritual blessings such as are connected therewith.

In the case of the Messianic Fish-meal, on the other hand, the parallel is striking; in both cases it is a communal meal, in both cases the privilege of sharing it is the reward of the faithful, in both cases it is a foretaste of the bliss of Paradise.

---

40. Hucher, *Le Saint Graal*, Vol. I. pp. 251 et seq., 315 *et seq.*
41. Cf. A. Nutt, *Studies in the Legend of the Holy Grail*, p. 209.

IX. The Fisher King

Furthermore, as remarked above, the practice was at one time of very widespread prevalence.

Now whence did Borron derive his knowledge, from Jewish, Christian or Mystery sources?

This is a question not very easy to decide. In view of the pronounced Christian tone of Borron's romance I should feel inclined to exclude the first, also the Jewish Fish-meal seems to have been of a more open, general and less symbolic character than the Christian; it was frankly an anticipation of a promised future bliss, obtainable by all.

Orthodox Christianity, on the other hand, knows nothing of the Sacred Fish-meal, so far as I am aware it forms no part of any Apocalyptic expectation, and where this special symbolism does occur it is often under conditions which place its interpretation outside the recognized category of Christian belief.

A noted instance in point is the famous epitaph of Bishop Aberkios, over the correct interpretation of which scholars have spent much time and ingenuity.[42] In this curious text Aberkios, after mentioning his journeys, says:

> [p125] "Paul I had as my guide,
> Faith however always went ahead and set before me as food a *Fish*
>   from a *Fountain*, a huge one, a clean one,
> Which a Holy Virgin has caught.
> This she gave to the friends ever to eat as food,
> Having good *Wine*, and offering it watered together with *Bread*.
> Aberkios had this engraved when 72 years of age in truth.
> *Whoever can understand this* let him pray for Aberkios."

Eisler (I am here quoting from the *Quest* article) remarks, "As the last line of our quotation gives us quite plainly to understand, a number of words which we have italicized are obviously used in an unusual, metaphorical, sense, that is to say as terms of the Christian Mystery language." While Harnack, admitting that the Christian character of the text is indisputable, adds significantly: "*aber das Christentum der Grosskirche ist es nicht.*"

---

42. Cf. Eisler, *The Mystic Epitaph of Bishop Aberkios* (*The Quest*, Vol. V. pp. 302–312); Scheftelowitz, *op. cit.* p. 8.

IX. The Fisher King

Thus it is possible that, to the various points of doubtful orthodoxy which scholars have noted as characteristic of the Grail romances, Borron's Fish-meal should also be added.

Should it be objected that the dependence of a medieval romance upon a Jewish tradition of such antiquity is scarcely probable, I would draw attention to the *Voyage of Saint Brandan,* where the monks, during their prolonged wanderings, annually 'kept their Resurrection,' *i.e.,* celebrate their Easter Mass, on the back of a great Fish.[43] On their first meeting with this monster Saint Brandan tells them it is the greatest of all fishes, and is named Jastoni, a name which bears a curious resemblance to the Jhasa of the Indian tradition cited above.[44] In this last instance the connection of the Fish with life, renewed and sustained, is undeniable.

[p126] The original source of such a symbol is most probably to be found in the belief, referred to in a previous chapter,[45] that all life comes from the water, but that a more sensual and less abstract idea was also operative appears from the close connection of the Fish with the goddess Astarte or Atargatis, a connection here shared by the Dove. Cumont, in his *Les Religions Orientales dans le Paganisme Romain,* says: "Two animals were held in general reverence, namely, Dove and Fish. Countless flocks of Doves greeted the traveller when he stepped on shore at Askalon, and in the outer courts of all the temples of Astarte one might see the flutter of their white wings. The Fish were preserved in ponds near to the Temple, and superstitious dread forbade their capture, for the goddess punished such sacrilege, smiting the offender with ulcers and tumours."[46]

But at certain mystic banquets priests and initiates partook of this otherwise forbidden food, in the belief that they thus partook of the flesh of the goddess. Eisler and other scholars are of the opinion that it was the familiarity with this ritual gained by the Jews during the Captivity that led to the adoption of the Friday Fish-meal, already referred to, Friday being the day dedicated to the goddess and, later, to her equivalent, Venus. From the Jews the custom spread to the Christian Church, where it still flourishes, its true origin, it is needless to say, being wholly unsuspected.[47]

---

43. Cf. *The Voyage of Saint Brandan,* ll. 372, *et seq.,* 660 *et seq.*
44. *Op. cit.* ll. 170 *et seq.,* and *supra,* p. 119.
45. *Vide supra,* p. 70.
46. *Op. cit.* p. 168.
47. Cf. *The Messianic Fish-meal.*

IX. The Fisher King

Dove and Fish also appear together in ancient iconography. In Comte Goblet d'Alviella's work *The Migration of Symbols* there is an illustration of a coin of Cyzicus, on which is represented an Omphalus, flanked by two Doves, with a Fish beneath;[48] and a whole section is devoted to the discussion of the representations of two Doves on either side of a Temple entrance, or of an Omphalus. In the [p127] author's opinion the origin of the symbol may be found in the sacred dove-cotes of Phoenicia, referred to by Cumont.

Scheftelowitz instances the combination of Fish-meal and Dove, found on a Jewish tomb of the first century at Syracuse, and remarks that the two are frequently found in combination on Christian tombstones.[49]

Students of the Grail romances will not need to be reminded that the Dove makes its appearance in certain of our texts. In the *Parzival* it plays a somewhat important *rôle;* every Good Friday a Dove brings from Heaven a Host, which it lays upon the Grail; and the Dove is the badge of the Grail Knights.[50] In the prose *Lancelot* the coming of the Grail procession is heralded by the entrance through the window of a Dove, bearing a censer in its beak.[51] Is it not possible that it was the already existing connection in Nature ritual of these two, Dove and Fish, which led to the introduction of the former into our romances, where its *rôle* is never really adequately motivated? It is further to be noted that besides Dove and Fish the Syrians reverenced Stones, more especially meteoric Stones, which they held to be endowed with life potency, another point of contact with our romances.[52]

That the Fish was considered a potent factor in ensuring fruitfulness is proved by certain prehistoric tablets described by Scheftelowitz, where Fish, Horse, and Swastika, or in another instance Fish and Reindeer, are found in a combination which unmistakeably denotes that the object of the [p128] votive tablet was to ensure the fruitfulness of flocks and herds.[53]

---

48. *Op. cit.* p. 92, fig. 42 *a.*
49. *Op. cit.* p. 23, and note, p. 29.
50. *Parzival,* Bk. IX. ll., 1109 et seq., Bk. XVI. ll. 175 et seq.
51. Cf. *Sir Gawain at the Grail Castle,* p. 55. Certain of the *Lancelot* MSS., e.g., B.N., f. Fr. 123, give two doves.
52. Cf. Scheftelowitz, p. 338. Haven, *Der Gral,* has argued that Wolfram's stone is such a meteoric stone, a Boetylus. I am not prepared to take up any position as to the exact nature of the stone itself, whether precious stone or meteor; the real point of importance being its Life-giving potency.
53. *Op. cit.* p. 381.

IX. The Fisher King

With this intention its influence was also invoked in marriage ceremonies. The same writer points out that the Jews in Poland were accustomed to hold a Fish feast immediately on the conclusion of the marriage ceremony and that a similar practice can be prove for the ancient Greeks.[54] At the present day the Jews of Tunis exhibit a Fish's tail on a cushion at their weddings.[55] In some parts of India the newly-wedded pair waded knee-deep into the water, and caught fish in a new garment. During the ceremony a Brahmin student, from the shore, asked solemnly, "What seest thou?" to which the answer was returned, "Sons and Cattle."[56] In all these cases there can be no doubt that it was the prolific nature of the Fish, a feature which it shares in common with the Dove, which inspired practice and intention.

Surely the effect of this cumulative body of evidence is to justify us in the belief that Fish and Fisher, being, as they undoubtedly are, Life symbols of immemorial antiquity, are, by virtue of their origin, entirely in their place in a sequence of incidents which there is solid ground for believing derive ultimately from a Cult of this nature. That Borron's Fish-meal, that the title of Fisher King, are not accidents of literary invention but genuine and integral parts of the common body of tradition which has furnished the incidents and *mise-en-scène* of the Grail drama. Can it be denied that, while from the standpoint of a Christian interpretation the character of the Fisher King is simply incomprehensible, from the standpoint of Folk-tale inadequately explained, from that of a Ritual survival it assumes a profound meaning and significance? He is not merely a deeply symbolic [p129] figure, but the essential centre of the whole cult, a being semi-divine, semi-human, standing between his people and land, and the unseen forces which control their destiny. If the Grail story be based upon a Life ritual the character of the Fisher King is of the very essence of the tale, and his title, so far from being meaningless, expresses, for those who are at pains to seek, the intention and object of the perplexing whole. The Fisher King is, as I suggested above, the very heart and centre of the whole mystery, and I contend that with an adequate interpretation of this enigmatic character the soundness of the theory providing such an interpretation may be held to be definitely proved. [p130]

---

54. *Ibid.* p. 376 et seq.
55. *Ibid.* p. 20.
56. *Ibid.* p. 377.

X. The Secret of the Grail (1)

The Mysteries

The Grail regarded as an object of awe. Danger of speaking of Grail or revealing Its secrets. Passages in illustration. Why, if survival of Nature cults, popular, and openly performed? A two-fold element in these cults, Exoteric, Esoteric. *The Mysteries. Their influence on Christianity to be sought in the Hellenized rather than the Hellenic cults. Cumont. Rohde. Radical difference between Greek and Oriental conceptions. Lack of evidence as regards Mysteries on the whole. Best attested form that connected with Nature cults. Attis-Adonis. Popularity of the Phrygian cult in Rome. Evidence as to Attis Mysteries. Utilized by Neo-Platonists as vehicle for teaching. Close connection with Mithraism. The Taurobolium. Details of Attis Mysteries. Parallels with the Grail romances.*

Students of the Grail literature cannot fail to have been impressed by a certain atmosphere of awe and mystery which surrounds that enigmatic Vessel. There is a secret connected with it, the revelation of which will entail dire misfortune on the betrayer. If spoken of at all it must be with scrupulous accuracy. It is so secret a thing that no woman, be she wife or maid, may venture to speak of it. A priest, or a man of holy life might indeed tell the marvel of the Grail, but none can hearken to the recital without shuddering, trembling, and changing colour for very fear.

> "C'est del Graal dont nus ne doit
> Le secret dire ne conter;
> Car tel chose poroit monter
> Li contes ains qu'il fust tos dis
> Que teus hom en seroit maris
> Qui ne l'aroit mie fourfait.
> . . . .

X. The Secret of the Grail (1)

> Car, se Maistre Blihis ne ment
> Nus ne doit dire le secré."[1]

> "Mais la mervelle qu'il trova
> Dont maintes fois s'espoenta
> Ne doit nus hom conter ne dire
> Cil ki le dist en a grant ire
> Car c'est li signes del Graal (other texts secrés)
> S'en puet avoir et paine et mal (Li fet grant pechié et grant mal)
> Cil qui s'entremet del conter
> Fors ensi com it doit aler."[2]

[p131] The above refers to Gawain's adventure at the Black Chapel, *en route* for the Grail Castle.

The following is the answer given to Perceval by the maiden of the White Mule, after he has been overtaken by a storm in the forest. She tells him the mysterious light he beheld proceeded from the Grail, but on his enquiry as to what the Grail may be, refuses to give him any information.

> "Li dist 'Sire, ce ne puet estre
> Que je plus vos en doie dire
> Si vous .c. fois esties me sire
> N'en oseroie plus conter,
> Ne de mon labor plus parler (other texts, ma bouche)
> Car ce est chose trop secrée
> Si ne doit estre racontée
> Par dame ne par damoisele,
> Par mescine ne par puciele,
> Ne par nul home qui soit nés
> Si prouvoires n'est ordenés,
> U home qui maine sainte vie,
> . . . .
> Cil poroit del Graal parler,
> Et la mervelle raconter,

---

1. *Elucidation*, ll. 4–9 and 12, 13.
2. Potvin, ll. 19933–40. I quote from Potvin's edition as more accessible than the MSS., but the version of Mons is, on the whole, an inferior one.

X. The Secret of the Grail (1)

> Que nus hom nel poroit oïr
> Que il ne l'estuece fremir
> Trambler et remuer color,
> Et empalir de la paour.[3]

From this evidence there is no doubt that to the romance writers the Grail was something secret, mysterious and awful, the exact knowledge of which was reserved to a select few, and which was only to be spoken of with bated breath, and a careful regard to strict accuracy.

But how does this agree with the evidence set forth in our preceding chapters? There we have been led rather to [p132] emphasize the close parallels existing between the characters and incidents of the Grail story, and a certain well-marked group of popular beliefs and observances, now very generally recognized as fragments of a once widespread Nature Cult. These beliefs and observances, while dating from remotest antiquity, have, in their modern survivals, of recent years, attracted the attention of scholars by their persistent and pervasive character, and their enduring vitality.

Yet, so far as we have hitherto dealt with them, these practices were, and are, popular in character, openly performed, and devoid of the special element of mystery which is so characteristic a feature of the Grail.

Nor, in these public Folk-ceremonies, these Spring festivals, Dances, and Plays, is there anything which, on the face of it, appears to bring them into touch with the central mystery of the Christian Faith. Yet the men who wrote these romances saw no incongruity in identifying the mysterious Food-providing Vessel of the *Bleheris-Gawain* version with the Chalice of the Eucharist, and in ascribing the power of bestowing Spiritual Life to that which certain modern scholars have identified as a *Wunsch-Ding*, a Folk-tale Vessel of Plenty.

If there be a mystery of the Grail surely the mystery lies here, in the possibility of identifying two objects which, apparently, lie at the very opposite poles of intellectual conception. What brought them together? Where shall we seek a connecting link? By what road did the romancers reach so strangely unexpected a goal?

It is, of course, very generally recognized that in the case of most of the pre-Christian religions, upon the nature and character of whose rites we possess reliable information, such rites possessed a two-fold

---

3. Potvin, ll. 28108-28.

X. The Secret of the Grail (1)

character—*exoteric;* in celebrations openly and publicly performed, in which all adherents of that particular cult could join freely, the object of such [p133] public rites being to obtain some external and material benefit, whether for the individual worshipper, or for the community as a whole—*esoteric;* rites open only to a favoured few, the initiates, the object of which appears, as a rule, to have been individual rather than social, and non-material. In some cases, certainly, the object aimed at was the attainment of a conscious, ecstatic, union with the god, and the definite assurance of a future life. In other words there was the public worship, and there were the Mysteries.

Of late years there has been a growing tendency among scholars to seek in the Mysteries the clue which shall enable us to read aright the baffling riddle of the Grail, and there can be little doubt that, in so doing, we are on the right path. At the same time I am convinced that to seek that clue in those Mysteries which are at once the most famous, and the most familiar to the classical scholar, *i.e.,* the Eleusinian, is a fatal mistake. There are, as we shall see, certain essential, and radical, differences between the Greek and the Christian religious conceptions which, affecting as they do the root conceptions of the two groups, render it quite impossible that any form of the Eleusinian Mystery cult could have given such results as we find in the Grail legend.[4]

Cumont in his *Les Religions Orientales dans le Paganisme Romain,* speaking of the influence of the Mysteries upon Christianity, remarks acutely, "Or, lorsqu'on parle de mystères on doit songer à l'Asie hellénisée, bien plus qu'à la Grèce propre, malgré tout le prestige qui entourait Eleusis, car d'abord les premières communautés Chrétiennes se font fondées, formées, développées, au milieu de populations Orientales, Sémites, Phrygiens, Egyptiens."[5]

[p134] This is perfectly true, but it was not only the influence of *milieu,* not only the fact that the 'hellenized' faiths were, as Cumont points out, more advanced, richer in ideas and sentiments, more pregnant, more poignant, than the more strictly 'classic' faiths, but they possessed, in common with Christianity, certain distinctive features lacking in these latter.

If we were asked to define the special characteristic of the central Christian rite, should we not state it as being a Sacred meal of Communion in which the worshipper, not merely symbolically, but actually,

---

4. This is to my mind the error vitiating much of Dr Nitze's later work, *e.g.,* the studies entitled *The Fisher-King in the Grail Romances* and *The Sister's Son, and the Conte del Graal.*
5. *Op. cit.* Introduction, p. x.

partakes of, and becomes one with, his God, receiving thereby the assurance of eternal life? (*The Body of Our Lord Jesus Christ preserve thy body and soul unto everlasting life.*)

But it is precisely this conception which is lacking in the Greek Mysteries, and that inevitably, as Rohde points out: "The Eleusinian Mysteries in common with all Greek religion, differentiated clearly between gods and men, *eins ist der Menschen, ein andres der Götter-Geschlecht*— ἐνἀνδρ ων,ἐν θε ων γένος.' The attainment of union with the god, by way of ecstasy, as in other Mystery cults, is foreign to the Eleusinian idea. As Cumont puts it "The Greco-Roman deities rejoice in the perpetual calm and youth of Olympus, the Eastern deities die to live again."[6] In other words Greek religion lacks the Sacramental idea.

Thus even if we set aside the absence of a parallel between the ritual of the Greek Mysteries and the *mise-en-scène* of the Grail stories, Eleusis would be unable to offer us those essential elements which would have rendered possible a translation of the incidents of those stories into terms of high Christian symbolism. Yet we cannot refrain from the conclusion that there was something in the legend that not merely rendered possible, but actually invited, such a translation.

[p135] If we thus dismiss, as fruitless for our investigation, the most famous representative of the Hellenic Mysteries proper, how does the question stand with regard to those faiths to which Cumont is referring, the hellenized cults of Asia Minor?

Here the evidence, not merely of the existence of Mysteries, but of their widespread popularity, and permeating influence, is overwhelming; the difficulty is not so much to prove our case, as to select and co-ordinate the evidence germane to our enquiry.

Regarding the question as a whole it is undoubtedly true that, as Anrich remarks, "the extent of the literature devoted to the Mysteries stands in no relation whatever (*gar keinem Verhältniss*) to the importance in reality attached to them."[7] Later in the same connection, after quoting Clement of Alexandria's dictum "Geheime Dinge wie die Gottheit, werden der Rede anvertraut, nicht der Schrift," he adds, "*Schriftliche Fixierung ist schon beinahe Entweihung.*"[8] A just remark which it would be well if certain critics who make a virtue of refusing to

---

6. Rohde, *Psyche*, p. 293, and Cumont, *op. cit.* p. 44.
7. Anrich, *Das alte Mysterien-Wesen in seinem Verhältniss zum Christentum*, p. 46.
8. *Op. cit.* p. 136.

X. The Secret of the Grail (1)

accept as evidence anything short of a direct and positive literary statement would bear in mind. There are certain lines of research in which, as Bishop Butler long since emphasized, probability must be our guide.

Fortunately, however, so far as our present research is concerned, we have more than probability to rely upon; not only did these Nature Cults with which we are dealing express themselves in Mystery terms, but as regards these special Mysteries we possess clear and definite information, and we know, moreover, that in the Western world they were, of all the Mystery faiths, the most widely spread, and the most influential.

[p136] As Sir J. G. Frazer has before now pointed out, there are parallel and over-lapping forms of this cult, the name of the god, and certain details of the ritual, may differ in different countries, but whether he hails from Babylon, Phrygia, or Phoenicia, whether he be called Tammuz, Attis, or Adonis, the main lines of the story are fixed, and invariable. Always he is young and beautiful, always the beloved of a great goddess; always he is the victim of a tragic and untimely death, a death which entails bitter loss and misfortune upon a mourning world, and which, for the salvation of that world, is followed by a resurrection. Death and Resurrection, mourning and rejoicing, present themselves in sharp antithesis in each and all of the forms.

We know the god best as Adonis, for it was under that name that, though not originally Greek, he became known to the Greek world, was adopted by them with ardour, carried by them to Alexandria, where his feast assumed the character of a State solemnity; under that name his story has been enshrined in Art, and as Adonis he is loved and lamented to this day. The Adonis ritual may be held to be the classic form of the cult.

But in Rome, the centre of Western civilization, it was otherwise: there it was the Phrygian god who was in possession; the dominating position held by the cult of Attis and the *Magna Mater*, and the profound influence exercised by that cult over better known, but subsequently introduced, forms of worship, have not, so far, been sufficiently realized.

The first of the Oriental cults to gain a footing in the Imperial city, the worship of the *Magna Mater* of Pessinonte was, for a time, rigidly confined within the limits of her sanctuary. The orgiastic ritual of the priests of Kybele made at first little appeal to the more disciplined temperament of the Roman population. By degrees, however, it won its [p137] way, and by the reign of Claudius had become so popular that the emperor instituted public feasts in honour of Kybele and Attis, feasts which were celebrated at the Spring solstice, March 15th-27th.[9]

As the public feast increased in popularity, so did the Mystery feast, of which the initiated alone were privileged to partake, acquire a symbolic significance: the foods partaken of became "un aliment de vie spirituelle, et doivent soutenir dans les épreuves de la vie l'initié." Philosophers boldly utilized the framework of the Attis cult as the vehicle for imparting their own doctrines, "Lorsque le Nèoplatonisme triomphera la fable Phrygienne deviendra le moule traditionnel dans lequel des exégètes subtils verseront hardiment leurs spéculations philosophiques sur les forces créatrices fécondantes, principes de toutes les formes matérielles, et sur la délivrance de l'âme divine plongée dans la corruption de ce monde terrestre."[10]

Certain of the Gnostic sects, both pre- and post-Christian, appear to have been enthusiastic participants in the Attis mysteries;[11] Hepding, in his *Attis* study, goes so far as to refer to Bishop Aberkios, to whose enigmatic epitaph our attention was directed in the last chapter, as "*der Attis-Preister.*"[12]

Another element aided in the diffusion of the ritual. Of all the Oriental cults which journeyed Westward under the aegis of Rome none was so deeply rooted or so widely spread as the originally Persian cult of Mithra—the popular religion of the Roman legionary. But between the cults of Mithra and of Attis there was a close and intimate alliance. In parts of Asia Minor the Persian god had early taken over features of the Phrygian deity. "Aussitôt que nous pouvons constater la présence du culte Persique en Italie [p138] nous le trouvons étroitement uni à celui de la Grande Mére de Pessinonte."[13] The union between Mithra and the goddess Anâhita was held to be the equivalent of that subsisting between the two great Phrygian deities Attis-Kybele. The most ancient Mithreum known, that at Ostia, was attached to the Metroon, the temple of Kybele. At Saalburg the ruins of the two temples are but a few steps apart. "L'on a tout lieu de croire que le culte du dieu Iranien et celui de la déesse Phrygienne vécurent en communion intime sur toute l'étendue de l'Empire."[14]

---

9. Cumont, *op. cit.* p. 84.
10. *Op. cit.* pp. 104, 105.
11. Cf. Anrich, *op. cit.* p. 81.
12. Hepding, *Attis,* p. 189.
13. Cumont, Mystères de Mithra, pp. 19 and 78.
14. Ibid. p. 188.

X. The Secret of the Grail (1)

A proof of the close union of the two cults is afforded by the mystic rite of the Taurobolium, which was practised by both, and which, in the West, at least, seems to have passed from the temples of the Mithra to those of the *Magna Mater*. At the same time Cumont remarks that the actual rite seems to have been practised in Asia from a great antiquity, before Mithraism had attributed to it a spiritual significance. It is thus possible that the rite had earlier formed a part of the Attis initiation, and had been temporarily disused.[15]

We shall see that the union of the Mithra-Attis cults becomes of distinct importance when we examine, (*a*) the spiritual significance of these rituals, and their elements of affinity with Christianity, (*b*) their possible diffusion in the British Isles.

But now what do we know of the actual details of the Attis mysteries? The first and most important point was a Mystic Meal, at which the food partaken of was served in the sacred vessels, the tympanum, and the cymbals. The formula of an Attis initiate was "*I have eaten from the tympanum, I have drunk from the cymbals.*" As I have remarked above, the food thus partaken of was a Food of Life—"*Die Attis-Diener* [p139] *in der Tat eine magische Speise des Lebens aus ihren Kult-Geräten zu essen meinten.*"[16]

Dieterich in his interesting study entitled *Eine Mithras-liturgie* refers to this meal as the centre of the whole religious action.

Further, in some mysterious manner, the fate of the initiate was connected with, and dependent upon, the death and resurrection of the god. The Christian writer Firmicius Maternus, at one time himself an initiate, has left an account of the ceremony, without, however, specifying whether the deity in question was Attis or Adonis—as Dieterich remarks "*Was er erzählt kann sich auf Attis-gemeinden, und auf Adonis-gemeinden beziehen.*"

This is what he says: "*Nocte quadam simulacrum in lectica supinum ponitur, et per numeros digestis fletibus plangitur: deinde cum se ficta lamentatione satiaverint lumen infertur: tunc a sacerdote omnium qui flebant fauces unguentur, quibus perunctis sacerdos hoc lento murmure susurrit:*

Θάρρετεμ ύςται του θεού ςεςωςμένου

---
15. Ibid. pp. 190 et seq.
16. *Vide* Hepding, *Attis*, Chap. 4, for details.

X. The Secret of the Grail (1)

Ἐϲται γα'ρ ἡμιν ἐκ πόνων ϲωτηρία—

on which Dieterich remarks: "Das Heil der Mysten hängt an der Rettung des Gottes."[17]

Hepding holds that in some cases there was an actual burial, and awakening with the god to a new life.[18] In any case it is clear that the successful issue of the test of initiation was dependent upon the resurrection and revival of the god.

Now is it not clear that we have here a close parallel with the Grail romances? In each case we have a common, and mystic, meal, in which the food partaken of stands in close connection with the holy vessels. In the Attis feast the [p140] initiates actually ate and drank from these vessels; in the romances the Grail community never actually eat from the Grail itself, but the food is, in some mysterious and unexplained manner, supplied by it. In both cases it is a *Lebens-Speise,* a Food of Life. This point is especially insisted upon in the *Parzival,* where the Grail community never become any older than they were on the day they first beheld the Talisman.[19] In the Attis initiation the proof that the candidate has successfully passed the test is afforded by the revival of the god—in the Grail romances the proof lies in the healing of the Fisher King.

Thus, while deferring for a moment any insistence on the obvious points of parallelism with the Sacrament of the Eucharist, and the possibilities of Spiritual teaching inherent in the ceremonies, necessary links in our chain of argument, we are, I think, entitled to hold that, even when we pass beyond the outward *mise-en-scène* of the story—the march of incident, the character of the King, his title, his disability, and relation to his land and folk—to the inner and deeper significance of the tale, the Nature Cults still remain reliable guides; it is their inner, their esoteric, ritual which will enable us to bridge the gulf between what appears at first sight the wholly irreconcilable elements of Folk-tale and high Spiritual mystery. [p141]

---

17. Dieterich, *Eine Mithrasliturgie,* p. 174.
18. Hepding, *op. cit.* p. 196.
19. Cf. my *Legend of Sir Perceval,* Vol. II. p. 313. Hepding mentions (op. cit. p. 174) among the *sacra* of the goddess *Phrygium ferrum,* which he suggests was the knife from which the Archigallus wounded himself on the 'Blood' day. Thus it is possible that the primitive ritual may have contained a knife.

XI. The Secret of the Grail (2)

The Naassene Document

Relations between early Christianity, and pre-Christian cults. Early Heresies. Hippolytus, and The Refutation of all Heresies. *Character of the work. The Naassene Document. Mr Mead's analysis of text. A synthesis of Mysteries. Identification of Life Principle with the Logos. Connection between Drama and Mysteries of Attis. Importance of the Phrygian Mysteries. Naassene claim to be sole Christians. Significance of evidence. Vegetation cults as vehicle of high spiritual teaching. Exoteric and Esoteric parallels with the Grail tradition. Process of evolution sketched. Bleheris. Perlesvaus. Borron and the Mystery tradition. Christian Legendary, and Folk-tale, secondary, not primary, features.*

We have now seen that the Ritual which, as we have postulated, lies, in a fragmentary and distorted condition, at the root of our existing Grail romances, possessed elements capable of assimilation with a religious system which the great bulk of its modern adherents would unhesitatingly declare to be its very antithesis. That Christianity might have borrowed from previously existing cults certain outward signs and symbols, might have accommodated itself to already existing Fasts and Feasts, may be, perforce has had to be, more or less grudgingly admitted; that such a *rapprochement* should have gone further, that it should even have been inherent in the very nature of the Faith, that, to some of the deepest thinkers of old, Christianity should have been held for no new thing but a fulfilment of the promise enshrined in the Mysteries from the beginning of the world, will to many be a strange and startling thought. Yet so it was, and I firmly believe that it is only in the recognition of this one-time claim of essential kinship between Christianity and the Pagan Mysteries that we shall find the key to the Secret of the Grail.

And here at the outset I would ask those readers who are inclined to turn with feelings of contemptuous impatience from what they deem

XI. The Secret of the Grail (2)

an unprofitable discussion of idle speculations which have little or nothing to do with a problem they hold to be one of purely literary interest, to be [p142] solved by literary comparison and criticism, and by no other method, to withhold their verdict till they have carefully examined the evidence I am about to bring forward, evidence which has never so far been examined in this connection, but which if I am not greatly mistaken provides us with clear and unmistakable proof of the actual existence of a ritual in all points analogous to that indicated by the Grail romances.

In the previous chapter we have seen that there is evidence, and abundant evidence, not merely of the existence of Mysteries connected with the worship of Adonis-Attis, but of the high importance assigned to such Mysteries; at the time of the birth of Christianity they were undoubtedly the most popular and the most influential of the foreign cults adopted by Imperial Rome. In support of this statement I quoted certain passages from Cumont's *Religions Orientales,* in which he touches on the subject: here are two other quotations which may well serve as introduction to the evidence we are about to examine. "Researches on the doctrines and practices common to Christianity and the Oriental Mysteries almost invariably go back, beyond the limits of the Roman Empire, to the Hellenized East. It is there we must seek the key of enigmas still unsolved—The essential fact to remember is that the Eastern religions had diffused, first anterior to, then parallel with, Christianity, doctrines which acquired with this latter a universal authority in the decline of the ancient world. The preaching of Asiatic priests prepared in their own despite the triumph of the Church."[1]

But the triumph of the new Faith once assured the organizing, dominating, influence of Imperial Rome speedily came into play. Christianity, originally an Eastern, became a Western, religion, the 'Mystery' elements were frowned upon, kinship with pre-Christian faiths ignored, or denied; [p143] where the resemblances between the cults proved too striking for either of these methods such resemblances were boldly attributed to the invention of the Father of Lies himself, a cunning snare whereby to deceive unwary souls. Christianity was carefully trimmed, shaped, and forced into an Orthodox mould, and anything that refused to adapt itself to this drastic process became by that very refusal anathema to the righteous.

---

1. Cumont, *op. cit.* Introd. pp. xx and xxi.

XI. The Secret of the Grail (2)

Small wonder that, under such conditions, the early ages of the Church were marked by a fruitful crop of Heresies, and heresy-hunting became an intellectual pastime in high favour among the strictly orthodox. Among the writers of this period whose works have been preserved Hippolytus, Bishop of Portus in the early years of the third century, was one of the most industrious. He compiled a voluminous treatise, entitled *Philosophumena*, or *The Refutation of all Heresies*, of which only one MS. and that of the fourteenth century, has descended to us. The work was already partially known by quotations, the first Book had been attributed to Origen, and published in the *editio princeps* of his works. The text originally consisted of ten Books, but of these the first three, and part of the fourth, are missing from the MS. The Origen text supplies part of the lacuna, but two entire Books, and part of a third are missing.

Now these special Books, we learn from the Introduction, dealt with the doctrines and Mysteries of the Egyptians and Chaldaeans, whose most sacred secrets Hippolytus boasts that he has divulged. Curiously enough, not only are these Books lacking but in the Epitome at the beginning of Book X. the summary of their contents is also missing, a significant detail, which, as has been suggested by critics, looks like a deliberate attempt on the part of some copyist to suppress the information contained in the Books in question. Incidentally this would seem to suggest that the [p144] worthy bishop was not making an empty boast when he claimed to be a revealer of secrets.

But what is of special interest to us is the treatment meted out to the Christian Mystics, whom Hippolytus stigmatizes as heretics, and whose teaching he deliberately asserts to be simply that of the Pagan Mysteries. He had come into possession of a secret document belonging to one of these sects, whom he calls the Naassenes; this document he gives in full, and it certainly throws a most extraordinary light upon the relation which this early Christian sect held to exist between the New, and the Old, Faith. Mr G. R. S. Mead, in his translation of the Hermetic writings entitled *Thrice-Greatest Hermes*, has given a careful translation and detailed analysis of this most important text, and it is from his work that I shall quote.

So far as the structure of the document is concerned Mr Mead distinguishes three stages.

(*a*) An original Pagan source, possibly dating from the last half of the first century B.C., but containing material of earlier date.

XI. The Secret of the Grail (2)

(*b*) The working over of this source by a Jewish Mystic whom the critic holds to have been a contemporary of Philo.

(*c*) A subsequent working over, with additions, by a Christian Gnostic (Naassene), in the middle of the second century A.D. Finally the text was edited by Hippolytus, in the *Refutation,* about 222 A.D. Thus the ground covered is roughly from 50 B.C. to 220 A.D.[2]

In the translation given by Mr Mead these successive layers are distinguished by initial letters and difference of type, but these distinctions are not of importance for us; what we desire to know is what was really held and taught by these mystics of the Early Church. Mr Mead, in his [p145] introductory remarks, summarizes the evidence as follows: "The claim of these Gnostics was practically that Christianity, or rather the Good News of The Christ, was precisely the consummation of the inner doctrine of the Mystery-institutions of all the nations: the end of them all was the revelation of the Mystery of Man."[3] In other words the teaching of these Naassenes was practically a synthesis of all the Mystery-religions, and although Hippolytus regards them as nothing more than devotees of the cult of the *Magna Mater,* we shall see that, while their doctrine and teaching were undoubtedly based mainly upon the doctrine and practices of the Phrygian Mysteries, they practically identified the deity therein worshipped, *i.e.,* Attis, with the presiding deity of all the other Mysteries.

Mr Mead draws attention to the fact that Hippolytus places these Naassenes in the fore-front of his *Refutation;* they are the first group of Heretics with whom he deals, and we may therefore conclude that he considered them, if not the most important, at least the oldest, of such sectaries.[4]

With these prefatory remarks it will be well to let the document speak for itself. It is of considerable length, and, as we have seen, of intricate construction. I shall therefore quote only those sections which bear directly upon the subject of our investigation; any reader desirous of fuller information can refer to Mr Mead's work, or to the original text published by Reitzenstein.[5]

---

2. *Thrice-Greatest Hermes,* Vol. I, p. 195.
3. *Op. cit.* p. 141.
4. *Op. cit.* p. 142.
5. *Op. cit.* pp. 146 *et seq.* Reitzenstein, *Die Hellenistischen Mysterien Religionen,* Leipzig, 1910, gives the document in the original. There is also a translation of Hippolytus in the *Ante-Nicene Library.*

XI. The Secret of the Grail (2)

At the outset it will be well to understand that the central doctrine of all these Mysteries is what Reitzenstein sums up as "the doctrine of the Man, the Heavenly Man, the Son of God, who descends and becomes a slave of the Fate [p146] Sphere: the Man who, though originally endowed with all power, descends into weakness and bondage, and has to win his own freedom, and regain his original state. This doctrine is not Egyptian, but seems to have been in its origin part and parcel of the Chaldean Mystery-tradition and was widely spread in Hellenistic circles."[6]

Thus, in the introductory remarks prefixed by Hippolytus to the document he is quoting he asserts that the Naassenes honour as the Logos of all universals Man, and Son of Man—"and they divide him into three, for they say he has a mental, psychic, and choïc aspect; and they think that the Gnosis of this Man is the beginning of the possibility of knowing God, saying, 'The beginning of Perfection is the Gnosis of Man, but the Gnosis of God is perfected Perfection.' All these, mental, psychic, and earthy, descended together into one Man, Jesus, the Son of Mary."[7]

Thus the *Myth of Man,* the Mystery of Generation, is the subject matter of the document in question, and this myth is set forth with reference to all the Mysteries, beginning with the Assyrian.

Paragraph 5 runs: "Now the Assyrians call this Mystery Adonis, and whenever it is called Adonis it is Aphrodite who is in love with and desires Soul so-called, and Aphrodite is Genesis according to them."[8]

But in the next section the writer jumps from the Assyrian to the Phrygian Mysteries, saying, "But if the Mother of the Gods emasculates Attis, she too regarding him as the object of her love, it is the Blessed Nature above of the super-Cosmic, and Aeonian spaces which calls back the masculine power of Soul to herself."[9]

[p147] In a note to this Mr Mead quotes from *The Life of Isidorus:* "I fell asleep and in a vision Attis seemed to appear to me, and on behalf of the Mother of gods to initiate me into the feast called Hilario, a mystery which discloses the way of our salvation from Hades." Throughout the document reference is continually made to the Phrygians and their

---

6. Quoted by Mead, *op. cit.* p. 138.
7. *Op. cit.* pp. 146, 147.
8. *Op. cit.* p. 151.
9. *Op. cit.* p. 152. Mr Mead concludes that there is here a lacuna of the original.

XI. The Secret of the Grail (2)

doctrine of Man. The Eleusinian Mysteries are then treated of as subsequent to the Phrygian, "after the Phrygians, the Athenians," but the teaching is represented as being essentially identical.

We have then a passage of great interest for our investigation, in which the Mysteries are sharply divided into two classes, and their separate content clearly defined. There are—"the little Mysteries, those of the Fleshly Generation, and after men have been initiated into them they should cease for a while and become initiated in the Great, Heavenly, Mysteries—for this is the Gate of Heaven, and this is the House of God, where the Good God dwells alone, into which House no impure man shall come."[10] Hippolytus remarks that "these Naassenes say that the performers in theatres, they too, neither say nor do anything without design—for example, when the people assemble in the theatre, and a man comes on the stage clad in a robe different from all others, with lute in hand on which he plays, and thus chants the Great Mysteries, not knowing what he says:

'Whether blest Child of Kronos, or of Zeus, or of Great Rhea,
Hail Attis, thou mournful song of Rhea!
Assyrians call thee thrice-longed-for Adonis;
All Egypt calls thee Osiris;
The Wisdom of Hellas names thee Men's Heavenly Horn;
The Samothracians call thee august Adama;
The Haemonians, Korybas;
[p148] The Phrygians name thee Papa sometimes;
At times again Dead, or God, or Unfruitful, or Aipolos;
Or Green Reaped Wheat-ear;
Or the Fruitful that Amygdalas brought forth,
Man, Piper—Attis!'

This is the Attis of many forms, of whom they sing as follows:

'Of Attis will I sing, of Rhea's Beloved,
Not with the booming of bells,
Nor with the deep-toned pipe of Idaean Kuretes;
But I will blend my song with Phoebus' music of the lyre;

---

10. *Op. cit.* p. 181. In a note Mr Mead says of the Greater Mysteries, "presumably the candidate went through some symbolic rite of death and resurrection."

XI. The Secret of the Grail (2)

Evoi, Evan,—for thou art Pan, thou Bacchus art, and Shepherd of bright stars!'"[11]

On this Hippolytus comments: "For these and suchlike reasons these Naassenes frequent what are called the Mysteries of the Great Mother, believing that they obtain the clearest view of the universal Mystery from the things done in them."

And after all this evidence of elaborate syncretism, this practical identification of all the Mystery-gods with the Vegetation deity Adonis-Attis, we are confronted in the concluding paragraph, after stating that "the True Gate is Jesus the Blessed," with this astounding claim, from the pen of the latest redactor, "And of all men we alone are Christians, accomplishing the Mystery at the Third Gate."[12]

Now what conclusions are to be drawn from this document which, in its entirety, Mr Mead regards as "the most [p149] important source we have for the higher side (regeneration) of the Hellenistic Mysteries"?

First of all, does it not provide a complete and overwhelming justification of those scholars who have insisted upon the importance of these Vegetation cults—a justification of which, from the very nature of their studies, they could not have been aware?

Sir James Frazer, and those who followed him, have dealt with the public side of the cult, with its importance as a recognized vehicle for obtaining material advantages; it was the social, rather than the individual, aspect which appealed to them. Now we find that in the immediate *pre-* and *post*-Christian era these cults were considered not only most potent factors for assuring the material prosperity of land and folk, but were also held to be the most appropriate vehicle for imparting the highest religious teaching. The Vegetation deities, Adonis-Attis, and more especially the Phrygian god, were the chosen guides to the knowledge of, and union with, the supreme Spiritual Source of Life, of which they were the communicating medium.

We must remember that though the document before us is, in its actual form, the expression of faith of a discredited 'Christian-Gnostic' sect, the essential groundwork upon which it is elaborated belongs to

---

11. *Op. cit.* pp. 185, 186. I would draw especial attention to this passage in view of the present controversy as to the Origin of Drama. It looks as if the original writer of the document (and this section is in the Pagan Source) would have inclined to the views of Sir Gilbert Murray, Miss Harrison, and Mr Cornford rather than to those championed by their sarcastic critic, Sir W. Ridgeway.

12. *Op. cit.* p. 190.

XI. The Secret of the Grail (2)

a period anterior to Christianity, and that the Ode in honour of Attis quoted above not only forms part of the original source, but is, in the opinion of competent critics, earlier than the source itself.

I would also recall to the memory of the reader the passage previously quoted from Cumont, in which he refers to the use made by the Neo-Platonist philosophers of the Attis legend, as the mould into which they poured their special theories of the universe, and of generation.[13] Can the [p150] importance of a cult capable of such far-reaching developments be easily exaggerated? Secondly, and of more immediate importance for our investigation, is it not evident that we have here all the elements necessary for a mystical development of the Grail tradition? The Exoteric side of the cult gives us the Human, the Folk-lore, elements—the Suffering King; the Waste Land; the effect upon the Folk; the task that lies before the hero; the group of Grail symbols. The Esoteric side provides us with the Mystic Meal, the Food of Life, connected in some mysterious way with a Vessel which is the centre of the cult; the combination of that vessel with a Weapon, a combination bearing a well-known 'generative' significance; a double initiation into the source of the lower and higher spheres of Life; the ultimate proof of the successful issue of the final test in the restoration of the King. I would ask any honest-minded critic whether any of the numerous theories previously advanced has shown itself capable of furnishing so comprehensive a solution of the ensemble problem?

At the same time it should be pointed out that the acceptance of this theory of the origin of the story in no way excludes the possibility of the introduction of other elements during the period of romantic evolution. As I have previously insisted,[14] not all of those who handled the theme knew the real character of the material with which they were dealing, while even among those who did know there were some who allowed themselves considerable latitude in their methods of composition; who did not scruple to introduce elements foreign to the original *Stoff*, but which would make an appeal to the public of the day. Thus while Bleheris who, I believe, really held a tradition of the original cult, contented himself with a practically simple [p151] recital of the initiations, later redactors, under the influence of the Crusades, and the Longinus legend—possibly also actuated by a desire to substitute a more edifying explanation than that originally offered—added a

---

13. *Vide supra*, p. 137.
14. Cf. *Legend of Sir Perceval*, Vol. II. Chapters 10 and 11.

XI. The Secret of the Grail (2)

directly Christian interpretation of the Lance. As it is concerning the Lance alone that Gawain asks, the first modification must have been at this point; the bringing into line of the twin symbol, the Vase, would come later.

The fellowship, it may even be, the rivalry, between the two great Benedictine houses of Fescamp and Glastonbury, led to the redaction, in the interests of the latter, of a *Saint-Sang* legend, parallel to that which was the genuine possession of the French house.[15] For we must emphasize the fact that the original Joseph-Glastonbury story is a *Saint-Sang*, and not a *Grail* legend. A phial containing the Blood of Our Lord was said to have been buried in the tomb of Joseph—surely a curious fate for so precious a relic—and the Abbey never laid claim to the possession of the Vessel of the Last Supper.[16] Had it done so it would certainly have become a noted centre of pilgrimage—as Dr Brugger acutely remarks such relics are *besucht,* not *gesucht.*

But there is reason to believe that the kindred Abbey of Fescamp had developed its genuine *Saint-Sang* legend into a Grail romance, and there is critical evidence to lead us to suppose that the text we know as *Perlesvaus* was, in its original form, now it is to be feared practically impossible to reconstruct, connected with that Abbey. As we have it, this alone, of all the Grail romances, connects the hero alike with Nicodemus, and with Joseph of Arimathea, the respective protagonists of the *Saint-Sang* legends; while its assertion that the original Latin text was found in a holy [p152] house situated in marshes, the burial place of Arthur and Guenevere, unmistakably points to Glastonbury.

In any case, when Robert de Borron proposed to himself the task of composing a trilogy on the subject the Joseph legend was already in a developed form, and a fresh element, the combination of the Grail legend with the story of a highly popular Folk-tale hero, known in this connection as Perceval (though he has had many names), was established.

Borron was certainly aware of the real character of his material; he knew the Grail cult as Christianized Mystery, and, while following the romance development, handled the theme on distinctively religious lines, preserving the Mystery element in its three-fold development, and equating the Vessel of the Mystic Feast with the Christian Eucharist. From what we now know of the material it seems certain that

---

15. Cf. my *Quest of the Holy Grail*, Bell, 1913, Chap. 4, for summary of evidence on this point.
16. Cf. Heinzel, *Alt-Franz. Gral-Romanen*, p. 72.

XI. The Secret of the Grail (2)

the equation was already established, and that Borron was simply stating in terms of romance what was already known to him in terms of Mystery. In face of the evidence above set forth there can no longer be any doubt that the Mystic Feast of the Nature cults really had, and that at a very early date, been brought into touch with the Sacrament of the Eucharist.

But to Chrétien de Troyes the story was romance, pure and simple. There was still a certain element of awe connected with Grail, and Grail Feast, but of the real meaning and origin of the incidents he had, I am convinced, no idea whatever. Probably many modifications were already in his source, but the result so far as his poem is concerned is that he duplicated the character of the Fisher King; he separated both, Father and Son, from the Wasted Land, transferring the responsibility for the woes of Land and Folk to the Quester, who, although his failure might be responsible for their continuance, never had anything to do with their origin. He bestowed the wound of the Grail King, deeply [p153] significant in its original conception and connection, upon Perceval's father, a shadowy character, entirely apart from the Grail tradition. There is no trace of the Initiation elements in his poem, no Perilous Chapel, no welding of the Sword. We have here passed completely and entirely into the land of romance, the doors of the Temple are closed behind us. It is the story of Perceval li Gallois, not the Ritual of the Grail, which fills the stage, and with the story of Perceval there comes upon the scene a crowd of Folk-tale themes, absolutely foreign to the Grail itself.

Thus we have not only the central theme of the lad reared in woodland solitude, making his entrance into a world of whose ordinary relations he is absolutely and ludicrously ignorant, and the traditional illustrations of the results of that ignorance, such as the story of the Lady of the Tent and the stolen ring; but we have also the sinister figure of the Red Knight with his Witch Mother; the three drops of blood upon the snow, and the ensuing love trance; pure Folk-tale themes, mingled with the more chivalric elements of the rescue of a distressed maiden, and the vanquishing in single combat of doughty antagonists, Giant, or Saracen. One and all of them elements offering widespread popular parallels, and inviting the unwary critic into paths which lead him far astray from the goal of his quest, the Grail Castle. I dispute in no way the possible presence of Celtic elements in this complex. The Lance may well have borrowed at one time features from early Irish tradition,

XI. The Secret of the Grail (2)

at another details obviously closely related to the Longinus legend. It is even possible that, as Burdach insists, features of the Byzantine Liturgy may have coloured the representation of the Grail procession, although, for my own part, I consider such a theory highly improbable in view of the facts that (*a*) Chrétien's poem otherwise shows no traces of Oriental influence; (*b*) the 'Spear' in the Eastern rite is [p154] simply a small spear-shaped knife; (*c*) the presence of the lights is accounted for by the author of *Sone de Nansai* on the ground of a Nativity legend, the authenticity of which was pointed out by the late M. Gaston Paris; (*d*) it is only in the later prose form that we find any suggestion of a Grail Chapel, whereas were the source of the story really to be found in the Mass, such a feature would certainly have had its place in the earliest versions. But in each and all these cases the solution proposed has no relation to other features of the story; it is consequently of value in, and *per se,* only, and cannot be regarded as valid evidence for the source of the legend as a whole. In the process of transmutation from Ritual to Romance, the kernel, the Grail legend proper, may be said to have formed for itself a shell composed of accretions of widely differing *provenance*. It is the legitimate task of criticism to analyse such accretions, and to resolve them into their original elements, but they are accretions, and should be treated as such, not confounded with the original and essential material. After upwards of thirty years spent in careful study of the Grail legend and romances I am firmly and entirely convinced that the root origin of the whole bewildering complex is to be found in the Vegetation Ritual, treated from the esoteric point of view as a Life-Cult, and *in that alone*. Christian Legend, and traditional Folk-tale, have undoubtedly contributed to the perfected romantic *corpus,* but they are in truth subsidiary and secondary features; a criticism that would treat them as original and primary can but defeat its own object; magnified out of proportion they become stumbling-blocks upon the path, instead of sign-posts towards the goal. [p155]

XII. Mithra and Attis

Problem of close connection of cults. Their apparent divergence. Nature of deities examined. Attis. Mithra. The Messianic Feast. Dieterich, Eine Mithrasliturgie. *Difference between the two initiations. Link between Phrygian, Mithraic, and Christian, Mysteries to be found in their higher, esoteric, teaching. Women not admitted to Mithraic initiation. Possible survival in Grail text. Joint diffusion through the Roman Empire. Cumont's evidence. Traces of cult in British Isles. Possible explanation of unorthodox character of Grail legend. Evidence of survival of cult in fifth century. The* Elucidation *a possible record of historic facts. Reason for connecting Grail with Arthurian tradition.*

The fact that there was, at a very early date, among a certain sect of Christian Gnostics, a well-developed body of doctrine, based upon the essential harmony existing between the Old Faith and the New, which claimed by means of a two-fold Initiation to impact to the inner circle of its adherents the secret of life, physical and spiritual, being, in face of the evidence given in the previous chapter, placed beyond any possible doubt, we must now ask, is there any evidence that such teaching survived for any length of time, or could have penetrated to the British Isles, where, in view of the priority of the *Bleheris-Gawain* form, the Grail legend, as we know it, seems to have originated? I think there is at least presumptive evidence of such preservation, and transmission. I have already alluded to the close connection existing between the Attis cult, and the worship of the popular Persian deity, Mithra, and have given quotations from Cumont illustrating this connection; it will be worth while to study the question somewhat more closely, and discover, if possible, the reason for this intimate alliance.

On the face of it there seems to be absolutely no reason for the connection of these cults; the two deities in no way resemble each other; the stories connected with them have no possible analogy; the root conception is widely divergent.

With the character of the deity we know as Adonis, or Attis, we are now thoroughly familiar. In the first instance it seems to be the human

XII. Mithra and Attis

element in the myth which is most insisted upon. He is a mortal youth beloved by a [p156] great goddess; only after his tragic death does he appear to assume divine attributes, and, alike in death and resurrection, become the accepted personification of natural energies.

Baudissin, *Adonis und Esmun,* remarks that Adonis belongs to "einer Klasse von Wesen sehr unbestimmter Art der wohl über den Menschen aber unter den grossen Göttern stehen, und weniger Individualität besitzen als diese."[1] Such a criticism applies of course equally to Attis.

Mithra, on the other hand, occupies an entirely different position. Cumont, in his *Mystères de Mithra,* thus describes him; he is "le génie de la lumière céleste. Il n'est ni le soleil, ni la lune, ni les étoiles, mais à l'aide de ces mille oreilles, et de ces deux milles yeux, il surveille le monde."[2]

His beneficent activities might seem to afford a meeting ground with the Vegetation goods—"Il donne l'accroissement, il donne l'abondance, il donne les troupeaux, il donne la progéniture et la vie."[3]

This summary may aptly be compared with the lament for Tammuz, quoted in Chapter 3.

But the worship of Mithra in the form in which it spread throughout the Roman Empire, Mithra as the god of the Imperial armies, the deity beloved of the Roman legionary, was in no sense of this concrete and material type.

This is how Cumont sums up the main features. Mithra is the Mediator, who stands between "le Dieu inaccessible, et inconnaissable, qui règne dans les sphères éthérées, et le genre humain qui s'agite ici-bas."—"Il est le Logos émané de Dieu, et participant à sa toute puissance, qui après avoir formé le monde comme démiurge continue à veiller sur lui." The initiates must practice a strict chastity—"La résistance à la sensualité était un des aspects du combat contre le [p157] principe du mal—le dualisme Mithraique servait de fondement à une morale très pure et très efficace."[4]

Finally, Mithraism taught the resurrection of the body—Mithra will descend upon earth, and will revive all men. All will issue from their graves, resume their former appearance and recognize each other. All will be united in one great assembly, and the good will be separated

---

1. *Op. cit.* p. 71.
2. *Op. cit.* p. 3.
3. *Op. cit.* p. 4.
4. Cumont, *op. cit.* pp. 129–141 et seq.

XII. Mithra and Attis

from the evil. Then in one supreme sacrifice Mithra will immolate the divine bull, and mixing its fat with the consecrated wine will offer to the righteous the cup of Eternal Life.[5]

The final parallel with the Messianic Feast described in Chapter 9 is too striking to be overlooked.

The celestial nature of the deity is also well brought out in the curious text edited by Dieterich from the great Magic Papyrus of the Bibliothèque Nationale, and referred to in a previous chapter. This text purports to be a formula of initiation, and we find the aspirant ascending through the Seven Heavenly Spheres, to be finally met by Mithra who brings him to the presence of God. So in the Mithraic temples we find seven ladders, the ascent of which by the Initiate typified his passage to the seventh and supreme Heaven.[6]

Bousset points out that the original idea was that of three Heavens above which was Paradise; the conception of Seven Heavens, ruled by the seven Planets, which we find in Mithraism, is due to the influence of Babylonian sidereal cults.[7]

There is thus a marked difference between the two initiations; [p158] the Attis initiate dies, is possibly buried, and revives with his god; the Mithra initiate rises direct to the celestial sphere, where he is met and welcomed by his god. There is here no evidence of the death and resurrection of the deity.

What then is the point of contact between the cults that brought them into such close and intimate relationship?

I think it must be sought in the higher teaching, which, under widely differing external mediums, included elements common to both. In both cults the final aim was the attainment of spiritual and eternal life. Moreover, both possessed essential features which admitted, if they did not encourage, an assimilation with Christianity. Both of them, if forced to yield ground to their powerful rival, could, with a fair show of reason, claim that they had been not vanquished, but fulfilled, that their teaching had, in Christianity, attained its normal term.

The extracts given above will show the striking analogy between the higher doctrine of Mithraism, and the fundamental teaching of its great rival, a resemblance that was fully admitted, and which became the subject of heated polemic. Greek philosophers did not hesitate to establish

---

5. *Op. cit.* p. 148.
6. Dieterich, *Eine Mithrasliturgie,* the text is given with translation and is followed by an elaborate commentary. The whole study is most interesting and suggestive.
7. Cf. Bousset, *Der Himmelfahrt der Seele, Archiv für Religionswissenschaft,* Vol. IV.

XII. Mithra and Attis

a parallel entirely favourable to Mithraism, while Christian apologists insisted that such resemblances were the work of the Devil, a line of argument which, as we have seen above, they had already adopted with regard to the older Mysteries. It is a matter of historical fact that at one moment the religious fate of the West hung in the balance, and it was an open question whether Mithraism or Christianity would be the dominant Creed.[8]

On the other hand we have also seen that certainly one early Christian sect, the Naassenes, while equally regarding the Logos as the centre of their belief, held the equivalent deity to be Attis, and frequented the Phrygian Mysteries as [p159] the most direct source of spiritual enlightenment, while the teaching as to the Death and Resurrection of the god, and the celebration of a Mystic Feast, in which the worshippers partook of the Food and Drink of Eternal Life, offered parallels to Christian doctrine and practice to the full as striking as any to be found in the Persian faith.

I would therefore submit that it was rather through the medium of their inner, Esoteric, teaching, that the two faiths, so different in their external practice, preserved so close and intimate a connection and that, by the medium of that same Esoteric teaching, both alike came into contact with Christianity, and, in the case of the Phrygian cult, could, and actually did, claim identity with it.

Baudissin in his work above referred to suggests that the Adonis cult owed its popularity to its higher, rather than to its lower, elements, to its suggestion of ever-renewing life, rather than to the satisfaction of physical desire to be found in it.[9] Later evidence seems to prove that he judged correctly.

We may also note that the Attis Mysteries were utilized by the priests of Mithra for the initiation of women who were originally excluded from the cult of the Persian god. Cumont remarks that this, an absolute rule in the Western communities, seems to have had exceptions in the Eastern.[10] Is it possible that the passage quoted in the previous chapter, in which Perceval is informed that no woman may speak of the Grail, is due to contamination with the Mithra worship? It does not appear to be in harmony with the prominent position assigned to women in the Grail ritual, the introduction of a female Grail messenger, or the

---

8. Cumont, *op. cit.* pp. 199 *et seq.*
9. *Adonis und Esmun*, p. 521.
10. Cf. Mead, *op. cit.* p. 179, note; Cumont, *Mystères de Mithra*, p. 183.

XII. Mithra and Attis

fact that (with the exception of Merlin in the Borron text) it is invariably a maiden who directs the hero on his road to the Grail castle, or reproaches him for his failure there.

[p160] But there is little doubt that, separately, or in conjunction, both cults travelled to the furthest borders of the Roman Empire. The medium of transmission is very fully discussed by Cumont in both of the works referred to. The channel appears to have been three-fold. First, commercial, through the medium of Syrian merchants. As ardently religious as practically business-like, the Syrians introduced their native deities wherever they penetrated, "founding their chapels at the same time as their counting-houses."[11]

Secondly, there was social penetration—by means of the Asiatic slaves, who formed a part of most Roman households, and the State *employés,* such as officers of customs, army paymasters, etc., largely recruited from Oriental sources.

Thirdly, and most important, were the soldiers, the foreign legions, who, drawn mostly from the Eastern parts of the Empire, brought their native deities with them. Cumont signalizes as the most active agents of the dispersion of the cult of Mithra, Soldiers, Slaves, and Merchants.[12]

As far North as Hadrian's Dyke there has been found an inscription in verse in honour of the goddess of Hierapolis, the author a prefect, probably, Cumont remarks, the officer of a cohort of Hamii, stationed in this distant spot. Dedications to Melkart and Astarte have been found at Corbridge near Newcastle. The Mithraic remains are practically confined to garrison centres, London, York, Chester, Caerleon-on-Usk, and along Hadrian's Dyke.[13] From the highly interesting map attached to the Study, giving the sites of ascertained Mithraic remains, there seems to have been such a centre in Pembrokeshire.

Now in view of all this evidence is it not at least possible that the higher form of the Attis cult, that in which it was [p161] known and practised by early Gnostic Christians, may have been known in Great Britain? Scholars have been struck by the curiously unorthodox tone of the Grail romances, their apparent insistence on a succession quite other than the accredited Apostolic tradition, and yet, according to the writers, directly received from Christ Himself. The late M. Paulin Paris believed that the source of this peculiar feature was to be found in the

---

11. Cumont, *Les Religions Orientales,* pp. 160 et seq.
12. *Mystères de Mithra,* p. 77.
13. *Les Religions Orientales,* pp. 166, 167, *Mystères de Mithra,* p. 57.

XII. Mithra and Attis

struggle for independence of the early British Church; but, after all, the differences of that Church with Rome affected only minor points of discipline: the date of Easter, the fashion of tonsure of the clergy, nothing which touched vital doctrines of the Faith. Certainly the British Church never claimed the possession of a revelation *à part*. But if the theory based upon the evidence of the Naassene document be accepted such a presentation can be well accounted for. According to Hippolytus the doctrines of the sect were derived from James, the brother of Our Lord, and Clement of Alexandria asserts that "The Lord imparted the Gnosis to James the Just, to John and to Peter, after His Resurrection; these delivered it to the rest of the Apostles, and they to the Seventy."[14] Thus the theory proposed in these pages will account not only for the undeniable parallels existing between the Vegetation cults and the Grail romances, but also for the Heterodox colouring of the latter, two elements which at first sight would appear to be wholly unconnected, and quite incapable of relation to a common source.

Nor in view of the persistent vitality and survival, even to our own day, of the Exoteric practices can there be anything improbable in the hypothesis of a late survival of the Esoteric side of the ritual. Cumont points out that the worship of Mithra was practised in the fifth century in certain remote cantons of the Alps and the Vosges—*i.e.*, at the [p162] date historically assigned to King Arthur. Thus it would not be in any way surprising if a tradition of the survival of these semi-Christian rites at this period also existed.[15] In my opinion it is the tradition of such a survival which lies at the root, and explains the confused imagery, of the text we know as the *Elucidation*. I have already, in my short study of the subject, set forth my views; as I have since found further reasons for maintaining the correctness of the solution proposed, I will repeat it here.[16]

The text in question is found in three of our existing Grail versions: in the MS. of Mons; in the printed edition of 1530; and in the German translation of Wisse-Colin. It is now prefixed to the poem of Chrétien de Troyes, but obviously, from the content, had originally nothing to do with that version.

---

14. Mead, *op. cit.* pp. 147, 148, and note.
15. Without entering into indiscreet details I may say that students of the Mysteries are well aware of the continued survival of this ritual under circumstances which correspond exactly with the indications of two of our Grail romances.
16. *The Quest of the Holy Grail*, pp. 110 *et seq.*

XII. Mithra and Attis

It opens with the passage quoted above (p. 130) in which Master Blihis utters his solemn warning against revealing the secret of the Grail. It goes on to tell how aforetime there were maidens dwelling in the hills[17] who brought forth to the passing traveller food and drink. But King Amangons outraged one of these maidens, and took away from her her golden Cup:

"Des puceles une esforcha
Et la coupe d'or li toli—."[18]

His knights, when they saw their lord act thus, followed his evil example, forced the fairest of the maidens, and [p163] robbed them of their cups of gold. As a result the springs dried up, the land became waste, and the court of the Rich Fisher, which had filled the land with plenty, could no longer be found.

For 1000 years the land lies waste, till, in the days of King Arthur, his knights find maidens wandering in the woods, each with her attendant knight. They joust, and one, Blihos-Bliheris, vanquished by Gawain, comes to court and tells how these maidens are the descendants of those ravished by King Amangons and his men, and how, could the court of the Fisher King, and the Grail, once more be found, the land would again become fertile. Blihos-Bliheris is, we are told, so entrancing a story-teller that none at court could ever weary of listening to his words.

The natural result, which here does not immediately concern us, was that Arthur's knights undertook the quest, and Gawain achieved it. Now at first sight this account appears to be nothing but a fantastic fairy-tale (as such Professor Brown obviously regarded it), and although the late Dr Sebastian Evans attempted in all seriousness to find a historical basis for the story in the events which provoked the pronouncement of the Papal Interdict upon the realm of King John, and the consequent deprivation of the Sacraments, I am not aware that anyone took the solution seriously. Yet, on the basis of the theory now set forth, is it not possible that there may be a real foundation of historical fact at the root

---

17. Professor A. C. L. Brown, *Notes on Celtic Cauldrons of Plenty*, n. p. 249, translates this 'wells,' an error into which the late Mr Alfred Nutt had already fallen. Wisse Colin translates this correctly, *berg, gebirge*.

18. I suspect that the robbery of the Golden Cup was originally a symbolic expression for the outrage being offered.

XII. Mithra and Attis

of this wildly picturesque tale? May it not be simply a poetical version of the disappearance from the land of Britain of the open performance of an ancient Nature ritual? A ritual that lingered on in the hills and mountains of Wales as the Mithra worship did in the Alps and Vosges, celebrated as that cult habitually was, in natural caverns, and mountain hollows? That it records the outrage offered by some, probably local, chieftain to a [p164] priestess of the cult, an evil example followed by his men, and the subsequent cessation of the public celebration of the rites, a cessation which in the folk-belief would certainly be held sufficient to account for any subsequent drought that might affect the land? But the ritual, in its higher, esoteric, form was still secretly observed, and the tradition, alike of its disappearance as a public cult, and of its persistence in some carefully hidden strong-hold, was handed on in the families of those who had been, perhaps still were, officiants of these rites.

That among the handers on of the torch would be the descendants of the outraged maidens, is most probable.

The sense of mystery, of a real danger to be faced, of an overwhelming Spiritual gain to be won, were of the essential nature of the tale. It was the very mystery of Life which lay beneath the picturesque wrappings; small wonder that the Quest of the Grail became the synonym for the highest achievement that could be set before men, and that when the romantic evolution of the Arthurian tradition reached its term, this supreme adventure was swept within the magic circle. The knowledge of the Grail was the utmost man could achieve, Arthur's knights were the very flower of manhood, it was fitting that to them the supreme test be offered. That the man who first told the story, and boldly, as befitted a born teller of tales, wedded it the Arthurian legend, was himself connected by descent with the ancient Faith, himself actually held the Secret of the Grail, and told, in purposely romantic form, that of which he knew, I am firmly convinced, nor do I think that the time is far distant when the missing links will be in our hand, and we shall be able to weld once more the golden chain which connects Ancient Ritual with Medieval Romance. [p165]

XIII. The Perilous Chapel

The adventure of the Perilous Chapel in Grail romances. Gawain *form.* Perceval *versions.* Queste. Perlesvaus. Lancelot. Chevalier à Deux Espées. *Perilous Cemetery. Earliest reference in* Chastel Orguellous. Âtre Perilleus. Prose Lancelot. *Adventure part of 'Secret of the Grail.' The Chapel of Saint Austin.* Histoire de Fulk Fitz-Warin. *Genuine record of an initiation. Probable locality North Britain. Site of remains of Mithra-Attis cults. Traces of Mystery tradition in Medieval romance.* Owain Miles. Bousset, Himmelfahrt der Seele. *Parallels with romance. Appeal to Celtic scholars. Otherworld journeys a possible survival of Mystery tradition. The Templars, were they Naassenes?*

Students of the Grail romances will remember that in many of the versions the hero—sometimes it is a heroine—meets with a strange and terrifying adventure in a mysterious Chapel, an adventure which, we are given to understand, is fraught with extreme peril to life. The details vary: sometimes there is a Dead Body laid on the altar; sometimes a Black Hand extinguishes the tapers; there are strange and threatening voices, and the general impression is that this is an adventure in which supernatural, and evil, forces are engaged.

Such an adventure befalls Gawain on his way to the Grail Castle.[1] He is overtaken by a terrible storm, and coming to a Chapel, standing at a crossways in the middle of a forest, enters for shelter. The altar is bare, with no cloth, or covering, nothing is thereon but a great golden candlestick with a tall taper burning within it. Behind the altar is a window, and as Gawain looks a Hand, black and hideous, comes through the window, and extinguishes the taper, while a voice makes lamentation loud and dire, beneath which the very building rocks. Gawain's horse shies for terror, and the knight, making the sign of the Cross, rides out of the Chapel, to find the storm abated, and the great wind fallen. Thereafter the night was calm and clear.

---

1. MS B.N. 12576, ff. 87vo et seq. A translation will be found in my *Sir Gawain at the Grail Castle*, pp. 13-15.

XIII. The Perilous Chapel

In the *Perceval* section of Wauchier and Manessier we find the same adventure in a dislocated form.[2]

[p166] Perceval, seeking the Grail Castle, rides all day through a heavy storm, which passes off at night-fall, leaving the weather calm and clear. He rides by moonlight through the forest, till he sees before him a great oak, on the branches of which are lighted candles, ten, fifteen, twenty, or twenty-five. The knight rides quickly towards it, but as he comes near the lights vanish, and he only sees before him a fair little Chapel, with a candle shining through the open door. He enters, and finds on the altar the body of a dead knight, covered with a rich samite, a candle burning at his feet.

Perceval remains some time, but nothing happens. At midnight he departs; scarcely has he left the Chapel when, to his great surprise, the light is extinguished.

The next day he reaches the castle of the Fisher King, who asks him where he passed the preceding night. Perceval tells him of the Chapel; the King sighs deeply, but makes no comment.

Wauchier's section breaks off abruptly in the middle of this episode; when Manessier takes up the story he gives explanations of the Grail, etc., at great length, explanations which do not at all agree with the indications of his predecessor. When Perceval asks of the Chapel he is told it was built by Queen Brangemore of Cornwall, who was later murdered by her son Espinogres, and buried beneath the altar. Many knights have since been slain there, none know by whom, save it be by the Black Hand which appeared and put out the light. (As we saw above it had not appeared.) The enchantment can only be put an end to if a valiant knight will fight the Black Hand, and, taking a veil kept in the Chapel, will dip it in holy water, and sprinkle the walls, after which the enchantment will cease.

At a much later point Manessier tells how Perceval, riding through the forest, is overtaken by a terrible storm. He takes refuge in a Chapel which he recognizes as that of [p167] the Black Hand. The Hand appears, Perceval fights against and wounds it; then appears a Head; finally the Devil in full form who seizes Perceval as he is about to seek the veil of which he has been told. Perceval makes the sign of the Cross, on which the Devil vanishes, and the knight falls insensible before the altar. On reviving he takes the veil, dips it in holy water, and sprinkles

---

2. MS B.N. 12576, ff. 150*vo*, 222, 238*vo*.

XIII. The Perilous Chapel

the walls within and without. He sleeps there that night, and the next morning, on waking, sees a belfry. He rings the bell, upon which an old man, followed by two others, appears. He tells Perceval he is a priest, and has buried 3000 knights slain by the Black Hand; every day a knight has been slain, and every day a marble tomb stands ready with the name of the victim upon it. Queen Brangemore founded the cemetery, and was the first to be buried within it. (But according to the version given earlier she was buried beneath the altar.) We have here evidently a combination of two themes, Perilous Chapel and Perilous Cemetery, originally independent of each other. In other MSS. the Wauchier adventure agrees much more closely with the Manessier sequel, the Hand appearing, and extinguishing the light. Sometimes the Hand holds a bridle, a feature probably due to contamination with a Celtic Folk-tale, in which a mysterious Hand (here that of a giant) steals on their birth-night a Child, and a foal.[3] These *Perceval* versions are manifestly confused and dislocated, and are probably drawn from more than one source.

In the *Queste* Gawain and Hector de Maris come to an old and ruined Chapel where they pass the night. Each has a marvellous dream. The next morning, as they are telling each other their respective visions, they see, "a Hand, showing unto the elbow, and was covered with red samite, and upon that hung a bridle, not rich, and held within the [p168] fist a great candle that burnt right clear, and so passed afore them, and entered into the Chapel, and then vanished away, and they wist not where."[4] This seems to be an unintelligent borrowing from the *Perceval* version.

We have, also, a group of visits to the Perilous Chapel, or Perilous Cemetery, which appear to be closely connected with each other. In each case the object of the visit is to obtain a portion of the cloth which covers the altar, or a dead body lying upon the altar. The romances in question are the *Perlesvaus,* the prose *Lancelot,* and the *Chevalier à deux Espées.*[5] The respective protagonists being Perceval's sister, Sir Lancelot, and the young Queen of Garadigan, whose city has been taken by King Ris and who dares the venture to win her freedom.

In the first case the peril appears to lie in the Cemetery, which is surrounded by the ghosts of knights slain in the forest, and buried in

---

3. Cf. here Prof. Kittredge's monograph *Arthur and Gorlagon.*
4. Cf. Malory, Book XVI. Chap. 2.
5. Cf. Perlesvaus, Branch XV. sections XII.-XX.; Malory, Book VI. Chap. 15; *Chevalier à deux Espées,* ll. 531 et seq.

XIII. The Perilous Chapel

unconsecrated ground. The *Lancelot* version is similar, but here the title is definitely *Perilous Chapel*. In the last version there is no hint of a Cemetery.

In the *Lancelot* version there is a dead knight on the altar, whose sword Lancelot takes in addition to the piece of cloth. In the poem a knight is brought in, and buried before the altar; the young queen, after cutting off a piece of the altar cloth, uncovers the body, and buckles on the sword. There is no mention of a Hand in any of the three versions, which appear to be late and emasculated forms of the theme.

The earliest mention of a Perilous Cemetery, as distinct from a Chapel, appears to be in the Chastel Orguellous section of the *Perceval*, a section probably derived from a very early stratum of Arthurian romantic tradition. Here [p169] Arthur and his knights, on their way to the siege of Chastel Orguellous, come to the *Vergier des Sepoltures*, where they eat with the Hermits, of whom there are a hundred and more.

> "ne me l'oïst or pas chi dire
> Les merveilles del chimetire
> car si sont diverses et grans
> qu'il n'est hom terriens vivans
> qui poist pas quidier ne croire
> que ce fust onques chose voire."[6]

But there is no hint of a Perilous Chapel here.

The adventures of Gawain in the *Atre Perilleus*,[7] and of Gawain and Hector in the *Lancelot* of the final cyclic prose version, are of the most *banal* description; the theme, originally vivid and picturesque, has become watered down into a meaningless adventure of the most conventional type.

But originally a high importance seems to have been attached to it. If we turn back to the first version given, that of which Gawain is the hero, we shall find that special stress is laid on this adventure, as being part of 'the Secret of the Grail,' of which no man may speak without grave danger.[8] We are told that, but for Gawain's loyalty and courtesy,

---

6. B.N. 12576, fo. 74*vo*.
7. Cf. B.N. MS 1433, ff. 10, 11, and the analysis and remarks in my *Legend of Sir Lancelot*, p. 219 and note.
8. Cf. passage in question quoted on p. 137.

XIII. The Perilous Chapel

he would not have survived the perils of that night. In the same way Perceval, before reaching the Fisher King's castle, meets a maiden, of whom he asks the meaning of the lighted tree, Chapel, etc. She tells him it is all part of the *saint secret* of the Grail.[9] Now what does this mean? Unless I am much mistaken the key is to be found in a very curious story related in the *Perlesvaus*, which is twice referred to in texts of a professedly historical [p170] character. The tale runs thus. King Arthur has fallen into slothful and *fainéant* ways, much to the grief of Guenevere, who sees her lord's fame and prestige waning day by day. In this crisis she urges him to visit the Chapel of Saint Austin, a perilous adventure, but one that may well restore his reputation. Arthur agrees; he will take with him only one squire; the place is too dangerous. He calls a youth named Chaus, the son of Yvain the Bastard, and bids him be ready to ride with him at dawn. The lad, fearful of over-sleeping, does not undress, but lies down as he is in the hall. He falls asleep—and it seems to him that the King has wakened and gone without him. He rises in haste, mounts and rides after Arthur, following, as he thinks, the track of his steed. Thus he comes to a forest glade, where he sees a Chapel, set in the midst of a grave-yard. He enters, but the King is not there; there is no living thing, only the body of a knight on a bier, with tapers burning in golden candlesticks at head and foot. Chaus takes out one of the tapers, and thrusting the golden candlestick betwixt hose and thigh, remounts and rides back in search of the King. Before he has gone far he meets a man, black, and foul-favoured, armed with a large two-edged knife. He asks, has he met King Arthur? The man answers, No, but he has met him, Chaus; he is a thief and a traitor; he has stolen the golden candlestick; unless he gives it up he shall pay for it dearly. Chaus refuses, and the man smites him in the side with the knife. With a loud cry the lad awakes, he is lying in the hall at Cardoil, wounded to death, the knife in his side and the golden candlestick still in his hose.

He lives long enough to tell the story, confess, and be shriven, and then dies. Arthur, with the consent of his father, gives the candlestick to the church of Saint Paul, then newly founded, "for he would that this marvellous [p171] adventure should everywhere be known, and that prayer should be made for the soul of the squire."[10]

---

9. B.N. 12576, fo. 150vo.
10. *Perlesvaus*, Branch I. sections III., IV.

XIII. The Perilous Chapel

The pious wish of the King seems to have been fulfilled, as the story was certainly well known, and appears to have been accepted as a genuine tradition. Thus the author of the *Histoire de Fulk Fitz-Warin* gives a *résumé* of the adventure, and asserts that the Chapel of Saint Austin referred to was situated in Fulk's patrimony, *i.e.*, in the tract known as the Blaunche Launde, situated in Shropshire, on the border of North Wales. As source for the tale he refers to *Le Graal, le lyvre de le Seint Vassal*, and goes on to state that here King Arthur recovered *sa bounté et sa valur* when he had lost his knighthood and fame. This obviously refers to the *Perlesvaus* romance, though whether in its present, or in an earlier form, it is impossible to say. In any case the author of the *Histoire* evidently thought that the Chapel in question really existed, and was to be located in Shropshire.[11] But John of Glastonbury also refers to the story, and he connects it with Glastonbury.[12]

Now how can we account for so wild, and at first sight so improbable, a tale assuming what we may term a semi-historical character, and becoming connected with a definite and precise locality?—a feature which is, as a rule, absent from the Grail stories.

At the risk of startling my readers I must express my opinion that it was because the incidents recorded were a reminiscence of something which had actually happened, and which, owing to the youth, and possible social position, of the victim, had made a profound impression upon the popular imagination.

For this is the story of an initiation (or perhaps it would [p172] be more correct to say the test of fitness for an initiation) *carried out on the astral plane, and reacting with fatal results upon the physical.*

We have already seen in the Naassene document that the Mystery ritual comprised a double initiation, the Lower, into the mysteries of generation, *i.e.*, of physical Life; the higher, into the Spiritual Divine Life, where man is made one with God.[13]

Some years ago I offered the suggestion that the test for the primary initiation, that into the sources of physical life, would probably consist in a contact with the horrors of physical death, and that the tradition of the Perilous Chapel, which survives in the Grail romances in confused and contaminated form, was a reminiscence of the test for

---

11. Cf. my notes on the subject, *Romania*, Vol. XLIII. pp. 420–426.
12. Cf. Nitze, *Glastonbury and the Holy Grail,* where the reference is given.
13. *Vide supra*, p. 147.

XIII. The Perilous Chapel

this lower initiation.[14] This would fully account for the importance ascribed to it in the *Bleheris-Gawain* form, and for the asserted connection with the Grail. It was not till I came to study the version of the *Perlesvaus*, with a view to determining its original *provenance*, that I recognized its extreme importance for critical purposes. The more one studies this wonderful legend the more one discovers significance in what seem at first to be entirely independent and unrelated details. If the reader will refer to my Notes on the *Perlesvaus*, above referred to, he will find that the result of an investigation into the evidence for *locale* pointed to the conclusion that the author of the *Histoire de Fulk Fitz-Warin* and most probably also the author of the *Perlesvaus* before him, were mistaken in their identification, that there [p173] was no tradition of any such Chapel in Shropshire, and consequently no tale of its foundation, such as the author of the *Histoire* relates. But I was also able to show that further north, in Northumberland, there was also a Blanchland, connected with the memory of King Arthur, numerous dedications to Saint Austin, and a tradition of that Saint driving out the local demons closely analogous to the tale told of the presumed Shropshire site. I therefore suggested that inasmuch as the *Perlesvaus* represented Arthur as holding his court at Cardoil (Carlisle), the Northern Blanchland, which possessed a Chapel of Saint Austin, and lay within easy reach, was probably the original site rather than the Shropshire Blaunche Launde, which had no Chapel, and was much further away.

Now in view of the evidence set forth in the last chapter, is it not clear that this was a locality in which these semi-Pagan, semi-Christian, rites, might, *prima facie*, be expected to linger on? It is up here, along the Northern border, that the Roman legionaries were stationed; it is here that we find monuments and memorials of their heathen cults; obviously this was a locality where the demon-hunting activities of the Saint might find full scope for action. I would submit that there is at least presumptive evidence that we may here be dealing with the survival of a genuine tradition.

And should any of my readers find it difficult to believe that, even did initiations take place, and even were they of a character that involved a

---

14. Cf. *Legend of Sir Perceval*, Vol. II. p. 261. I suggested then that the actual initiation would probably consist in enlightenment into the meaning of Lance and Cup, in their sexual juxtaposition. I would now go a step further, and suggest that the identification of the Lance with the weapon of Longinus may quite well have replaced the original explanation as given by Bleheris. In *The Quest*, Oct. 1916, I have given, under the title "The Ruined Temple," a hypothetical reconstruction of the Grail Initiation.

XIII. The Perilous Chapel

stern test of mental and physical endurance—and I imagine most scholars would admit that there was, possibly, more in the original institutions, than, let us say, in a modern admission to Free-Masonry—yet it is 'a far cry' from pre-Christian initiations to Medieval Romance, and a connection between the two is a rash postulate, I would draw their attention to the fact that, [p174] quite apart from our Grail texts, we possess a romance which is, plainly, and blatantly, nothing more or less than such a record. I refer, of course, to *Owain Miles*, or *The Purgatory of Saint Patrick*, where we have an account of the hero, after purification by fasting and prayer, descending into the Nether World, passing through the abodes of the Lost, finally reaching Paradise, and returning to earth after Three Days, a reformed and regenerated character.[15]

> "Then with his monks the Prior anon,
> With Crosses and with Gonfanon
> Went to that hole forthright,
> Thro' which Knight Owain went below,
> There, as of burning fire the glow,
> They saw a gleam of light;
> And right amidst that beam of light
> He came up, Owain, God's own knight,
> By this knew every man
> That he in Paradise had been,
> And Purgatory's pains had seen,
> And was a holy man."

Now if we turn to Bousset's article *Himmelfahrt der Seele*, to which I have previously referred (p. 157), we shall find abundant evidence that such a journey to the Worlds beyond was held to be a high spiritual adventure of actual possibility—a venture to be undertaken by those who, greatly daring, felt that the attainment of actual knowledge of the Future Life was worth all the risks, and they were great and terrible, which such an enterprise involved.

Bousset comments fully on Saint Paul's claim to have been 'caught up into the Third Heaven' and points out [p175] that such an experience was the property of the Rabbinical school to which Saul of Tarsus

---

15. *Owain Miles*, edited from the unique MS. by Turnbull and Laing, Edinburgh, 1837. *The Purgatory of Saint Patrick* will be found in Horstmann's Southern Legendary. I have given a modern English rendering of part of *Owain Miles* in my *Chief Middle-English Poets*, published by Houghton Mifflin Co., Boston, U.S.A.

XIII. The Perilous Chapel

had belonged, and was brought over by him from his Jewish past; such experiences were rare in Orthodox Christianity.[16] According to Jewish classical tradition but one Rabbi had successfully passed the test, other aspirants either failing at a preliminary stage, or, if they persevered, losing their senses permanently. The practice of this ecstatic ascent ceased among Jews in the second century A.D.

Bousset also gives instances of the soul leaving the body for three days, and wandering through other worlds, both good and evil, and also discusses the origin of the bridge which must be crossed to reach Paradise, both features characteristic of the *Owain* poem.[17] In fact the whole study is of immense importance for a critical analysis of the sources of the romance in question.

And here I would venture to beg the adherents of the 'Celtic' school to use a little more judgment in their attribution of sources. Visits to the Otherworld are not always derivations from Celtic Fairy-lore. Unless I am mistaken the root of this theme is far more deeply imbedded than in the shifting sands of Folk and Fairy tale. I believe it to be essentially a Mystery tradition; the Otherworld is not a myth, but a reality, and in all ages there have been souls who have been willing to brave the great adventure, and to risk all for the chance of bringing back with them some assurance of the future life. Naturally these ventures passed into tradition with the men who risked them. The early races of men became semi-mythic, their beliefs, their experiences, receded into a land of mist, where their figures assumed fantastic outlines, and the record of their deeds departed more and more widely from historic accuracy.

The poets and dreamers wove their magic webs, and a [p176] world apart from the world of actual experience came to life. But it was not all myth, nor all fantasy; there was a basis of truth and reality at the foundation of the mystic growth, and a true criticism will not rest content with wandering in these enchanted lands, and holding all it meets with for the outcome of human imagination.

The truth may lie very deep down, but it is there, and it is worth seeking, and Celtic fairy-tales, charming as they are, can never afford a satisfactory, or abiding, resting place. I, for one, utterly refuse to accept such as an adequate goal for a life's research. A path that leads but into a Celtic Twilight can only be a by-path, and not the King's Highway!

---

16. Cf. *op. cit.* pp. 148 *et seq.*
17. *Op. cit.* pp. 155 and 254.

XIII. The Perilous Chapel

The Grail romances repose eventually, not upon a poet's imagination, but upon the ruins of an august and ancient ritual, a ritual which once claimed to be the accredited guardian of the deepest secrets of Life. Driven from its high estate by the relentless force of religious evolution—for after all Adonis, Attis, and their congeners, were but the 'half-gods' who must needs yield place when 'the Gods' themselves arrive—it yet lingered on; openly, in Folk practice, in Fast and Feast, whereby the well-being of the land might be assured; secretly, in cave or mountain-fastness, or island isolation, where those who craved for a more sensible (not necessarily sensuous) contact with the unseen Spiritual forces of Life than the orthodox development of Christianity afforded, might, and did, find satisfaction.

Were the Templars such? Had they, when in the East, come into touch with a survival of the Naassene, or some kindred sect? It seems exceedingly probable. If it were so we could understand at once the puzzling connection of the Order with the Knights of the Grail, and the doom which fell upon them. That they were held to be Heretics [p177] is very generally admitted, but in what their Heresy consisted no one really knows; little credence can be attached to the stories of idol worship often repeated. If their Heresy, however, were such as indicated above, a Creed which struck at the very root and vitals of Christianity, we can understand at once the reason for punishment, and the necessity for secrecy. In the same way we can now understand why the Church knows nothing of the Grail; why that Vessel, surrounded as it is with an atmosphere of reverence and awe, equated with the central Sacrament of the Christian Faith, yet appears in no Legendary, is figured in no picture, comes on the scene in no Passion Play. The Church of the eleventh and twelfth centuries knew well what the Grail was, and we, when we realize its genesis and true lineage, need no longer wonder why a theme, for some short space so famous and so fruitful a source of literary inspiration, vanished utterly and completely from the world of literature.

Were Grail romances forbidden? Or were they merely discouraged? Probably we shall never know, but of this one thing we may be sure, the Grail is a living force, it will never die; it may indeed sink out of sight, and, for centuries even, disappear from the field of literature, but it will rise to the surface again, and become once more a theme of vital inspiration even as, after slumbering from the days of Malory, it woke to new life in the nineteenth century, making its fresh appeal through the genius of Tennyson and Wagner. [p178]

XIV. The Author

Provenance and authorship of Grail romantic tradition. Evidence points to Wales, probably Pembrokeshire. Earliest form contained in group of Gawain poems assigned to Bleheris. Of Welsh origin. Master Blihis, Blihos, Bliheris, Bréri, Bledhericus. Probably all references to same person. Conditions of identity. Mr E. Owen, and Bledri ap Cadivor. Evidence not complete but fulfils conditions of problem Professor Singer and possible character of Bleheris' text. Mr Alfred Nutt. Irish and Welsh parallels. Recapitulation of evolutionary process. Summary and conclusion.

Having now completed our survey of the various elements which have entered into the composite fabric of the Grail Legend, the question naturally arises where, and when, did that legend assume romantic form, and to whom should we ascribe its literary origin?

On these crucial points the evidence at our disposal is far from complete, and we can do little more than offer suggestions towards the solution of the problem.

With regard to the first point, that of locality, the evidence is unmistakably in favour of a Celtic, specifically a Welsh, source. As a literary theme the Grail is closely connected with the Arthurian tradition. The protagonist is one of Arthur's knights, and the hero of the earlier version, Gawain, is more closely connected with Arthur than are his successors, Perceval and Galahad. The Celtic origin of both Gawain and Perceval is beyond doubt; and the latter is not merely a Celt, but is definitely Welsh; he is always 'li Gallois.' Galahad I hold to be a literary, and not a traditional, hero; he is the product of deliberate literary invention, and has no existence outside the frame of the later cyclic redactions. It is not possible at the present moment to say whether the *Queste* was composed in the British Isles, or on the continent, but we may safely lay it down as a basic principle that the original Grail heroes are of insular origin, and that the Grail legend, in its romantic, and literary, form is closely connected with British pseudo-historical tradition.

[p179] The beliefs and practices of which, if the theory maintained in these pages be correct, the Grail stories offer a more or less coherent

XIV. The Author

survival can be shown, on the evidence of historic monuments, and surviving Folk-customs, to have been popular throughout the area of the British Isles; while, with regard to the higher teaching of which I hold these practices to have been the vehicle, Pliny comments upon the similarity existing between the ancient Magian Gnosis and the Druidical Gnosis of Gaul and Britain, an indication which, in the dearth of accurate information concerning the teaching of the Druids, is of considerable value.[1]

As we noted in the previous chapter, an interesting parallel exists between Wales, and localities, such as the Alps, and the Vosges, where we have definite proof that these Mystery cults lingered on after they had disappeared from public celebration. The Chart appended to Cumont's *Monuments de Mithra* shows Mithraic remains in precisely the locality where we have reason to believe certain of the *Gawain* and *Perceval* stories to have originated.

As to the date of origin, that, of course, is closely connected with the problem of authorship; if we can, with any possibility, identify the author we can approximately fix the date. So far as the literary evidence is concerned, we have no trace of the story before the twelfth century, but when we do meet with it, it is already in complete, and crystallized, form. More, there is already evidence of competing versions; we have no existing Grail romance which we can claim to be free from contamination, and representing in all respects the original form.

There is no need here to go over old, and well-trodden, ground; in my studies of the *Perceval* Legend, and in [p180] the later popular *résumé* of the evidence,[2] *The Quest of the Holy Grail*, I have analysed the texts, and shown that, while the poem of Chrétien de Troyes is our earliest surviving literary version, there is the strongest possible evidence that Chrétien, as he himself admits, was not inventing, but re-telling, an already popular tale.[3] The Grail Quest was a theme which had been treated not once nor twice, but of which numerous, and conflicting, versions were already current, and, when Wauchier de Denain undertook to complete Chrétien's unfinished work, he drew largely upon these already existing forms, regardless of the fact that they not only contradicted the version

---

1. Cf. Mead, *Thrice Greatest Hermes*, Vol. III. p. 295. On this point the still untranslated *corpus* of Bardic poetry may possibly throw light.

2. *The Quest of The Holy Grail* (Quest series, Bell, 1913).

3. On the point that Chrétien was treating an already popular theme, cf. Brugger, *Enserrement Merlin*, I. (*Zeitschrift für Franz. Sprache*, XXIX.).

they were ostensibly completing, but were impossible to harmonize with each other.

It is of importance for our investigation, however, to note that where Wauchier does refer to a definite source, it is to an evidently important and already famous collection of tales, *Le Grant Conte,* comprising several 'Branches,' the hero of the collection being not Chrétien's hero, Perceval, but Gawain, who, both in pseudo-historic and romantic tradition, is far more closely connected with the Arthurian legend, occupying, as he does, the traditional position of nephew, Sister's Son, to the monarch who is the centre of the cycle; even as Cuchullinn is sister's son to Conchobar, Diarmid to Finn, Tristan to Mark, and Roland to Charlemagne. In fact this relationship was so obviously required by tradition that we find Perceval figuring now as sister's son to Arthur, now to the Grail King, according as the Arthurian, or the Grail, tradition dominates the story.[4]

The actual existence of such a group of tales as those [p181] referred to by Wauchier derives confirmation from our surviving *Gawain* poems, as well as from the references in the *Elucidation,* and on the evidence at our disposal I have ventured to suggest the hypothesis of a group of poems, dealing with the adventures of Gawain, his son, and brother, the *ensemble* being originally known as *The Geste of Syr Gawayne,* a title which, in the inappropriate form *The Jest of Sir Gawain,* is preserved in the English version of that hero's adventure with the sister of Brandelis.[5] So keen a critic as Dr Brugger has not hesitated to accept the theory of the existence of this *Geste,* and is of opinion that the German poem *Diû Crône* may, in part at least, be derived from this source.

The central adventure ascribed to Gawain in this group of tales is precisely the visit to the Grail Castle to which we have already referred, and we have pointed out that the manner in which it is related, its directness, simplicity, and conformity with what we know of the Mystery teaching presumably involved, taken in connection with the personality of the hero, and his position in Arthurian romantic tradition, appear to warrant us in assigning to it the position of priority among the conflicting versions we possess.

---

4. That is, the relationship is due to romantic tradition, not to Mystery survival, as Dr Nitze maintains.
5. Cf. *Romania,* Vol. XXXIII. pp. 333 *et seq.*

XIV. The Author

At two points in the re-telling of these *Gawain* tales Wauchier definitely refers to the author by name, Bleheris. On the second occasion he states categorically that this Bleheris was of Welsh birth and origin, *né et engenuïs en Galles*, and that he told the tale in connection with which the statement is made to a certain Comte de Poitiers, whose favourite story it was, he loved it above all others, which would imply that it was not the only tale Bleheris had told him.[6]

[p182] As we have seen in a previous chapter, the *Elucidation* prefaces its account of the Grail Quest by a solemn statement of the gravity of the subject to be treated, and a warning of the penalties which would follow on a careless revelation of the secret. These warnings are put into the mouth of a certain Master Blihis, concerning whom we hear no more. A little further on in the poem we meet with a knight, Blihos-Bliheris, who, made prisoner by Gawain, reveals to Arthur and his court the identity of the maidens wandering in the woods, of the Fisher King, and the Grail, and is so good a story-teller that none can weary of listening to his tales.[7]

Again, in the fragmentary remains of Thomas's *Tristan* we have a passage in which the poet refers, as source, to a certain Bréri, who knew "all the feats, and all the tales, of all the kings, and all the counts who had lived in Britain."[8]

Finally, Giraldus Cambrensis refers to *famosus ille fabulator,* Bledhericus, who had lived "shortly before our time" and whose renown he evidently takes for granted was familiar to his readers.

Now are we to hold that the Bleheris who, according to Wauchier, had told tales concerning Gawain, and Arthur's court, one of which tales was certainly the Grail adventure; the Master Blihis, who knew the Grail mystery, and gave solemn warning against its revelation; the Blihos-Bliheris, who knew the Grail, and many other tales; the Bréri, who knew all the legendary tales concerning the princes of Britain; and the famous story-teller Bledhericus, of whom Giraldus speaks, are distinct and separate personages, or mere inventions of the separate writers, or do all these passages refer to one and the same individual, who, in that case, may well have deserved the title *famosus ille fabulator?*

---

6. Cf. *Legend of Sir Perceval*, Vol. I. Chap. 12, for the passages referred to, also article in *Romania*, XXXIII.
7. Cf. my *Quest of the Holy Grail*, pp. 110 *et seq.*
8. Cf. *Tristan* (Bédier's ed.), Vol. I. l. 2120.

XIV. The Author

[p183] With regard to the attitude taken up by certain critics, that no evidential value can be attached to these references, I would point out that when Medieval writers quote an authority for their statements they, as a rule, refer to a writer whose name carries weight, and will impress their readers; they are offering a guarantee for the authenticity of their statements. The special attribution may be purely fictitious but the individual referred to enjoys an established reputation. Thus, the later cyclic redactions of the Arthurian romances are largely attributed to Walter Map, who, in view of his public position, and political activities, could certainly never have had the leisure to compose one half of the literature with which he is credited! In the same way Robert de Borron, Chrétien de Troyes, Wolfram von Eschenbach, are all referred to as sources without any justification in fact. Nor is it probable that Wauchier, who wrote on the continent, and who, if he be really Wauchier de Denain, was under the patronage of the Count of Flanders, would have gone out of his way to invent a Welsh source.

Judging from analogy, the actual existence of a personage named Bleheris, who enjoyed a remarkable reputation as a story-teller, is, *prima facie*, extremely probable.[9]

[p184] But are these references independent, was there more than one Bleheris? I think not. The name is a proper, and not a family, name.

---

9. A critic of my *Quest* volume remarks that "we have as little faith in Wauchier's appeal to a Welshman Bleheris as source for his continuation of Chrétien's '*Perceval*' as we have in Layamon's similar appeal to Bede and St Austin at the beginning of the '*Brut*.'" The remark seems to me singularly inept, there is no parallel between the cases. In the first place Layamon does not refer to Bede and St Austin as *source*, but as *models*, a very different thing. Then the statement is discredited by the fact that we possess the writings of these men, and know them to be of another character than Metrical Chronicles. In the case of Wauchier his reference does not stand alone; it is one of a group, and that group marked by an extraordinary unanimity of statement; whoever Bleheris may have been he was certainly possessed of two definite qualifications—he knew a vast number of tales, and he possessed a remarkable gift of narration, *i.e.,* he was a story-teller, *par excellence.* Thus he was, *a priori,* a probable source for that section of Wauchier's work which is attributed to him, a section consisting of short, picturesque, and mutually independent tales, which formed part of a popular collection. It is misleading to speak as if Wauchier refers to him as general source for his *Perceval* continuation; the references are clearly marked and refer to *Gawain* tales. Apart from the fact that Wauchier's reference does not stand alone we have independent evidence of the actual existence of such a group of tales, in our surviving Gawain poems, certain of which, such as *Kay and the Spit,* and *Golagros and Gawayne* are versions of the stories given by Wauchier, while the author of the *Elucidation* was also familiar with the same collection. If evidence for the identity of Bleheris is incomplete, that for his existence appears to be incontrovertible. Would it not be more honest if such a would-be critic as the writer referred to said, 'I do not choose to believe in the existence of Bleheris, because it runs counter to my pre-conceived theory of the evolution of the literature'? We should then know where we are. Such a parallel as that cited above has no value for those familiar with the literature but may easily mislead the general reader. I would also draw attention to the fact noted in the text—the extreme improbability of Wauchier, a continental writer, inventing an insular and Welsh source. This is a point critics carefully evade.

XIV. The Author

In the latter case it might be possible to argue that we were dealing with separate members of a family, or group, of bardic poets, whose office it was to preserve, and relate, the national legends. But we are dealing with variants of a proper name, and that of distinctly insular, and Welsh origin.[10]

The original form, Bledri, was by no means uncommon in Wales: from that point of view there might well have been four or five, or even more, of that name, but that each and all of these should have possessed the same qualifications, should have been equally well versed in popular traditions, equally dowered with the gift of story-telling, on equally friendly terms with the Norman invaders, and equally possessed of such a knowledge of the French language as should permit them to tell their stories in that tongue, is, I submit, highly improbable. This latter point, *i.e.*, the knowledge of French, seems to me to be of crucial importance. [p185] Given the relations between conqueror and conquered, and the *intransigeant* character of Welsh patriotism, the men who were on sufficiently friendly terms with the invaders to be willing to relate the national legends, with an assurance of finding a sympathetic hearing, must have been few and far between. I do not think the importance of this point has been sufficiently grasped by critics.

The problem then is to find a Welshman who, living at the end of the eleventh and commencement of the twelfth centuries, was well versed in the legendary lore of Britain; was of sufficiently good social status to be well received at court; possessed a good knowledge of the French tongue; and can be shown to have been on friendly terms with the Norman nobles.

Mr Edward Owen, of the Cymmrodorion Society, has suggested that a certain Welsh noble, Bledri ap Cadivor, fulfils, in a large measure, the conditions required. Some years ago I published in the *Revue Celtique* a letter in which Mr Owen summarized the evidence at his disposal. As the review in question may not be easily accessible to some of my readers I will recapitulate the principal points.[11]

The father of Bledri, Cadivor, was a great personage in West Wales, and is looked upon as the ancestor of the most important families in the ancient Dyfed, a division now represented by Pembrokeshire, and the Western portion of Carmarthen. (We may note here that the traditional

---

10. Cf. *Bledhericus de Cornouailles*, note contributed by M. Ferd. Lot, to *Romania*, Vol. XXVIII. p. 336. M. Lot remarks that he has not met with the name in Armorica; it thus appears to be insular.
11. Cf. *Revue Celtique*, 1911, *A note on the identification of Bleheris*.

XIV. The Author

tomb of Gawain is at Ross in Pembrokeshire, and that there is reason to believe that the *Perceval* story, in its earliest form, was connected with that locality.)

Cadivor had three sons, of whom Bledri was the eldest; thus, at his father's death, he would be head of this ancient and distinguished family. At the division of the paternal estates Bledri inherited, as his share, lands ranging along [p186] the right bank of the lower Towey, and the coast of South Pembrokeshire, extending as far as Manorbeer, the birthplace of Giraldus Cambrensis. (This is again a geographical indication which should be borne in mind.) Cadivor himself appears to have been on friendly terms with the Normans; he is said to have entertained William the Conqueror on his visit to St David's in 1080, while every reference we have to Bledri shows him in close connection with the invaders.

Thus, in 1113 the *Brut-y-Tywysogion* mentions his name as ally of the Norman knights in their struggle to maintain their ground in, and around, Carmarthen. In 1125 we find his name as donor of lands to the Augustinian Church of St John the Evangelist, and St Theuloc of Carmarthen, newly founded by Henry I. Here his name appears with the significant title *Latinarius* (The Interpreter), a qualification repeated in subsequent charters of the same collection. In one of these we find Griffith, the son of Bledri, confirming his father's gift. Professor Lloyd, in an article in *Archaeologia Cambrensis*, July 1907, has examined these charters, and considers the grant to have been made between 1129 and 1134, the charter itself being of the reign of Henry I, 1101–1135.[12]

In the Pipe Roll of Henry I, 1131, Bledri's name is entered as debtor for a fine incurred by the killing of a Fleming by his men; while a highly significant entry records the fine of 7 marks imposed upon a certain Bleddyn of Mabedrud and his brothers for outraging Bledri's daughter. When we take into consideration the rank of Bledri, this insult to his family by a fellow Welshman would seem to indicate that his relations with his compatriots were not of a specially friendly character.

Mr Owen also points out that portion of the *Brut-y-Tywysogion* [p187] which covers the years 1101–20 (especially the events of the year 1113, where we find Bledri, and other friendly Welsh nobles, holding the castle of Carmarthen for the Normans against the Welsh), is related at an altogether disproportionate length, and displays a strong bias in

---

12. Ed. Rhys-Evans, Vol. II. p. 297; cf. also *Revue Celtique*.

XIV. The Author

favour of the invaders. The year just referred to, for instance, occupies more than twice the space assigned to any other year. Mr Owen suggests that here Bledri himself may well have been the chronicler; a hypothesis which, if he really be the author we are seeking, is quite admissible.

So far as indications of date are concerned, Bledri probably lived between the years 1070-1150. His father Cadivor died in 1089, and his lands were divided between his sons of whom Bledri, as we have seen, was the eldest. Thus they cannot have been children at that date; Bledri, at least, would have been born before 1080. From the evidence of the Pipe Roll we know that he was living in 1131. The charter signed by his son, confirmatory of his grant, must have been subsequent to 1148, as it was executed during the Episcopate of David, Bishop of St David's 1148-1176. Thus the period of 80 years suggested above (1070-1150) may be taken as covering the extreme limit to be assigned to his life, and activity.

The passage in which Giraldus Cambrensis refers to *Bledhericus, famosus ille fabulator* who *tempora nostra paulo praevenit*, was written about 1194; thus it might well refer to a man who had died some 40 or 50 years previously. As we have noted above, Giraldus was born upon ground forming a part of Bledri's ancestral heritage, and thus might well be familiar with his fame.

The evidence is of course incomplete, but it does provide us with a personality fulfilling the main conditions of a complex problem. Thus, we have a man of the required name, and nationality; living at an appropriate date; of the [p188] requisite social position; on excellent terms with the French nobles, and so well acquainted with their language as to sign himself officially 'The Interpreter.' We have no direct evidence of his literary skill, or knowledge of the traditional history of his country, but a man of his birth could scarcely have failed to possess the latter, while certain peculiarities in that section of the national Chronicle which deals with the aid given by him to the Norman invaders would seem to indicate that Bledri himself may well have been responsible for the record. Again, we know him to have been closely connected with the locality from which came the writer who refers to the famous story-teller of the same name. I would submit that we have here quite sufficient evidence to warrant us in accepting Bledri ap Cadivor as, at least, the possible author of the romantic Grail tradition. In any case, so far, there is no other candidate in the field.[13]

---

13. In the course of 1915-16 I received letters from Mr Rogers Rees, resident at Stepaside,

XIV. The Author

Shortly after the publication of the second volume of my *Perceval* studies, I received a letter from Professor [p189] Singer, in which, after expressing his general acceptance of the theories there advanced, in especial of the suggested date and relation of the different versions, which he characterized as *"sehr gelungen, und zu meiner Alffassung der Entwickelung der Altfranzösischen Literatur sehr zu stimmen,"* he proceeded to comment upon the probable character of the literary activity of Bleheris. His remarks are so interesting and suggestive that I venture to submit them for the consideration of my readers.

Professor Singer points out that in Eilhart von Oberge's *Tristan* we find the name in the form of *Pleherin* attached to a knight of *Mark's* court. The same name in a slightly varied form, *Pfelerin,* occurs in the *Tristan* of Heinrich von Freiberg; both poems, Professor Singer considers, are derived from a French original. Under a compound form, *Blihos,* (or *Blio*)-*Bliheris,* he appears, in the *Gawain-Grail* compilation, as a knight at *Arthur's* court. Now *Bréri-Blihis-Bleheris* is referred to as authority alike in the *Tristan, Grail* and *Gawain* tradition, and Professor Singer makes the interesting suggestion that these references are originally due to Bleheris himself, who not only told the stories in the third person (a common device at that period, *v.* Chrétien's *Erec,* and Gerbert's continuation of the *Perceval*), but also introduced himself as eye-witness of, and actor, in a subordinate *rôle,* in, the incidents he recorded. Thus in the *Tristan* he is a knight of Mark's, in the *Elucidation* and the *Gawain* stories a knight of Arthur's, court. Professor Singer instances the case of Dares in the *De exidio Trojae,* and Bishop Pilgrim of Passau in the lost *Nibelungias* of his secretary Konrad, as illustrations of the theory.

Pembrokeshire, who informed me that he held definite proof of the connection of Bledri with both *Grail* and *Perceval* legends. The locality had been part of Bledri's estate, and the house in which he lived was built on the site of what had been Bledri's castle. Mr Rogers Rees maintained the existence of a living tradition connecting Bledri with the legends in question. At his request I sent him the list of the names of the brothers of Alain li Gros, as given in the 1516 edition of the *Perlesvaus,* a copy of which is in the Bibliothèque Nationale, and received in return a letter stating that the list must have been compiled by one familiar with the district. Unfortunately, for a year, from the autumn of 1916, I was debarred from work, and when, on resuming my studies, I wrote to my correspondent asking for the promised evidence I obtained no answer to my repeated appeal. On communicating with Mr Owen I found he had had precisely the same experience, and, for his part, was extremely sceptical as to there being any genuine foundation for our correspondent's assertions. While it is thus impossible to use the statements in question as elements in my argument, I think it right in the interests of scholarship to place them on record; they may afford a clue which some Welsh scholar may be able to follow up to a more satisfactory conclusion.

XIV. The Author

If this be the case such a statement as that which we find in Wauchier, regarding Bleheris's birth and origin, would have emanated from Bleheris himself, and simply been taken over by the later writer from his source; he incorporated [p190] the whole tale of the shield as it stood, a quite natural and normal proceeding.[14] Again, this suggestion would do away with the necessity for postulating a certain lapse of time before the story-teller Bleheris could be converted into an Arthurian knight—the two *rôles, Gewährsmann und Mithandelnden,* as Professor Singer expresses it, are coincident in date. I would also suggest that the double form, *Blihos-Bliheris,* would have been adopted by the author himself, to indicate the identity of the two, Blihis, and Bleheris. It is worthy of note that, when dealing directly with the Grail, he assumes the title of *Master,* which would seem to indicate that here he claimed to speak with special authority.

I sent the letter in question to the late Mr Alfred Nutt, who was forcibly struck with the possibilities involved in the suggestion, the full application of which he thought the writer had not grasped. I quote the following passages from the long letter I received from him in return.

"Briefly put we presuppose the existence of a set of semi-dramatic, semi-narrative, poems, in which a Bledri figures as an active, and at the same time a recording, personage. Now that such a body of literature *may* have existed we are entitled to assume from the fact that two such have survived, one from Wales, in the Llywarch Hen cycle, the other from Ireland, in the Finn Saga. In both cases, the fact that the descriptive poems are put in the mouth, in Wales of Llywarch, in Ireland largely of Oisin, led to the ascription at an early date of the whole literature to Llywarch and Oisin. It is therefore conceivable that a Welsh 'littérateur,' familiar as he must have been with the Llywarch, and as he quite possibly was with the Oisin, instance, should cast his version of the Arthurian stories in a similar form, [p191] and that the facts noted by you and Singer may be thus explained."

Now that both Professor Singer (who has an exceptionally wide knowledge of Medieval literature), and the late Mr Alfred Nutt, knew what they were talking about, does not need to be emphasized, and the fact that two such competent authorities should agree upon a possible solution of a puzzling literary problem, makes that solution worthy of

---

14. Had Wauchier really desired to *invent* an authority, in view of his date, and connection with the house of Flanders, he had a famous name at hand—that of Chrétien de Troyes.

XIV. The Author

careful consideration; it would certainly have the merit of simplifying the question and deserves to be placed upon record.

But while it would of course be far more satisfactory could one definitely place, and label, the man to whom we owe the original conception which gave birth and impetus to this immortal body of literature, yet the precise identity of the author of the earliest Grail romance is of the accident, rather than the essence, of our problem. Whether Bleheris the Welshman be, or be not, identical with Bledri ap Cadivor, Interpreter, and friend of the Norman nobles, the general hypothesis remains unaffected and may be thus summarized—

The Grail story is not *du fond en comble* the product of imagination, literary or popular. At its root lies the record, more or less distorted, of an ancient Ritual, having for its ultimate object the initiation into the secret of the sources of Life, physical and spiritual. This ritual, in its lower, exoteric, form, as affecting the processes of Nature, and physical life, survives to-day, and can be traced all over the world, in Folk ceremonies, which, however widely separated the countries in which they are found, show a surprising identity of detail and intention. In its esoteric 'Mystery' form it was freely utilized for the imparting of high spiritual teaching concerning the relation of Man to the Divine Source of his being, and the possibility of a [p192] sensible union between Man, and God. The recognition of the cosmic activities of the Logos appears to have been a characteristic feature of this teaching, and when Christianity came upon the scene it did not hesitate to utilize the already existing medium of instruction, but boldly identified the Deity of Vegetation, regarded as Life Principle, with the God of the Christian Faith. Thus, to certain of the early Christians, Attis was but an earlier manifestation of the Logos, Whom they held identical with Christ. The evidence of the Naassene document places this beyond any shadow of doubt, and is of inestimable value as establishing a link between pre-Christian, and Christian, Mystery tradition.

This curious synthetic belief, united as it was with the highly popular cult of Mithra, travelled with the foreign legionaries, adherents of that cult, to the furthest bounds of the Roman Empire, and when the struggle between Mithraism and Christianity ended in the definite triumph of the latter, by virtue of that dual synthetic nature, the higher ritual still survived, and was celebrated in sites removed from the centres of population—in caves, and mountain fastnesses; in islands, and on desolate sea-coasts.

XIV. The Author

The earliest version of the Grail story, represented by our Bleheris form, relates the visit of a wandering knight to one of these hidden temples; his successful passing of the test into the lower grade of Life initiation, his failure to attain to the highest degree. It matters little whether it were the record of an actual, or of a possible, experience; the casting into romantic form of an event which the story-teller knew to have happened, had, perchance, actually witnessed; or the objective recital of what he knew *might* have occurred; the essential fact is that the *mise-en-scène* of the story, the nomenclature, the march of incident, the character of the tests, correspond to what we know from [p193] independent sources of the details of this Nature Ritual. The Grail Quest was actually possible then, it is actually possible to-day, for the indication of two of our romances as to the final location of the Grail is not imagination, but the record of actual fact.

As first told the story preserved its primal character of a composite between Christianity and the Nature Ritual, as witnessed by the ceremony over the bier of the Dead Knight, the procession with Cross and incense, and the solemn Vespers for the Dead. This, I suspect, correctly represents the final stage of the process by which Attis-Adonis was identified with Christ. Thus, in its first form the story was the product of conscious intention.

But when the tale was once fairly launched as a romantic tale, and came into the hands of those unfamiliar with its Ritual origin (though the fact that it had such an origin was probably well understood), the influence of the period came into play. The Crusades, and the consequent traffic in relics, especially in relics of the Passion, caused the identification of the sex Symbols, Lance and Cup, with the Weapon of the Crucifixion, and the Cup of the Last Supper; but the Christianization was merely external, the tale, as a whole, retaining its pre-Christian character.

The conversion into a definitely Christian romance seems to have been due to two causes. First, the rivalry between the two great monastic houses of Glastonbury and Fescamp, the latter of which was already in possession of a genuine *Saint-Sang* relic, and fully developed tradition. There is reason to suppose that the initial combination of the Grail and *Saint-Sang* traditions took place at Fescamp, and was the work of some member of the minstrel Guild attached to that Abbey. But the Grail tradition was originally British; Glastonbury was from time immemorial a British sanctuary; it was the reputed burial place of Arthur, of [p194] whose court the Grail Quest was the crowning adventure; the story must be identified with British soil. Consequently a version was composed, now represented by our *Perlesvaus* text, in which the union of Nicodemus of Fescamp, and Joseph of Glastonbury, fame, as ancestors of the Grail hero, offers a significant hint of the *provenance* of the version.

Secondly, a no less important element in the process was due to the conscious action of Robert de Borron, who well understood the character of his material, and radically remodelled the whole on the basis of the triple Mystery tradition translated into terms of high Christian Mysticism. A notable feature of Borron's version is his utilization of the tradition of the final Messianic Feast, in combination with his Eucharistic symbolism, a combination thoroughly familiar to early Christian Mystics.

Once started on a definitely romantic career, the Grail story rapidly became a complex of originally divergent themes, the most important stage in its development being the incorporation of the popular tale of the Widow's Son, brought up in the wilderness, and launched into the world in a condition of absolute ignorance of men, and manners. The *Perceval* story is a charming story, but it has originally nothing whatever to do with the Grail. The original tale, now best represented by our English *Syr Percyvelle of Galles*, has no trace of Mystery element; it is Folk-lore, pure and simple. I believe the connection with the Grail legend to be purely fortuitous, and due to the fact that the hero of the Folk-tale was known as 'The Widow's Son,' which he actually was, while this title represented in Mystery terminology a certain grade of Initiation, and as such is preserved to-day in Masonic ritual.[15]

[p195] Finally the rising tide of dogmatic Medievalism, with its crassly materialistic view of the Eucharist; its insistence on the saving grace of asceticism and celibacy; and its scarcely veiled contempt for women, overwhelmed the original conception. Certain of the features of the ancient ritual indeed survive, but they are factors of confusion, rather than clues to enlightenment. Thus, while the Grail still retains its character of a Feeding Vessel, comes and goes without visible agency,

---

15. Cf. *Legend of Sir Perceval*, Vol. II. p. 307 and note. I have recently received Dr Brugger's review of Mr R. H. Griffith's study of the English poem, and am glad to see that the critic accepts the independence of this version. If scholars can see their way to accept as *faits acquis* the mutual independence of the *Grail*, and *Perceval* themes, we shall, at last, have a solid basis for future criticism.

and supplies each knight with 'such food and drink as he best loved in the world,' it is none the less the Chalice of the Sacred Blood, and critics are sorely put to it to harmonize these conflicting aspects. In the same way Galahad's grandfather still bears the title of the Rich Fisher, and there are confused references to a Land laid Waste as the result of a Dolorous Stroke.

But while the terminology lingers on to our perplexity the characters involved lie outside the march of the story; practically no trace of the old Nature Ritual survives in the final *Queste* form. The remodelling is so radical that it seems most reasonable to conclude that it was purposeful, that the original author of the *Queste* had a very clear idea of the real nature of the Grail, and was bent upon a complete restatement in terms of current orthodoxy. I advisedly use this term, as I see no trace in the *Queste* of a genuine Mystic conception, such as that of Borron. So far as criticism of the literature is concerned I adhere to my previously expressed opinion that the *Queste* should be treated rather as a *Lancelot* than as a *Grail* romance. It is of real importance in the evolution of the Arthurian romantic cycle; as a factor in determining the true character and origins of the Grail legend it is worse than useless; what remains of the [p196] original features is so fragmentary, and so distorted, that any attempt to use the version as basis for argument, or comparison, can only introduce a further element of confusion into an already more than sufficiently involved problem.

I am also still of opinion that the table of descent given on p. 283 of Volume II. of my *Perceval* studies, represents the most probable evolution of the literature; at the same time, in the light of further research, I should feel inclined to add the Grail section of *Sone de Nansai* as deriving from the same source which gave us Kiot's poem, and the *Perlesvaus*.[16] As evidence for a French original combining important features of these two versions, and at the same time retaining unmistakably archaic elements which have disappeared from both, I hold this section of the poem to be of extreme value for the criticism of the cycle.

While there are still missing links in the chain of descent, versions to be reconstructed, writers to be identified, I believe that in its *ensemble* the theory set forth in these pages will be found to be the only one which will satisfactorily meet all the conditions of the problem; which will cover the whole ground of investigation, omitting no element, evading no difficulty; which will harmonize apparently hopeless

---

16. Cf. my Notes, *Romania*, Vol. XLIII. pp. 403 *et seq.*

contradictions, explain apparently meaningless terminology, and thus provide a secure foundation for the criticism of a body of literature as important as it is fascinating.

The study and the criticism of the Grail literature will possess an even deeper interest, a more absorbing fascination, when it is definitely recognized that we possess in that literature a unique example of the restatement of an ancient and august Ritual in terms of imperishable Romance.

The Adonis, Attis, and Osiris Chapters from *The Golden Bough*

XXIX. The Myth of Adonis

The spectacle of the great changes which annually pass over the face of the earth has powerfully impressed the minds of men in all ages, and stirred them to meditate on the causes of transformations so vast and wonderful. Their curiosity has not been purely disinterested; for even the savage cannot fail to perceive how intimately his own life is bound up with the life of nature, and how the same processes which freeze the stream and strip the earth of vegetation menace him with extinction. At a certain stage of development men seem to have imagined that the means of averting the threatened calamity were in their own hands, and that they could hasten or retard the flight of the seasons by magic art. Accordingly they performed ceremonies and recited spells to make the rain to fall, the sun to shine, animals to multiply, and the fruits of the earth to grow. In course of time the slow advance of knowledge, which has dispelled so many cherished illusions, convinced at least the more thoughtful portion of mankind that the alternations of summer and winter, of spring and autumn, were not merely the result of their own magical rites, but that some deeper cause, some mightier power, was at work behind the shifting scenes of nature. They now pictured to themselves the growth and decay of vegetation, the birth and death of living creatures, as effects of the waxing or waning strength of divine beings, of gods and goddesses, who were born and died, who married and begot children, on the pattern of human life.

Thus the old magical theory of the seasons was displaced, or rather supplemented, by a religious theory. For although men now attributed the annual cycle of change primarily to corresponding changes in their deities, they still thought that by performing certain magical rites they could aid the god who was the principle of life, in his struggle with the opposing principle of death. They imagined that they could recruit his failing energies and even raise him from the dead. The ceremonies which they observed for this purpose were in substance a dramatic representation of the natural processes which they wished to facilitate; for

XXIX. The Myth of Adonis

it is a familiar tenet of magic that you can produce any desired effect by merely imitating it. And as they now explained the fluctuations of growth and decay, of reproduction and dissolution, by the marriage, the death, and the rebirth or revival of the gods, their religious or rather magical dramas turned in great measure on these themes. They set forth the fruitful union of the powers of fertility, the sad death of one at least of the divine partners, and his joyful resurrection. Thus a religious theory was blended with a magical practice. The combination is familiar in history. Indeed, few religions have ever succeeded in wholly extricating themselves from the old trammels of magic. The inconsistency of acting on two opposite principles, however it may vex the soul of the philosopher, rarely troubles the common man; indeed he is seldom even aware of it. His affair is to act, not to analyse the motives of his action. If mankind had always been logical and wise, history would not be a long chronicle of folly and crime.

Of the changes which the seasons bring with them, the most striking within the temperate zone are those which affect vegetation. The influence of the seasons on animals, though great, is not nearly so manifest. Hence it is natural that in the magical dramas designed to dispel winter and bring back spring the emphasis should be laid on vegetation, and that trees and plants should figure in them more prominently than beasts and birds. Yet the two sides of life, the vegetable and the animal, were not dissociated in the minds of those who observed the ceremonies. Indeed they commonly believed that the tie between the animal and the vegetable world was even closer than it really is; hence they often combined the dramatic representation of reviving plants with a real or a dramatic union of the sexes for the purpose of furthering at the same time and by the same act the multiplication of fruits, of animals, and of men. To them the principle of life and fertility, whether animal or vegetable, was one and indivisible. To live and to cause to live, to eat food and to beget children, these were the primary wants of men in the past, and they will be the primary wants of men in the future so long as the world lasts. Other things may be added to enrich and beautify human life, but unless these wants are first satisfied, humanity itself must cease to exist. These two things, therefore, food and children, were what men chiefly sought to procure by the performance of magical rites for the regulation of the seasons.

Nowhere, apparently, have these rites been more widely and solemnly celebrated than in the lands which border the Eastern Mediterranean. Under the names of Osiris, Tammuz, Adonis, and Attis, the

XXIX. The Myth of Adonis

peoples of Egypt and Western Asia represented the yearly decay and revival of life, especially of vegetable life, which they personified as a god who annually died and rose again from the dead. In name and detail the rites varied from place to place: in substance they were the same. The supposed death and resurrection of this oriental deity, a god of many names but of essentially one nature, is now to be examined. We begin with Tammuz or Adonis.

The worship of Adonis was practised by the Semitic peoples of Babylonia and Syria, and the Greeks borrowed it from them as early as the seventh century before Christ. The true name of the deity was Tammuz: the appellation of Adonis is merely the Semitic *Adon*, "lord," a title of honour by which his worshippers addressed him. But the Greeks through a misunderstanding converted the title of honour into a proper name. In the religious literature of Babylonia Tammuz appears as the youthful spouse or lover of Ishtar, the great mother goddess, the embodiment of the reproductive energies of nature. The references to their connexion with each other in myth and ritual are both fragmentary and obscure, but we gather from them that every year Tammuz was believed to die, passing away from the cheerful earth to the gloomy subterranean world, and that every year his divine mistress journeyed in quest of him "to the land from which there is no returning, to the house of darkness, where dust lies on door and bolt." During her absence the passion of love ceased to operate: men and beasts alike forgot to reproduce their kinds: all life was threatened with extinction. So intimately bound up with the goddess were the sexual functions of the whole animal kingdom that without her presence they could not be discharged. A messenger of the great god Ea was accordingly despatched to rescue the goddess on whom so much depended. The stern queen of the infernal regions, Allatu or Eresh-Kigal by name, reluctantly allowed Ishtar to be sprinkled with the Water of Life and to depart, in company probably with her lover Tammuz, that the two might return together to the upper world, and that with their return all nature might revive.

Laments for the departed Tammuz are contained in several Babylonian hymns, which liken him to plants that quickly fade. He is

> "*A tamarisk that in the garden has drunk no water,*
> *Whose crown in the field has brought forth no blossom.*
> *A willow that rejoiced not by the watercourse,*
> *A willow whose roots were torn up.*

XXIX. The Myth of Adonis

A herb that in the garden had drunk no water."

His death appears to have been annually mourned, to the shrill music of flutes, by men and women about midsummer in the month named after him, the month of Tammuz. The dirges were seemingly chanted over an effigy of the dead god, which was washed with pure water, anointed with oil, and clad in a red robe, while the fumes of incense rose into the air, as if to stir his dormant senses by their pungent fragrance and wake him from the sleep of death. In one of these dirges, inscribed *Lament of the Flutes for Tammuz*, we seem still to hear the voices of the singers chanting the sad refrain and to catch, like far-away music, the wailing notes of the flutes:

> "At his vanishing away she lifts up a lament,
> 'Oh my child!' at his vanishing away she lifts up a lament;
> 'My Damu!' at his vanishing away she lifts up a lament.
> 'My enchanter and priest!' at his vanishing away she lifts up a lament,
> At the shining cedar, rooted in a spacious place,
> In Eanna, above and below, she lifts up a lament.
> Like the lament that a house lifts up for its master, lifts she up a lament,
> Like the lament that a city lifts up for its lord, lifts she up a lament.
> Her lament is the lament for a herb that grows not in the bed,
> Her lament is the lament for the corn that grows not in the ear.
> Her chamber is a possession that brings not forth a possession,
> A weary woman, a weary child, forspent.
> Her lament is for a great river, where no willows grow,
> Her lament is for a field, where corn and herbs grow not.
> Her lament is for a pool, where fishes grow not.
> Her lament is for a thickest of reeds, where no reeds grow.
> Her lament is for woods, where tamarisks grow not.
> Her lament is for a wilderness where no cypresses (?) grow.
> Her lament is for the depth of a garden of trees, where honey and wine grow not.
> Her lament is for meadows, where no plants grow.
> Her lament is for a palace, where length of life grows not."

The tragical story and the melancholy rites of Adonis are better known to us from the descriptions of Greek writers than from the fragments of Babylonian literature or the brief reference of the prophet

XXIX. The Myth of Adonis

Ezekiel, who saw the women of Jerusalem weeping for Tammuz at the north gate of the temple. Mirrored in the glass of Greek mythology, the oriental deity appears as a comely youth beloved by Aphrodite. In his infancy the goddess hid him in a chest, which she gave in charge to Persephone, queen of the nether world. But when Persephone opened the chest and beheld the beauty of the babe, she refused to give him back to Aphrodite, though the goddess of love went down herself to hell to ransom her dear one from the power of the grave. The dispute between the two goddesses of love and death was settled by Zeus, who decreed that Adonis should abide with Persephone in the under world for one part of the year, and with Aphrodite in the upper world for another part. At last the fair youth was killed in hunting by a wild boar, or by the jealous Ares, who turned himself into the likeness of a boar in order to compass the death of his rival. Bitterly did Aphrodite lament her loved and lost Adonis. In this form of the myth, the contest between Aphrodite and Persephone for the possession of Adonis clearly reflects the struggle between Ishtar and Allatu in the land of the dead, while the decision of Zeus that Adonis is to spend one part of the year under ground and another part above ground is merely a Greek version of the annual disappearance and reappearance of Tammuz.

XXX. Adonis in Syria

The myth of Adonis was localised and his rites celebrated with much solemnity at two places in Western Asia. One of these was Byblus on the coast of Syria, the other was Paphos in Cyprus. Both were great seats of the worship of Aphrodite, or rather of her Semitic counterpart, Astarte; and of both, if we accept the legends, Cinyras, the father of Adonis, was king. Of the two cities Byblus was the more ancient; indeed it claimed to be the oldest city in Phoenicia, and to have been founded in the early ages of the world by the great god El, whom Greeks and Romans identified with Cronus and Saturn respectively. However that may have been, in historical times it ranked as a holy place, the religious capital of the country, the Mecca or Jerusalem of the Phoenicians. The city stood on a height beside the sea, and contained a great sanctuary of Astarte, where in the midst of a spacious open court, surrounded by cloisters and approached from below by staircases, rose a tall cone or obelisk, the holy image of the goddess. In this sanctuary the rites of Adonis were celebrated. Indeed the whole city was sacred to him, and the river Nahr Ibrahim, which falls into the sea a little to the south of Byblus, bore in antiquity the name of Adonis. This was the kingdom of Cinyras. From the earliest to the latest times the city appears to have been ruled by kings, assisted perhaps by a senate or council of elders.

The last king of Byblus bore the ancient name of Cinyras, and was beheaded by Pompey the Great for his tyrannous excesses. His legendary namesake Cinyras is said to have founded a sanctuary of Aphrodite, that is, of Astarte, at a place on Mount Lebanon, distant a day's journey from the capital. The spot was probably Aphaca, at the source of the river Adonis, half-way between Byblus and Baalbec; for at Aphaca there was a famous grove and sanctuary of Astarte which Constantine destroyed on account of the flagitious character of the worship. The site of the temple has been discovered by modern travellers near the miserable village which still bears the name of Afka at the head of

XXX. Adonis in Syria

the wild, romantic, wooded gorge of the Adonis. The hamlet stands among groves of noble walnut-trees on the brink of the lyn. A little way off the river rushes from a cavern at the foot of a mighty amphitheatre of towering cliffs to plunge in a series of cascades into the awful depths of the glen. The deeper it descends, the ranker and denser grows the vegetation, which, sprouting from the crannies and fissures of the rocks, spreads a green veil over the roaring or murmuring stream in the tremendous chasm below. There is something delicious, almost intoxicating, in the freshness of these tumbling waters, in the sweetness and purity of the mountain air, in the vivid green of the vegetation. The temple, of which some massive hewn blocks and a fine column of Syenite granite still mark the site, occupied a terrace facing the source of the river and commanding a magnificent prospect. Across the foam and the roar of the waterfalls you look up to the cavern and away to the top of the sublime precipices above. So lofty is the cliff that the goats which creep along its ledges to browse on the bushes appear like ants to the spectator hundreds of feet below. Seaward the view is especially impressive when the sun floods the profound gorge with golden light, revealing all the fantastic buttresses and rounded towers of its mountain rampart, and falling softly on the varied green of the woods which clothe its depths. It was here that, according to the legend, Adonis met Aphrodite for the first or the last time, and here his mangled body was buried. A fairer scene could hardly be imagined for a story of tragic love and death. Yet, sequestered as the valley is and must always have been, it is not wholly deserted. A convent or a village may be observed here and there standing out against the sky on the top of some beetling crag, or clinging to the face of a nearly perpendicular cliff high above the foam and the din of the river; and at evening the lights that twinkle through the gloom betray the presence of human habitations on slopes which might seem inaccessible to man. In antiquity the whole of the lovely vale appears to have been dedicated to Adonis, and to this day it is haunted by his memory; for the heights which shut it in are crested at various points by ruined monuments of his worship, some of them overhanging dreadful abysses, down which it turns the head dizzy to look and see the eagles wheeling about their nests far below. One such monument exists at Ghineh. The face of a great rock, above a roughly hewn recess, is here carved with figures of Adonis and Aphrodite. He is portrayed with spear in rest, awaiting the attack of a bear, while she is seated in an attitude of sorrow. Her grief-stricken figure may well be the mourning Aphrodite of the Lebanon described by Macrobius, and the recess in the rock is perhaps her lover's tomb. Every year, in the belief of his worshippers, Adonis was wounded to death on the mountains, and every year the face of nature itself was dyed with his sacred blood. So year by year the Syrian damsels lamented his untimely fate, while the red anemone, his flower, bloomed among the cedars of Lebanon, and the river ran red to the sea, fringing the winding shores of the blue Mediterranean, whenever the wind set inshore, with a sinuous band of crimson.

XXXI. Adonis in Cyprus

The island of Cyprus lies but one day's sail from the coast of Syria. Indeed, on fine summer evenings its mountains may be descried looming low and dark against the red fires of sunset. With its rich mines of copper and its forests of firs and stately cedars, the island naturally attracted a commercial and maritime people like the Phoenicians; while the abundance of its corn, its wine, and its oil must have rendered it in their eyes a Land of Promise by comparison with the niggardly nature of their own rugged coast, hemmed in between the mountains and the sea. Accordingly they settled in Cyprus at a very early date and remained there long after the Greeks had also established themselves on its shores; for we know from inscriptions and coins that Phoenician kings reigned at Citium, the Chittim of the Hebrews, down to the time of Alexander the Great. Naturally the Semitic colonists brought their gods with them from the mother-land. They worshipped Baal of the Lebanon, who may well have been Adonis, and at Amathus on the south coast they instituted the rites of Adonis and Aphrodite, or rather Astarte. Here, as at Byblus, these rites resembled the Egyptian worship of Osiris so closely that some people even identified the Adonis of Amathus with Osiris.

But the great seat of the worship of Aphrodite and Adonis in Cyprus was Paphos on the south-western side of the island. Among the petty kingdoms into which Cyprus was divided from the earliest times until the end of the fourth century before our era Paphos must have ranked with the best. It is a land of hills and billowy ridges, diversified by fields and vineyards and intersected by rivers, which in the course of ages have carved for themselves beds of such tremendous depth that travelling in the interior is difficult and tedious. The lofty range of Mount Olympus (the modern Troodos), capped with snow the greater part of the year, screens Paphos from the northerly and easterly winds and cuts it off from the rest of the island. On the slopes of the range the last pine-woods of Cyprus linger, sheltering here and there monasteries in scenery not unworthy of the Apennines. The old city of Paphos occupied the summit of a hill about a mile from the sea; the newer city sprang up at the harbour some ten miles off. The sanctuary of Aphrodite at Old Paphos (the modern Kuklia) was one of the most celebrated shrines in the ancient world. According to Herodotus, it was founded by Phoenician colonists from Ascalon; but it is possible that a native goddess of fertility was worshipped on the spot before the arrival of the Phoenicians, and that the newcomers identified her with their own Baalath or Astarte, whom she may have closely resembled. If two deities were thus fused in one, we may suppose that they were both varieties of that great goddess of motherhood and fertility whose worship appears to have been spread all over Western Asia from a very early time. The supposition is confirmed as well by the archaic shape of her image as by the licentious character of her rites; for both that shape and those rites were shared by her with other Asiatic deities. Her image was simply a white cone or pyramid. In like manner, a cone was the emblem of Astarte at Byblus, of the native goddess whom the Greeks called Artemis at Perga in Pamphylia, and of the sun-god Heliogabalus at Emesa in Syria. Conical stones, which apparently served as idols, have also been found at Golgi in Cyprus, and in the Phoenician temples of Malta; and cones of sandstone came to light at the shrine of the "Mistress of Torquoise" among the barren hills and frowning precipices of Sinai.

In Cyprus it appears that before marriage all women were formerly obliged by custom to prostitute themselves to strangers at the sanctuary of the goddess, whether she went by the name of Aphrodite, Astarte, or what not. Similar customs prevailed in many parts of Western Asia. Whatever its motive, the practice was clearly regarded, not as an orgy of lust, but as a solemn religious duty performed in the service of that great Mother Goddess of Western Asia whose name varied, while her type remained constant, from place to place. Thus at Babylon every woman, whether rich or poor, had once in her life to submit to the embraces of a stranger at the temple of Mylitta, that is, of Ishtar or Astarte, and to dedicate to the goddess the wages earned by this sanctified harlotry. The sacred precinct was crowded with women waiting to observe the custom. Some of them had to wait there for years. At Heliopolis or Baalbec in Syria, famous for the imposing grandeur of its ruined temples, the custom of the country required that every maiden

XXXI. Adonis in Cyprus

should prostitute herself to a stranger at the temple of Astarte, and matrons as well as maids testified their devotion to the goddess in the same manner. The emperor Constantine abolished the custom, destroyed the temple, and built a church in its stead. In Phoenician temples women prostituted themselves for hire in the service of religion, believing that by this conduct they propitiated the goddess and won her favour. "It was a law of the Amorites, that she who was about to marry should sit in fornication seven days by the gate." At Byblus the people shaved their heads in the annual mourning for Adonis. Women who refused to sacrifice their hair had to give themselves up to strangers on a certain day of the festival, and the money which they thus earned was devoted to the goddess. A Greek inscription found at Tralles in Lydia proves that the practice of religious prostitution survived in that country as late as the second century of our era. It records of a certain woman, Aurelia Aemilia by name, not only that she herself served the god in the capacity of a harlot at his express command, but that her mother and other female ancestors had done the same before her; and the publicity of the record, engraved on a marble column which supported a votive offering, shows that no stain attached to such a life and such a parentage. In Armenia the noblest families dedicated their daughters to the service of the goddess Anaitis in her temple of Acilisena, where the damsels acted as prostitutes for a long time before they were given in marriage. Nobody scrupled to take one of these girls to wife when her period of service was over. Again, the goddess Ma was served by a multitude of sacred harlots at Comana in Pontus, and crowds of men and women flocked to her sanctuary from the neighbouring cities and country to attend the biennial festivals or to pay their vows to the goddess.

If we survey the whole of the evidence on this subject, some of which has still to be laid before the reader, we may conclude that a great Mother Goddess, the personification of all the reproductive energies of nature, was worshipped under different names but with a substantial similarity of myth and ritual by many peoples of Western Asia; that associated with her was a lover, or rather series of lovers, divine yet mortal, with whom she mated year by year, their commerce being deemed essential to the propagation of animals and plants, each in their several kind; and further, that the fabulous union of the divine pair was simulated and, as it were, multiplied on earth by the real, though temporary, union of the human sexes at the sanctuary of the goddess for the sake of thereby ensuring the fruitfulness of the ground and the increase of man and beast.

XXXI. Adonis in Cyprus

At Paphos the custom of religious prostitution is said to have been instituted by King Cinyras, and to have been practised by his daughters, the sisters of Adonis, who, having incurred the wrath of Aphrodite, mated with strangers and ended their days in Egypt. In this form of the tradition the wrath of Aphrodite is probably a feature added by a later authority, who could only regard conduct which shocked his own moral sense as a punishment inflicted by the goddess instead of as a sacrifice regularly enjoined by her on all her devotees. At all events the story indicates that the princesses of Paphos had to conform to the custom as well as women of humble birth.

Among the stories which were told of Cinyras, the ancestor of the priestly kings of Paphos and the father of Adonis, there are some that deserve our attention. In the first place, he is said to have begotten his son Adonis in incestuous intercourse with his daughter Myrrha at a festival of the corn-goddess, at which women robed in white were wont to offer corn-wreaths as first-fruits of the harvest and to observe strict chastity for nine days. Similar cases of incest with a daughter are reported of many ancient kings. It seems unlikely that such reports are without foundation, and perhaps equally improbable that they refer to mere fortuitous outbursts of unnatural lust. We may suspect that they are based on a practice actually observed for a definite reason in certain special circumstances. Now in countries where the royal blood was traced through women only, and where consequently the king held office merely in virtue of his marriage with an hereditary princess, who was the real sovereign, it appears to have often happened that a prince married his own sister, the princess royal, in order to obtain with her hand the crown which otherwise would have gone to another man, perhaps to a stranger. May not the same rule of descent have furnished a motive for incest with a daughter? For it seems a natural corollary from such a rule that the king was bound to vacate the throne on the death of his wife, the queen, since he occupied it only by virtue of his marriage with her. When that marriage terminated, his right to the throne terminated with it and passed at once to his daughter's husband. Hence if the king desired to reign after his wife's death, the only way in which he could legitimately continue to do so was by marrying his daughter, and thus prolonging through her the title which had formerly been his through her mother.

Cinyras is said to have been famed for his exquisite beauty and to have been wooed by Aphrodite herself. Thus it would appear, as scholars have already observed, that Cinyras was in a sense a duplicate of his handsome son Adonis, to whom the inflammable goddess also lost her heart. Further, these stories of the love of Aphrodite for two members of the royal house of Paphos can hardly be dissociated from the corresponding legend told of Pygmalion, a Phoenician king of Cyprus, who is said to have fallen in love with an image of Aphrodite and taken it to his bed. When we consider that Pygmalion was the father-in-law of Cinyras, that the son of Cinyras was Adonis, and that all three, in successive generations, are said to have been concerned in a love-intrigue with Aphrodite, we can hardly help concluding that the early Phoenician kings of Paphos, or their sons, regularly claimed to be not merely the priests of the goddess but also her lovers, in other words, that in their official capacity they personated Adonis. At all events Adonis is said to have reigned in Cyprus, and it appears to be certain that the title of Adonis was regularly borne by the sons of all the Phoenician kings of the island. It is true that the title strictly signified no more than "lord"; yet the legends which connect these Cyprian princes with the goddess of love make it probable that they claimed the divine nature as well as the human dignity of Adonis. The story of Pygmalion points to a ceremony of a sacred marriage in which the king wedded the image of Aphrodite, or rather of Astarte. If that was so, the tale was in a sense true, not of a single man only, but of a whole series of men, and it would be all the more likely to be told of Pygmalion, if that was a common name of Semitic kings in general, and of Cyprian kings in particular. Pygmalion, at all events, is known as the name of the king of Tyre from whom his sister Dido fled; and a king of Citium and Idalium in Cyprus, who reigned in the time of Alexander the Great, was also called Pygmalion, or rather Pumiyathon, the Phoenician name which the Greeks corrupted into Pygmalion. Further, it deserves to be noted that the names Pygmalion and Astarte occur together in a Punic inscription on a gold medallion which was found in a grave at Carthage; the characters of the inscription are of the earliest type. As the custom of religious prostitution at Paphos is said to have been founded by king Cinyras and observed by his daughters, we may surmise that the kings of Paphos played the part of the divine bridegroom in a less innocent rite than the form of marriage with a statue; in fact, that at certain festivals each of them had to mate with one or more of the sacred harlots of the temple, who played Astarte to his Adonis. If that was so, there is more truth than has commonly been supposed in the reproach cast by the Christian fathers that the Aphrodite worshipped by Cinyras was a

XXXI. Adonis in Cyprus

common whore. The fruit of their union would rank as sons and daughters of the deity, and would in time become the parents of gods and goddesses, like their fathers and mothers before them. In this manner Paphos, and perhaps all sanctuaries of the great Asiatic goddess where sacred prostitution was practised, might be well stocked with human deities, the offspring of the divine king by his wives, concubines, and temple harlots. Any one of these might probably succeed his father on the throne or be sacrificed in his stead whenever stress of war or other grave junctures called, as they sometimes did, for the death of a royal victim. Such a tax, levied occasionally on the king's numerous progeny for the good of the country, would neither extinguish the divine stock nor break the father's heart, who divided his paternal affection among so many. At all events, if, as there seems reason to believe, Semitic kings were often regarded at the same time as hereditary deities, it is easy to understand the frequency of Semitic personal names which imply that the bearers of them were the sons or daughters, the brothers or sisters, the fathers or mothers of a god, and we need not resort to the shifts employed by some scholars to evade the plain sense of the words. This interpretation is confirmed by a parallel Egyptian usage; for in Egypt, where the kings were worshipped as divine, the queen was called "the wife of the god" or "the mother of the god," and the title "father of the god" was borne not only by the king's real father but also by his father-in-law. Similarly, perhaps, among the Semites any man who sent his daughter to swell the royal harem may have been allowed to call himself "the father of the god."

If we may judge by his name, the Semitic king who bore the name of Cinyras was, like King David, a harper; for the name of Cinyras is clearly connected with the Greek *cinyra*, "a lyre," which in its turn comes from the Semitic *kinnor*, "a lyre," the very word applied to the instrument on which David played before Saul. We shall probably not err in assuming that at Paphos as at Jerusalem the music of the lyre or harp was not a mere pastime designed to while away an idle hour, but formed part of the service of religion, the moving influence of its melodies being perhaps set down, like the effect of wine, to the direct inspiration of a deity. Certainly at Jerusalem the regular clergy of the temple prophesied to the music of harps, of psalteries, and of cymbals; and it appears that the irregular clergy also, as we may call the prophets, depended on some such stimulus for inducing the ecstatic state which they took for immediate converse with the divinity. Thus we read of

XXXI. Adonis in Cyprus

a band of prophets coming down from a high place with a psaltery, a timbrel, a pipe, and a harp before them, and prophesying as they went. Again, when the united forces of Judah and Ephraim were traversing the wilderness of Moab in pursuit of the enemy, they could find no water for three days, and were like to die of thirst, they and the beasts of burden. In this emergency the prophet Elisha, who was with the army, called for a minstrel and bade him play. Under the influence of the music he ordered the soldiers to dig trenches in the sandy bed of the waterless waddy through which lay the line of march. They did so, and next morning the trenches were full of the water that had drained down into them underground from the desolate, forbidding mountains on either hand. The prophet's success in striking water in the wilderness resembles the reported success of modern dowsers, though his mode of procedure was different. Incidentally he rendered another service to his countrymen. For the skulking Moabites from their lairs among the rocks saw the red sun of the desert reflected in the water, and taking it for the blood, or perhaps rather for an omen of the blood, of their enemies, they plucked up heart to attack the camp and were defeated with great slaughter.

Again, just as the cloud of melancholy which from time to time darkened the moody mind of Saul was viewed as an evil spirit from the Lord vexing him, so on the other hand the solemn strains of the harp, which soothed and composed his troubled thoughts, may well have seemed to the hag-ridden king the very voice of God or of his good angel whispering peace. Even in our own day a great religious writer, himself deeply sensitive to the witchery of music, has said that musical notes, with all their power to fire the blood and melt the heart, cannot be mere empty sounds and nothing more; no, they have escaped from some higher sphere, they are outpourings of eternal harmony, the voice of angels, the Magnificat of saints. It is thus that the rude imaginings of primitive man are transfigured and his feeble lispings echoed with a rolling reverberation in the musical prose of Newman. Indeed the influence of music on the development of religion is a subject which would repay a sympathetic study. For we cannot doubt that this, the most intimate and affecting of all the arts, has done much to create as well as to express the religious emotions, thus modifying more or less deeply the fabric of belief to which at first sight it seems only to minister. The musician has done his part as well as the prophet and the thinker in the making of religion. Every faith has its appropriate music, and the difference between

XXXI. Adonis in Cyprus

the creeds might almost be expressed in musical notation. The interval, for example, which divides the wild revels of Cybele from the stately ritual of the Catholic Church is measured by the gulf which severs the dissonant clash of cymbals and tambourines from the grave harmonies of Palestrina and Handel. A different spirit breathes in the difference of the music.

XXXII. The Ritual of Adonis

At the festivals of Adonis, which were held in Western Asia and in Greek lands, the death of the god was annually mourned, with a bitter wailing, chiefly by women; images of him, dressed to resemble corpses, were carried out as to burial and then thrown into the sea or into springs; and in some places his revival was celebrated on the following day. But at different places the ceremonies varied somewhat in the manner and apparently also in the season of their celebration. At Alexandria images of Aphrodite and Adonis were displayed on two couches; beside them were set ripe fruits of all kinds, cakes, plants growing in flower-pots, and green bowers twined with anise. The marriage of the lovers was celebrated one day, and on the morrow women attired as mourners, with streaming hair and bared breasts, bore the image of the dead Adonis to the sea-shore and committed it to the waves. Yet they sorrowed not without hope, for they sang that the lost one would come back again. The date at which this Alexandrian ceremony was observed is not expressly stated; but from the mention of the ripe fruits it has been inferred that it took place in late summer. In the great Phoenician sanctuary of Astarte at Byblus the death of Adonis was annually mourned, to the shrill wailing notes of the flute, with weeping, lamentation, and beating of the breast; but next day he was believed to come to life again and ascend up to heaven in the presence of his worshippers. The disconsolate believers, left behind on earth, shaved their heads as the Egyptians did on the death of the divine bull Apis; women who could not bring themselves to sacrifice their beautiful tresses had to give themselves up to strangers on a certain day of the festival, and to dedicate to Astarte the wages of their shame.

This Phoenician festival appears to have been a vernal one, for its date was determined by the discoloration of the river Adonis, and this has been observed by modern travellers to occur in spring. At that season the red earth washed down from the mountains by the rain tinges the water of the river, and even the sea, for a great way with a blood-red hue, and the crimson stain was believed to be the blood of Adonis, annually wounded to death by the boar on Mount Lebanon. Again, the scarlet anemone is said to have sprung from the blood of Adonis, or to have been stained by it; and as the anemone blooms in Syria about Easter, this may be thought to show that the festival of Adonis, or at least one of his festivals, was held in spring. The name of the flower is probably derived from Naaman ("darling"), which seems to have been an epithet of Adonis. The Arabs still call the anemone "wounds of the Naaman." The red rose also was said to owe its hue to the same sad occasion; for Aphrodite, hastening to her wounded lover, trod on a bush of white roses; the cruel thorns tore her tender flesh, and her sacred blood dyed the white roses for ever red. It would be idle, perhaps, to lay much weight on evidence drawn from the calendar of flowers, and in particular to press an argument so fragile as the bloom of the rose. Yet so far as it counts at all, the tale which links the damask rose with the death of Adonis points to a summer rather than to a spring celebration of his passion. In Attica, certainly, the festival fell at the height of summer. For the fleet which Athens fitted out against Syracuse, and by the destruction of which her power was permanently crippled, sailed at midsummer, and by an ominous coincidence the sombre rites of Adonis were being celebrated at the very time. As the troops marched down to the harbour to embark, the streets through which they passed were lined with coffins and corpse-like effigies, and the air was rent with the noise of women wailing for the dead Adonis. The circumstance cast a gloom over the sailing of the most splendid armament that Athens ever sent to sea. Many ages afterwards, when the Emperor Julian made his first entry into Antioch, he found in like manner the gay, the luxurious capital of the East plunged in mimic grief for the annual death of Adonis; and if he had any presentiment of coming evil, the voices of lamentation which struck upon his ear must have seemed to sound his knell.

The resemblance of these ceremonies to the Indian and European ceremonies which I have described elsewhere is obvious. In particular, apart from the somewhat doubtful date of its celebration, the Alexandrian ceremony is almost identical with the Indian. In both of them the marriage of two divine beings, whose affinity with vegetation seems indicated by the fresh plants with which they are surrounded, is celebrated in effigy, and the effigies are afterwards mourned over and thrown into the water. From the similarity of these customs to each other and to the spring and midsummer customs of modern Europe we should naturally expect that they all admit of a common explanation. Hence, if the explanation which I have adopted of the latter is correct, the ceremony of the death and resurrection of Adonis must also have been a dramatic representation of the decay and revival of plant life. The inference thus based on the resemblance of the customs is confirmed by the following features in the legend and ritual of Adonis. His affinity with vegetation comes out at once in the common story of his birth. He was said to have been born from a myrrh-tree, the bark of which bursting, after a ten months' gestation, allowed the lovely infant to come forth. According to some, a boar rent the bark with his tusk and so opened a passage for the babe. A faint rationalistic colour was given to the legend by saying that his mother was a woman named Myrrh, who had been turned into a myrrh-tree soon after she had conceived the child. The use of myrrh as incense at the festival of Adonis may have given rise to the fable. We have seen that incense was burnt at the corresponding Babylonian rites, just as it was burnt by the idolatrous Hebrews in honour of the Queen of Heaven, who was no other than Astarte. Again, the story that Adonis spent half, or according to others a third, of the year in the lower world and the rest of it in the upper world, is explained most simply and naturally by supposing that he represented vegetation, especially the corn, which lies buried in the earth half the year and reappears above ground the other half. Certainly of the annual phenomena of nature there is none which suggests so obviously the idea of death and resurrection as the disappearance and reappearance of vegetation in autumn and spring. Adonis has been taken for the sun; but there is nothing in the sun's annual course within the temperate and tropical zones to suggest that he is dead for half or a third of the year and alive for the other half or two-thirds. He might, indeed, be conceived as weakened in winter, but dead he could not be thought to be; his daily reappearance contradicts the supposition. Within the Arctic Circle, where the sun annually disappears for a continuous period which varies from twenty-four hours to six months according to the latitude, his yearly death and resurrection would certainly be an obvious idea; but no one except the unfortunate astronomer Bailly has maintained that the Adonis worship came from the Arctic regions. On the other hand, the annual death and revival of vegetation is a conception which readily presents itself to men in every

XXXII. The Ritual of Adonis

stage of savagery and civilisation; and the vastness of the scale on which this ever-recurring decay and regeneration takes place, together with man's intimate dependence on it for subsistence, combine to render it the most impressive annual occurrence in nature, at least within the temperate zones. It is no wonder that a phenomenon so important, so striking, and so universal should, by suggesting similar ideas, have given rise to similar rites in many lands. We may, therefore, accept as probable an explanation of the Adonis worship which accords so well with the facts of nature and with the analogy of similar rites in other lands. Moreover, the explanation is countenanced by a considerable body of opinion amongst the ancients themselves, who again and again interpreted the dying and reviving god as the reaped and sprouting grain.

The character of Tammuz or Adonis as a corn-spirit comes out plainly in an account of his festival given by an Arabic writer of the tenth century. In describing the rites and sacrifices observed at the different seasons of the year by the heathen Syrians of Harran, he says: "Tammuz (July). In the middle of this month is the festival of el-Bûgât, that is, of the weeping women, and this is the Tâ-uz festival, which is celebrated in honour of the god Tâ-uz. The women bewail him, because his lord slew him so cruelly, ground his bones in a mill, and then scattered them to the wind. The women (during this festival) eat nothing which has been ground in a mill, but limit their diet to steeped wheat, sweet vetches, dates, raisins, and the like." Tâ-uz, who is no other than Tammuz, is here like Burns's John Barleycorn:

> "*They wasted o'er a scorching flame*
> *The marrow of his bones;*
> *But a miller us'd him worst of all—*
> *For he crush'd him between two stones.*"

This concentration, so to say, of the nature of Adonis upon the cereal crops is characteristic of the stage of culture reached by his worshippers in historical times. They had left the nomadic life of the wandering hunter and herdsman far behind them; for ages they had been settled on the land, and had depended for their subsistence mainly on the products of tillage. The berries and roots of the wilderness, the grass of the pastures, which had been matters of vital importance to their ruder forefathers, were now of little moment to them: more and more their thoughts and energies were engrossed by the staple of their life,

XXXII. The Ritual of Adonis

the corn; more and more accordingly the propitiation of the deities of fertility in general and of the corn-spirit in particular tended to become the central feature of their religion. The aim they set before themselves in celebrating the rites was thoroughly practical. It was no vague poetical sentiment which prompted them to hail with joy the rebirth of vegetation and to mourn its decline. Hunger, felt or feared, was the mainspring of the worship of Adonis.

It has been suggested by Father Lagrange that the mourning for Adonis was essentially a harvest rite designed to propitiate the corngod, who was then either perishing under the sickles of the reapers, or being trodden to death under the hoofs of the oxen on the threshing-floor. While the men slew him, the women wept crocodile tears at home to appease his natural indignation by a show of grief for his death. The theory fits in well with the dates of the festivals, which fell in spring or summer; for spring and summer, not autumn, are the seasons of the barley and wheat harvests in the lands which worshipped Adonis. Further, the hypothesis is confirmed by the practice of the Egyptian reapers, who lamented, calling upon Isis, when they cut the first corn; and it is recommended by the analogous customs of many hunting tribes, who testify great respect for the animals which they kill and eat.

Thus interpreted the death of Adonis is not the natural decay of vegetation in general under the summer heat or the winter cold; it is the violent destruction of the corn by man, who cuts it down on the field, stamps it to pieces on the threshing-floor, and grinds it to powder in the mill. That this was indeed the principal aspect in which Adonis presented himself in later times to the agricultural peoples of the Levant, may be admitted; but whether from the beginning he had been the corn and nothing but the corn, may be doubted. At an earlier period he may have been to the herdsman, above all, the tender herbage which sprouts after rain, offering rich pasture to the lean and hungry cattle. Earlier still he may have embodied the spirit of the nuts and berries which the autumn woods yield to the savage hunter and his squaw. And just as the husband-man must propitiate the spirit of the corn which he consumes, so the herdsman must appease the spirit of the grass and leaves which his cattle munch, and the hunter must soothe the spirit of the roots which he digs, and of the fruits which he gathers from the bough. In all cases the propitiation of the injured and angry, sprite would naturally comprise elaborate excuses and apologies, accompanied by loud lamentations at his decease whenever, through some deplorable accident or necessity, he happened to be murdered as well as robbed. Only

XXXII. The Ritual of Adonis

we must bear in mind that the savage hunter and herdsman of those early days had probably not yet attained to the abstract idea of vegetation in general; and that accordingly, so far as Adonis existed for them at all, he must have been the *Adon* or lord of each individual tree and plant rather than a personification of vegetable life as a whole. Thus there would be as many Adonises as there were trees and shrubs, and each of them might expect to receive satisfaction for any damage done to his person or property. And year by year, when the trees were deciduous, every Adonis would seem to bleed to death with the red leaves of autumn and to come to life again with the fresh green of spring.

There is some reason to think that in early times Adonis was sometimes personated by a living man who died a violent death in the character of the god. Further, there is evidence which goes to show that among the agricultural peoples of the Eastern Mediterranean, the corn-spirit, by whatever name he was known, was often represented, year by year, by human victims slain on the harvest-field. If that was so, it seems likely that the propitiation of the corn-spirit would tend to fuse to some extent with the worship of the dead. For the spirits of these victims might be thought to return to life in the ears which they had fattened with their blood, and to die a second death at the reaping of the corn. Now the ghosts of those who have perished by violence are surly and apt to wreak their vengeance on their slayers whenever an opportunity offers. Hence the attempt to appease the souls of the slaughtered victims would naturally blend, at least in the popular conception, with the attempt to pacify the slain corn-spirit. And as the dead came back in the sprouting corn, so they might be thought to return in the spring flowers, waked from their long sleep by the soft vernal airs. They had been laid to their rest under the sod. What more natural than to imagine that the violets and the hyacinths, the roses and the anemones, sprang from their dust, were empurpled or incarnadined by their blood, and contained some portion of their spirit?

> "*I sometimes think that never blows so red*
> *The Rose as where some buried Caesar bled;*
> *That every Hyacinth the Garden wears*
> *Dropt in her Lap from some once lovely Head.*
>
> "*And this reviving Herb whose tender Green*
> *Fledges the River-Lip on which we lean—*

XXXII. The Ritual of Adonis

Ah, lean upon it lightly, for who knows
From what once lovely Lip it springs unseen?"

In the summer after the battle of Landen, the most sanguinary battle of the seventeenth century in Europe, the earth, saturated with the blood of twenty thousand slain, broke forth into millions of poppies, and the traveller who passed that vast sheet of scarlet might well fancy that the earth had indeed given up her dead. At Athens the great Commemoration of the Dead fell in spring about the middle of March, when the early flowers are in bloom. Then the dead were believed to rise from their graves and go about the streets, vainly endeavouring to enter the temples and dwellings, which were barred against these perturbed spirits with ropes, buckthorn, and pitch. The name of the festival, according to the most obvious and natural interpretation, means the Festival of Flowers, and the title would fit well with the substance of the ceremonies if at that season the poor ghosts were indeed thought to creep from the narrow house with the opening flowers. There may therefore be a measure of truth in the theory of Renan, who saw in the Adonis worship a dreamy voluptuous cult of death, conceived not as the King of Terrors, but as an insidious enchanter who lures his victims to himself and lulls them into an eternal sleep. The infinite charm of nature in the Lebanon, he thought, lends itself to religious emotions of this sensuous, visionary sort, hovering vaguely between pain and pleasure, between slumber and tears. It would doubtless be a mistake to attribute to Syrian peasants the worship of a conception so purely abstract as that of death in general. Yet it may be true that in their simple minds the thought of the reviving spirit of vegetation was blent with the very concrete notion of the ghosts of the dead, who come to life again in spring days with the early flowers, with the tender green of the corn and the many-tinted blossoms of the trees. Thus their views of the death and resurrection of nature would be coloured by their views of the death and resurrection of man, by their personal sorrows and hopes and fears. In like manner we cannot doubt that Renan's theory of Adonis was itself deeply tinged by passionate memories, memories of the slumber akin to death which sealed his own eyes on the slopes of the Lebanon, memories of the sister who sleeps in the land of Adonis never again to wake with the anemones and the roses.

XXXIII. The Gardens of Adonis

Perhaps the best proof that Adonis was a deity of vegetation, and especially of the corn, is furnished by the gardens of Adonis, as they were called. These were baskets or pots filled with earth, in which wheat, barley, lettuces, fennel, and various kinds of flowers were sown and tended for eight days, chiefly or exclusively by women. Fostered by the sun's heat, the plants shot up rapidly, but having no root they withered as rapidly away, and at the end of eight days were carried out with the images of the dead Adonis, and flung with them into the sea or into springs.

These gardens of Adonis are most naturally interpreted as representatives of Adonis or manifestations of his power; they represented him, true to his original nature, in vegetable form, while the images of him, with which they were carried out and cast into the water, portrayed him in his later human shape. All these Adonis ceremonies, if I am right, were originally intended as charms to promote the growth or revival of vegetation; and the principle by which they were supposed to produce this effect was homoeopathic or imitative magic. For ignorant people suppose that by mimicking the effect which they desire to produce they actually help to produce it; thus by sprinkling water they make rain, by lighting a fire they make sunshine, and so on. Similarly, by mimicking the growth of crops they hope to ensure a good harvest. The rapid growth of the wheat and barley in the gardens of Adonis was intended to make the corn shoot up; and the throwing of the gardens and of the images into the water was a charm to secure a due supply of fertilising rain. The same, I take it, was the object of throwing the effigies of Death and the Carnival into water in the corresponding ceremonies of modern Europe. Certainly the custom of drenching with water a leaf-clad person, who undoubtedly personifies vegetation, is still resorted to in Europe for the express purpose of producing rain. Similarly the custom of throwing water on the last corn cut at harvest, or on the person who brings it home (a custom observed in Germany and France,

XXXIII. The Gardens of Adonis

and till lately in England and Scotland), is in some places practised with the avowed intent to procure rain for the next year's crops. Thus in Wallachia and amongst the Roumanians in Transylvania, when a girl is bringing home a crown made of the last ears of corn cut at harvest, all who meet her hasten to throw water on her, and two farm-servants are placed at the door for the purpose; for they believe that if this were not done, the crops next year would perish from drought. At the spring ploughing in Prussia, when the ploughmen and sowers returned in the evening from their work in the fields, the farmer's wife and the servants used to splash water over them. The ploughmen and sowers retorted by seizing every one, throwing them into the pond, and ducking them under the water. The farmer's wife might claim exemption on payment of a forfeit, but every one else had to be ducked. By observing this custom they hoped to ensure a due supply of rain for the seed.

The opinion that the gardens of Adonis are essentially charms to promote the growth of vegetation, especially of the crops, and that they belong to the same class of customs as those spring and mid-summer folk-customs of modern Europe which I have described else-where, does not rest for its evidence merely on the intrinsic probability of the case. Fortunately we are able to show that gardens of Adonis (if we may use the expression in a general sense) are still planted, first, by a primitive race at their sowing season, and, second, by European peasants at midsummer. Amongst the Oraons and Mundas of Bengal, when the time comes for planting out the rice which has been grown in seed-beds, a party of young people of both sexes go to the forest and cut a young Karma-tree, or the branch of one. Bearing it in triumph they return dancing, singing, and beating drums, and plant it in the middle of the village dancing-ground. A sacrifice is offered to the tree; and next morning the youth of both sexes, linked arm-in-arm, dance in a great circle round the Karma-tree, which is decked with strips of coloured cloth and sham bracelets and necklets of plaited straw. As a preparation for the festival, the daughters of the headman of the village cultivate blades of barley in a peculiar way. The seed is sown in moist, sandy soil, mixed with turmeric, and the blades sprout and unfold of a pale-yellow or primrose colour. On the day of the festival the girls take up these blades and carry them in baskets to the dancing-ground, where, prostrating themselves reverentially, they place some of the plants before the Karma-tree. Finally, the Karma-tree is taken away and thrown into a stream or tank. The meaning of planting these barley blades and then presenting them

XXXIII. The Gardens of Adonis

to the Karma-tree is hardly open to question. Trees are supposed to exercise a quickening influence upon the growth of crops, and amongst the very people in question—the Mundas or Mundaris— "the grove deities are held responsible for the crops." Therefore, when at the season for planting out the rice the Mundas bring in a tree and treat it with so much respect, their object can only be to foster thereby the growth of the rice which is about to be planted out; and the custom of causing barley blades to sprout rapidly and then presenting them to the tree must be intended to subserve the same purpose, perhaps by reminding the tree-spirit of his duty towards the crops, and stimulating his activity by this visible example of rapid vegetable growth. The throwing of the Karma-tree into the water is to be interpreted as a rain-charm. Whether the barley blades are also thrown into the water is not said; but if my interpretation of the custom is right, probably they are so. A distinction between this Bengal custom and the Greek rites of Adonis is that in the former the tree-spirit appears in his original form as a tree; whereas in the Adonis worship he appears in human form, represented as a dead man, though his vegetable nature is indicated by the gardens of Adonis, which are, so to say, a secondary manifestation of his original power as a tree-spirit.

Gardens of Adonis are cultivated also by the Hindoos, with the intention apparently of ensuring the fertility both of the earth and of mankind. Thus at Oodeypoor in Rajputana a festival is held in honour of Gouri, or Isani, the goddess of abundance. The rites begin when the sun enters the sign of the Ram, the opening of the Hindoo year. An image of the goddess Gouri is made of earth, and a smaller one of her husband Iswara, and the two are placed together. A small trench is next dug, barley is sown in it, and the ground watered and heated artificially till the grain sprouts, when the women dance round it hand in hand, invoking the blessing of Gouri on their husbands. After that the young corn is taken up and distributed by the women to the men, who wear it in their turbans. In these rites the distribution of the barley shoots to the men, and the invocation of a blessing on their husbands by the wives, point clearly to the desire of offspring as one motive for observing the custom. The same motive probably explains the use of gardens of Adonis at the marriage of Brahmans in the Madras Presidency. Seeds of five or nine sorts are mixed and sown in earthen pots, which are made specially for the purpose and are filled with earth. Bride and bridegroom water the seeds both morning and evening for four days; and on the fifth day the seedlings are thrown, like the real gardens of Adonis, into a tank or river.

In Sardinia the gardens of Adonis are still planted in connexion with the great midsummer festival which bears the name of St. John. At the end of March or on the first of April a young man of the village presents himself to a girl, and asks her to be his *comare* (gossip or sweetheart), offering to be her *compare*. The invitation is considered as an honour by the girl's family, and is gladly accepted. At the end of May the girl makes a pot of the bark of the cork-tree, fills it with earth, and sows a handful of wheat and barley in it. The pot being placed in the sun and often watered, the corn sprouts rapidly and has a good head by Midsummer Eve (St. John's Eve, the twenty-third of June). The pot is then called *Erme* or *Nenneri*. On St. John's Day the young man and the girl, dressed in their best, accompanied by a long retinue and preceded by children gambolling and frolicking, move in procession to a church outside the village. Here they break the pot by throwing it against the door of the church. Then they sit down in a ring on the grass and eat eggs and herbs to the music of flutes. Wine is mixed in a cup and passed round, each one drinking as it passes. Then they join hands and sing "Sweethearts of St. John" (*Compare e comare di San Giovanni*) over and over again, the flutes playing the while. When they tire of singing they stand up and dance gaily in a ring till evening. This is the general Sardinian custom. As practised at Ozieri it has some special features. In May the pots are made of cork-bark and planted with corn, as already described. Then on the Eve of St. John the window-sills are draped with rich cloths, on which the pots are placed, adorned with crimson and blue silk and ribbons of various colours. On each of the pots they used formerly to place a statuette or cloth doll dressed as a woman, or a Priapus-like figure made of paste; but this custom, rigorously forbidden by the Church, has fallen into disuse. The village swains go about in a troop to look at the pots and their decorations and to wait for the girls, who assemble on the public square to celebrate the festival. Here a great bonfire is kindled, round which they dance and make merry. Those who wish to be "Sweethearts of St. John" act as follows. The young man stands on one side of the bonfire and the girl on the other, and they, in a manner, join hands by each grasping one end of a long stick, which they pass three times backwards and forwards across the fire, thus thrusting their hands thrice rapidly into the flames. This seals their relationship to each other. Dancing and music go on till late at night. The correspondence of

XXXIII. The Gardens of Adonis

these Sardinian pots of grain to the gardens of Adonis seems complete, and the images formerly placed in them answer to the images of Adonis which accompanied his gardens.

Customs of the same sort are observed at the same season in Sicily. Pairs of boys and girls become gossips of St. John on St. John's Day by drawing each a hair from his or her head and performing various ceremonies over them. Thus they tie the hairs together and throw them up in the air, or exchange them over a potsherd, which they afterwards break in two, preserving each a fragment with pious care. The tie formed in the latter way is supposed to last for life. In some parts of Sicily the gossips of St. John present each other with plates of sprouting corn, lentils, and canary seed, which have been planted forty days before the festival. The one who receives the plate pulls a stalk of the young plants, binds it with a ribbon, and preserves it among his or her greatest treasures, restoring the platter to the giver. At Catania the gossips exchange pots of basil and great cucumbers; the girls tend the basil, and the thicker it grows the more it is prized.

In these midsummer customs of Sardinia and Sicily it is possible that, as Mr. R. Wünsch supposes, St. John has replaced Adonis. We have seen that the rites of Tammuz or Adonis were commonly celebrated about midsummer; according to Jerome, their date was June.

In Sicily gardens of Adonis are still sown in spring as well as in summer, from which we may perhaps infer that Sicily as well as Syria celebrated of old a vernal festival of the dead and risen god. At the approach of Easter, Sicilian women sow wheat, lentils, and canaryseed in plates, which they keep in the dark and water every two days. The plants soon shoot up; the stalks are tied together with red ribbons, and the plates containing them are placed on the sepulchres which, with the effigies of the dead Christ, are made up in Catholic and Greek churches on Good Friday, just as the gardens of Adonis were placed on the grave of the dead Adonis. The practice is not confined to Sicily, for it is observed also at Cosenza in Calabria, and perhaps in other places. The whole custom—sepulchres as well as plates of sprouting grain—may be nothing but a continuation, under a different name, of the worship of Adonis.

Nor are these Sicilian and Calabrian customs the only Easter ceremonies which resemble the rites of Adonis. "During the whole of Good Friday a waxen effigy of the dead Christ is exposed to view in the middle of the Greek churches and is covered with fervent kisses

XXXIII. The Gardens of Adonis

by the thronging crowd, while the whole church rings with melancholy, monotonous dirges. Late in the evening, when it has grown quite dark, this waxen image is carried by the priests into the street on a bier adorned with lemons, roses, jessamine, and other flowers, and there begins a grand procession of the multitude, who move in serried ranks, with slow and solemn step, through the whole town. Every man carries his taper and breaks out into doleful lamentation. At all the houses which the procession passes there are seated women with censers to fumigate the marching host. Thus the community solemnly buries its Christ as if he had just died. At last the waxen image is again deposited in the church, and the same lugubrious chants echo anew. These lamentations, accompanied by a strict fast, continue till midnight on Saturday. As the clock strikes twelve, the bishop appears and announces the glad tidings that 'Christ is risen,' to which the crowd replies, 'He is risen indeed,' and at once the whole city bursts into an uproar of joy, which finds vent in shrieks and shouts, in the endless discharge of carronades and muskets, and the explosion of fire-works of every sort. In the very same hour people plunge from the extremity of the fast into the enjoyment of the Easter lamb and neat wine."

In like manner the Catholic Church has been accustomed to bring before its followers in a visible form the death and resurrection of the Redeemer. Such sacred dramas are well fitted to impress the lively imagination and to stir the warm feelings of a susceptible southern race, to whom the pomp and pageantry of Catholicism are more congenial than to the colder temperament of the Teutonic peoples.

When we reflect how often the Church has skilfully contrived to plant the seeds of the new faith on the old stock of paganism, we may surmise that the Easter celebration of the dead and risen Christ was grafted upon a similar celebration of the dead and risen Adonis, which, as we have seen reason to believe, was celebrated in Syria at the same season. The type, created by Greek artists, of the sorrowful goddess with her dying lover in her arms, resembles and may have been the model of the *Pietà* of Christian art, the Virgin with the dead body of her divine Son in her lap, of which the most celebrated example is the one by Michael Angelo in St. Peters. That noble group, in which the living sorrow of the mother contrasts so wonderfully with the languor of death in the son, is one of the finest compositions in marble. Ancient Greek art has bequeathed to us few works so beautiful, and none so pathetic.

XXXIII. The Gardens of Adonis

In this connexion a well-known statement of Jerome may not be without significance. He tells us that Bethlehem, the traditional birthplace of the Lord, was shaded by a grove of that still older Syrian Lord, Adonis, and that where the infant Jesus had wept, the lover of Venus was bewailed. Though he does not expressly say so, Jerome seems to have thought that the grove of Adonis had been planted by the heathen after the birth of Christ for the purpose of defiling the sacred spot. In this he may have been mistaken. If Adonis was indeed, as I have argued, the spirit of the corn, a more suitable name for his dwelling-place could hardly be found than Bethlehem, "the House of Bread," and he may well have been worshipped there at his House of Bread long ages before the birth of Him who said, "I am the bread of life." Even on the hypothesis that Adonis followed rather than preceded Christ at Bethlehem, the choice of his sad figure to divert the allegiance of Christians from their Lord cannot but strike us as eminently appropriate when we remember the similarity of the rites which commemorated the death and resurrection of the two. One of the earliest seats of the worship of the new god was Antioch, and at Antioch, as we have seen, the death of the old god was annually celebrated with great solemnity. A circumstance which attended the entrance of Julian into the city at the time of the Adonis festival may perhaps throw some light on the date of its celebration. When the emperor drew near to the city he was received with public prayers as if he had been a god, and he marvelled at the voices of a great multitude who cried that the Star of Salvation had dawned upon them in the East. This may doubtless have been no more than a fulsome compliment paid by an obsequious Oriental crowd to the Roman emperor. But it is also possible that the rising of a bright star regularly gave the signal for the festival, and that as chance would have it the star emerged above the rim of the eastern horizon at the very moment of the emperor's approach. The coincidence, if it happened, could hardly fail to strike the imagination of a superstitious and excited multitude, who might thereupon hail the great man as the deity whose coming was announced by the sign in the heavens. Or the emperor may have mistaken for a greeting to himself the shouts which were addressed to the star. Now Astarte, the divine mistress of Adonis, was identified with the planet Venus, and her changes from a morning to an evening star were carefully noted by the Babylonian astronomers, who drew omens from her alternate appearance and disappearance. Hence we may conjecture that the festival of Adonis was regularly timed to coincide with

XXXIII. The Gardens of Adonis

the appearance of Venus as the Morning or Evening Star. But the star which the people of Antioch saluted at the festival was seen in the East; therefore, if it was indeed Venus, it can only have been the Morning Star. At Aphaca in Syria, where there was a famous temple of Astarte, the signal for the celebration of the rites was apparently given by the flashing of a meteor, which on a certain day fell like a star from the top of Mount Lebanon into the river Adonis. The meteor was thought to be Astarte herself, and its flight through the air might naturally be interpreted as the descent of the amorous goddess to the arms of her lover. At Antioch and elsewhere the appearance of the Morning Star on the day of the festival may in like manner have been hailed as the coming of the goddess of love to wake her dead leman from his earthy bed. If that were so, we may surmise that it was the Morning Star which guided the wise men of the East to Bethlehem, the hallowed spot which heard, in the language of Jerome, the weeping of the infant Christ and the lament for Adonis.

XXXIV. The Myth and Ritual of Attis

Another of those gods whose supposed death and resurrection struck such deep roots into the faith and ritual of Western Asia is Attis. He was to Phrygia what Adonis was to Syria. Like Adonis, he appears to have been a god of vegetation, and his death and resurrection were annually mourned and rejoiced over at a festival in spring. The legends and rites of the two gods were so much alike that the ancients themselves sometimes identified them. Attis was said to have been a fair young shepherd or herdsman beloved by Cybele, the Mother of the Gods, a great Asiatic goddess of fertility, who had her chief home in Phrygia. Some held that Attis was her son. His birth, like that of many other heroes, is said to have been miraculous. His mother, Nana, was a virgin, who conceived by putting a ripe almond or a pomegranate in her bosom. Indeed in the Phrygian cosmogony an almond figured as the father of all things, perhaps because its delicate lilac blossom is one of the first heralds of the spring, appearing on the bare boughs before the leaves have opened. Such tales of virgin mothers are relics of an age of childish ignorance when men had not yet recognized the intercourse of the sexes as the true cause of offspring. Two different accounts of the death of Attis were current. According to the one he was killed by a boar, like Adonis. According to the other he unmanned himself under a pine-tree, and bled to death on the spot. The latter is said to have been the local story told by the people of Pessinus, a great seat of the worship of Cybele, and the whole legend of which the story forms a part is stamped with a character of rudeness and savagery that speaks strongly for its antiquity. Both tales might claim the support of custom, or rather both were probably invented to explain certain customs observed by the worshippers. The story of the self-mutilation of Attis is clearly an attempt to account for the self-mutilation of his priests, who regularly castrated themselves on entering the service of the goddess. The story of his death by the boar may have been told to explain why his worshippers, especially the

XXXIV. The Myth and Ritual of Attis

people of Pessinus, abstained from eating swine. In like manner the worshippers of Adonis abstained from pork, because a boar had killed their god. After his death Attis is said to have been changed into a pine-tree.

The worship of the Phrygian Mother of the Gods was adopted by the Romans in 204 B.C. towards the close of their long struggle with Hannibal. For their drooping spirits had been opportunely cheered by a prophecy, alleged to be drawn from that convenient farrago of nonsense, the Sibylline Books, that the foreign invader would be driven from Italy if the great Oriental goddess were brought to Rome. Accordingly ambassadors were despatched to her sacred city Pessinus in Phrygia. The small black stone which embodied the mighty divinity was entrusted to them and conveyed to Rome, where it was received with great respect and installed in the temple of Victory on the Palatine Hill. It was the middle of April when the goddess arrived, and she went to work at once. For the harvest that year was such as had not been seen for many a long day, and in the very next year Hannibal and his veterans embarked for Africa. As he looked his last on the coast of Italy, fading behind him in the distance, he could not foresee that Europe, which had repelled the arms, would yet yield to the gods, of the Orient. The vanguard of the conquerors had already encamped in the heart of Italy before the rearguard of the beaten army fell sullenly back from its shores.

We may conjecture, though we are not told, that the Mother of the Gods brought with her the worship of her youthful lover or son to her new home in the West. Certainly the Romans were familiar with the Galli, the emasculated priests of Attis, before the close of the Republic. These unsexed beings, in their Oriental costume, with little images suspended on their breasts, appear to have been a familiar sight in the streets of Rome, which they traversed in procession, carrying the image of the goddess and chanting their hymns to the music of cymbals and tambourines, flutes and horns, while the people, impressed by the fantastic show and moved by the wild strains, flung alms to them in abundance, and buried the image and its bearers under showers of roses. A further step was taken by the Emperor Claudius when he incorporated the Phrygian worship of the sacred tree, and with it probably the orgiastic rites of Attis, in the established religion of Rome. The great spring festival of Cybele and Attis is best known to us in the form in which it was celebrated at Rome; but as we are informed that the Roman ceremonies were also Phrygian, we may assume that they differed

XXXIV. The Myth and Ritual of Attis

hardly, if at all, from their Asiatic original. The order of the festival seems to have been as follows.

On the twenty-second day of March, a pine-tree was cut in the woods and brought into the sanctuary of Cybele, where it was treated as a great divinity. The duty of carrying the sacred tree was entrusted to a guild of Tree-bearers. The trunk was swathed like a corpse with woollen bands and decked with wreaths of violets, for violets were said to have sprung from the blood of Attis, as roses and anemones from the blood of Adonis; and the effigy of a young man, doubtless Attis himself, was tied to the middle of the stem. On the second day of the festival, the twenty-third of March, the chief ceremony seems to have been a blowing of trumpets. The third day, the twenty-fourth of March, was known as the Day of Blood: the Archigallus or highpriest drew blood from his arms and presented it as an offering. Nor was he alone in making this bloody sacrifice. Stirred by the wild barbaric music of clashing cymbals, rumbling drums, droning horns, and screaming flutes, the inferior clergy whirled about in the dance with waggling heads and streaming hair, until, rapt into a frenzy of excitement and insensible to pain, they gashed their bodies with potsherds or slashed them with knives in order to bespatter the altar and the sacred tree with their flowing blood. The ghastly rite probably formed part of the mourning for Attis and may have been intended to strengthen him for the resurrection. The Australian aborigines cut themselves in like manner over the graves of their friends for the purpose, perhaps, of enabling them to be born again. Further, we may conjecture, though we are not expressly told, that it was on the same Day of Blood and for the same purpose that the novices sacrificed their virility. Wrought up to the highest pitch of religious excitement they dashed the severed portions of themselves against the image of the cruel goddess. These broken instruments of fertility were afterwards reverently wrapt up and buried in the earth or in subterranean chambers sacred to Cybele, where, like the offering of blood, they may have been deemed instrumental in recalling Attis to life and hastening the general resurrection of nature, which was then bursting into leaf and blossom in the vernal sunshine. Some confirmation of this conjecture is furnished by the savage story that the mother of Attis conceived by putting in her bosom a pomegranate sprung from the severed genitals of a man-monster named Agdestis, a sort of double of Attis.

If there is any truth in this conjectural explanation of the custom, we can readily understand why other Asiatic goddesses of fertility were served in like manner by eunuch priests. These feminine deities required to receive from their male ministers, who personated the divine lovers, the means of discharging their beneficent functions: they had themselves to be impregnated by the life-giving energy before they could transmit it to the world. Goddesses thus ministered to by eunuch priests were the great Artemis of Ephesus and the great Syrian Astarte of Hierapolis, whose sanctuary, frequented by swarms of pilgrims and enriched by the offerings of Assyria and Babylonia, of Arabia and Phoenicia, was perhaps in the days of its glory the most popular in the East. Now the unsexed priests of this Syrian goddess resembled those of Cybele so closely that some people took them to be the same. And the mode in which they dedicated themselves to the religious life was similar. The greatest festival of the year at Hierapolis fell at the beginning of spring, when multitudes thronged to the sanctuary from Syria and the regions round about. While the flutes played, the drums beat, and the eunuch priests slashed themselves with knives, the religious excitement gradually spread like a wave among the crowd of onlookers, and many a one did that which he little thought to do when he came as a holiday spectator to the festival. For man after man, his veins throbbing with the music, his eyes fascinated by the sight of the streaming blood, flung his garments from him, leaped forth with a shout, and seizing one of the swords which stood ready for the purpose, castrated himself on the spot. Then he ran through the city, holding the bloody pieces in his hand, till he threw them into one of the houses which he passed in his mad career. The household thus honoured had to furnish him with a suit of female attire and female ornaments, which he wore for the rest of his life. When the tumult of emotion had subsided, and the man had come to himself again, the irrevocable sacrifice must often have been followed by passionate sorrow and lifelong regret. This revulsion of natural human feeling after the frenzies of a fanatical religion is powerfully depicted by Catullus in a celebrated poem.

The parallel of these Syrian devotees confirms the view that in the similar worship of Cybele the sacrifice of virility took place on the Day of Blood at the vernal rites of the goddess, when the violets, supposed to spring from the red drops of her wounded lover, were in bloom among the pines. Indeed the story that Attis unmanned himself under a pine-tree was clearly devised to explain why his priests did the same beside the sacred violet-wreathed tree at his festival. At all events, we can hardly doubt that the Day of Blood witnessed the mourning for

XXXIV. The Myth and Ritual of Attis

Attis over an effigy of him which was afterwards buried. The image thus laid in the sepulchre was probably the same which had hung upon the tree. Throughout the period of mourning the worshippers fasted from bread, nominally because Cybele had done so in her grief for the death of Attis, but really perhaps for the same reason which induced the women of Harran to abstain from eating anything ground in a mill while they wept for Tammuz. To partake of bread or flour at such a season might have been deemed a wanton profanation of the bruised and broken body of the god. Or the fast may possibly have been a preparation for a sacramental meal.

But when night had fallen, the sorrow of the worshippers was turned to joy. For suddenly a light shone in the darkness: the tomb was opened: the god had risen from the dead; and as the priest touched the lips of the weeping mourners with balm, he softly whispered in their ears the glad tidings of salvation. The resurrection of the god was hailed by his disciples as a promise that they too would issue triumphant from the corruption of the grave. On the morrow, the twenty-fifth day of March, which was reckoned the vernal equinox, the divine resurrection was celebrated with a wild outburst of glee. At Rome, and probably elsewhere, the celebration took the form of a carnival. It was the Festival of Joy (*Hilaria*). A universal licence prevailed. Every man might say and do what he pleased. People went about the streets in disguise. No dignity was too high or too sacred for the humblest citizen to assume with impunity. In the reign of Commodus a band of conspirators thought to take advantage of the masquerade by dressing in the uniform of the Imperial Guard, and so, mingling with the crowd of merrymakers, to get within stabbing distance of the emperor. But the plot miscarried. Even the stern Alexander Severus used to relax so far on the joyous day as to admit a pheasant to his frugal board. The next day, the twenty-sixth of March, was given to repose, which must have been much needed after the varied excitements and fatigues of the preceding days. Finally, the Roman festival closed on the twenty-seventh of March with a procession to the brook Almo. The silver image of the goddess, with its face of jagged black stone, sat in a waggon drawn by oxen. Preceded by the nobles walking barefoot, it moved slowly, to the loud music of pipes and tambourines, out by the Porta Capena, and so down to the banks of the Almo, which flows into the Tiber just below the walls of Rome. There the high-priest, robed in purple, washed the waggon, the image, and the other sacred objects in the water of the stream. On returning

XXXIV. The Myth and Ritual of Attis

from their bath, the wain and the oxen were strewn with fresh spring flowers. All was mirth and gaiety. No one thought of the blood that had flowed so lately. Even the eunuch priests forgot their wounds.

Such, then, appears to have been the annual solemnisation of the death and resurrection of Attis in spring. But besides these public rites, his worship is known to have comprised certain secret or mystic ceremonies, which probably aimed at bringing the worshipper, and especially the novice, into closer communication with his god. Our information as to the nature of these mysteries and the date of their celebration is unfortunately very scanty, but they seem to have included a sacramental meal and a baptism of blood. In the sacrament the novice became a partaker of the mysteries by eating out of a drum and drinking out of a cymbal, two instruments of music which figured prominently in the thrilling orchestra of Attis. The fast which accompanied the mourning for the dead god may perhaps have been designed to prepare the body of the communicant for the reception of the blessed sacrament by purging it of all that could defile by contact the sacred elements. In the baptism the devotee, crowned with gold and wreathed with fillets, descended into a pit, the mouth of which was covered with a wooden grating. A bull, adorned with garlands of flowers, its forehead glittering with gold leaf, was then driven on to the grating and there stabbed to death with a consecrated spear. Its hot reeking blood poured in torrents through the apertures, and was received with devout eagerness by the worshipper on every part of his person and garments, till he emerged from the pit, drenched, dripping, and scarlet from head to foot, to receive the homage, nay the adoration, of his fellows as one who had been born again to eternal life and had washed away his sins in the blood of the bull. For some time afterwards the fiction of a new birth was kept up by dieting him on milk like a new-born babe. The regeneration of the worshipper took place at the same time as the regeneration of his god, namely at the vernal equinox. At Rome the new birth and the remission of sins by the shedding of bull's blood appear to have been carried out above all at the sanctuary of the Phrygian goddess on the Vatican Hill, at or near the spot where the great basilica of St. Peter's now stands; for many inscriptions relating to the rites were found when the church was being enlarged in 1608 or 1609. From the Vatican as a centre this barbarous system of superstition seems to have spread to other parts of the Roman empire. Inscriptions found in Gaul and Germany prove that provincial sanctuaries modelled their ritual on that of the Vatican. From the same source we learn that the testicles as well as the blood of the bull played an important part in the ceremonies. Probably they were regarded as a powerful charm to promote fertility and hasten the new birth.

XXXV. Attis as a God of Vegetation

The original character of Attis as a tree-spirit is brought out plainly by the part which the pine-tree plays in his legend, his ritual, and his monuments. The story that he was a human being transformed into a pine-tree is only one of those transparent attempts at rationalising old beliefs which meet us so frequently in mythology. The bringing in of the pine-tree from the woods, decked with violets and woollen bands, is like bringing in the May-tree or Summer-tree in modern folk-custom; and the effigy which was attached to the pine-tree was only a duplicate representative of the tree-spirit Attis. After being fastened to the tree, the effigy was kept for a year and then burned. The same thing appears to have been sometimes done with the May-pole; and in like manner the effigy of the corn-spirit, made at harvest, is often preserved till it is replaced by a new effigy at next year's harvest. The original intention of such customs was no doubt to maintain the spirit of vegetation in life throughout the year. Why the Phrygians should have worshipped the pine above other trees we can only guess. Perhaps the sight of its changeless, though sombre, green cresting the ridges of the high hills above the fading splendour of the autumn woods in the valleys may have seemed to their eyes to mark it out as the seat of a diviner life, of something exempt from the sad vicissitudes of the seasons, constant and eternal as the sky which stooped to meet it. For the same reason, perhaps, ivy was sacred to Attis; at all events, we read that his eunuch priests were tattooed with a pattern of ivy leaves. Another reason for the sanctity of the pine may have been its usefulness. The cones of the stone-pine contain edible nut-like seeds, which have been used as food since antiquity, and are still eaten, for example, by the poorer classes in Rome. Moreover, a wine was brewed from these seeds, and this may partly account for the orgiastic nature of the rites of Cybele, which the ancients compared to those of Dionysus. Further, pine-cones were regarded as symbols or rather instruments of fertility. Hence at the festival of the Thesmophoria they were thrown, along with pigs and other

XXXV. Attis as a God of Vegetation

agents or emblems of fecundity, into the sacred vaults of Demeter for the purpose of quickening the ground and the wombs of women.

Like tree-spirits in general, Attis was apparently thought to wield power over the fruits of the earth or even to be identical with the corn. One of his epithets was "very fruitful": he was addressed as the "reaped green (or yellow) ear of corn"; and the story of his sufferings, death, and resurrection was interpreted as the ripe grain wounded by the reaper, buried in the granary, and coming to life again when it is sown in the ground. A statue of him in the Lateran Museum at Rome clearly indicates his relation to the fruits of the earth, and particularly to the corn; for it represents him with a bunch of ears of corn and fruit in his hand, and a wreath of pine-cones, pomegranates, and other fruits on his head, while from the top of his Phrygian cap ears of corn are sprouting. On a stone urn, which contained the ashes of an Archigallus or high-priest of Attis, the same idea is expressed in a slightly different way. The top of the urn is adorned with ears of corn carved in relief, and it is surmounted by the figure of a cock, whose tail consists of ears of corn. Cybele in like manner was conceived as a goddess of fertility who could make or mar the fruits of the earth; for the people of Augustodunum (Autun) in Gaul used to cart her image about in a waggon for the good of the fields and vineyards, while they danced and sang before it, and we have seen that in Italy an unusually fine harvest was attributed to the recent arrival of the Great Mother. The bathing of the image of the goddess in a river may well have been a rain-charm to ensure an abundant supply of moisture for the crops.

XXXVI. Human Representatives of Attis

From inscriptions it appears that both at Pessinus and Rome the high-priest of Cybele regularly bore the name of Attis. It is therefore a reasonable conjecture that he played the part of his namesake, the legendary Attis, at the annual festival. We have seen that on the Day of Blood he drew blood from his arms, and this may have been an imitation of the self-inflicted death of Attis under the pine-tree. It is not inconsistent with this supposition that Attis was also represented at these ceremonies by an effigy; for instances can be shown in which the divine being is first represented by a living person and afterwards by an effigy, which is then burned or otherwise destroyed. Perhaps we may go a step farther and conjecture that this mimic killing of the priest, accompanied by a real effusion of his blood, was in Phrygia, as it has been elsewhere, a substitute for a human sacrifice which in earlier times was actually offered.

A reminiscence of the manner in which these old representatives of the deity were put to death is perhaps preserved in the famous story of Marsyas. He was said to be a Phrygian satyr or Silenus, according to others a shepherd or herdsman, who played sweetly on the flute. A friend of Cybele, he roamed the country with the disconsolate goddess to soothe her grief for the death of Attis. The composition of the Mother's Air, a tune played on the flute in honour of the Great Mother Goddess, was attributed to him by the people of Celaenae in Phrygia. Vain of his skill, he challenged Apollo to a musical contest, he to play on the flute and Apollo on the lyre. Being vanquished, Marsyas was tied up to a pine-tree and flayed or cut limb from limb either by the victorious Apollo or by a Scythian slave. His skin was shown at Celaenae in historical times. It hung at the foot of the citadel in a cave from which the river Marsyas rushed with an impetuous and noisy tide to join the Maeander. So the Adonis bursts full-born from the precipices of the Lebanon; so the blue river of Ibreez leaps in a crystal jet from the red rocks of the Taurus; so the stream, which now rumbles deep underground, used to gleam for a moment on its passage from darkness to darkness in the dim light of the Corycian cave. In all these copious fountains, with their glad promise of fertility and life, men of old saw the hand of God and worshipped him beside the rushing river with the music of its tumbling waters in their ears. At Celaenae, if we can trust tradition, the piper Marsyas, hanging in his cave, had a soul for harmony even in death; for it is said that at the sound of his native Phrygian melodies the skin of the dead satyr used to thrill, but that if the musician struck up an air in praise of Apollo it remained deaf and motionless.

In this Phrygian satyr, shepherd, or herdsman who enjoyed the friendship of Cybele, practised the music so characteristic of her rites, and died a violent death on her sacred tree, the pine, may we not detect a close resemblance to Attis, the favourite shepherd or herdsman of the goddess, who is himself described as a piper, is said to have perished under a pine-tree, and was annually represented by an effigy hung, like Marsyas, upon a pine? We may conjecture that in old days the priest who bore the name and played the part of Attis at the spring festival of Cybele was regularly hanged or otherwise slain upon the sacred tree, and that this barbarous custom was afterwards mitigated into the form in which it is known to us in later times, when the priest merely drew blood from his body under the tree and attached an effigy instead of himself to its trunk. In the holy grove at Upsala men and animals were sacrificed by being hanged upon the sacred trees. The human victims dedicated to Odin were regularly put to death by hanging or by a combination of hanging and stabbing, the man being strung up to a tree or a gallows and then wounded with a spear. Hence Odin was called the Lord of the Gallows or the God of the Hanged, and he is represented sitting under a gallows tree. Indeed he is said to have been sacrificed to himself in the ordinary way, as we learn from the weird verses of the *Havamal*, in which the god describes how he acquired his divine power by learning the magic runes:

> "*I know that I hung on the windy tree*
> *For nine whole nights,*
> *Wounded with the spear, dedicated to Odin,*
> *Myself to myself.*"

XXXVI. Human Representatives of Attis

The Bagobos of Mindanao, one of the Philippine Islands, used annually to sacrifice human victims for the good of the crops in a similar way. Early in December, when the constellation Orion appeared at seven o'clock in the evening, the people knew that the time had come to clear their fields for sowing and to sacrifice a slave. The sacrifice was presented to certain powerful spirits as payment for the good year which the people had enjoyed, and to ensure the favour of the spirits for the coming season. The victim was led to a great tree in the forest; there he was tied with his back to the tree and his arms stretched high above his head, in the attitude in which ancient artists portrayed Marsyas hanging on the fatal tree. While he thus hung by the arms, he was slain by a spear thrust through his body at the level of the armpits. Afterwards the body was cut clean through the middle at the waist, and the upper part was apparently allowed to dangle for a little from the tree, while the under part wallowed in blood on the ground. The two portions were finally cast into a shallow trench beside the tree. Before this was done, anybody who wished might cut off a piece of flesh or a lock of hair from the corpse and carry it to the grave of some relation whose body was being consumed by a ghoul. Attracted by the fresh corpse, the ghoul would leave the mouldering old body in peace. These sacrifices have been offered by men now living.

In Greece the great goddess Artemis herself appears to have been annually hanged in effigy in her sacred grove of Condylea among the Arcadian hills, and there accordingly she went by the name of the Hanged One. Indeed a trace of a similar rite may perhaps be detected even at Ephesus, the most famous of her sanctuaries, in the legend of a woman who hanged herself and was thereupon dressed by the compassionate goddess in her own divine garb and called by the name of Hecate. Similarly, at Melite in Phthia, a story was told of a girl named Aspalis who hanged herself, but who appears to have been merely a form of Artemis. For after her death her body could not be found, but an image of her was discovered standing beside the image of Artemis, and the people bestowed on it the title of Hecaerge or Far-shooter, one of the regular epithets of the goddess. Every year the virgins sacrificed a young goat to the image by hanging it, because Aspalis was said to have hanged herself. The sacrifice may have been a substitute for hanging an image or a human representative of Artemis. Again, in Rhodes the fair Helen was worshipped under the title of Helen of the Tree, because the queen of the island had caused her handmaids, disguised as Furies, to string her up to a bough. That the Asiatic Greeks sacrificed animals in this fashion is proved by coins of Ilium, which represent an ox or cow hanging on a tree and stabbed with a knife by a man, who sits among the branches or on the animal's back. At Hierapolis also the victims were hung on trees before they were burnt. With these Greek and Scandinavian parallels before us we can hardly dismiss as wholly improbable the conjecture that in Phrygia a man-god may have hung year by year on the sacred but fatal tree.

XXXVII. Oriental Religions in the West

The worship of the Great Mother of the Gods and her lover or son was very popular under the Roman Empire. Inscriptions prove that the two received divine honours, separately or conjointly, not only in Italy, and especially at Rome, but also in the provinces, particularly in Africa, Spain, Portugal, France, Germany, and Bulgaria. Their worship survived the establishment of Christianity by Constantine; for Symmachus records the recurrence of the festival of the Great Mother, and in the days of Augustine her effeminate priests still paraded the streets and squares of Carthage with whitened faces, scented hair, and mincing gait, while, like the mendicant friars of the Middle Ages, they begged alms from the passers-by. In Greece, on the other hand, the bloody orgies of the Asiatic goddess and her consort appear to have found little favour. The barbarous and cruel character of the worship, with its frantic excesses, was doubtless repugnant to the good taste and humanity of the Greeks, who seem to have preferred the kindred but gentler rites of Adonis. Yet the same features which shocked and repelled the Greeks may have positively attracted the less refined Romans and barbarians of the West. The ecstatic frenzies, which were mistaken for divine inspiration, the mangling of the body, the theory of a new birth and the remission of sins through the shedding of blood, have all their origin in savagery, and they naturally appealed to peoples in whom the savage instincts were still strong. Their true character was indeed often disguised under a decent veil of allegorical or philosophical interpretation, which probably sufficed to impose upon the rapt and enthusiastic worshippers, reconciling even the more cultivated of them to things which otherwise must have filled them with horror and disgust.

The religion of the Great Mother, with its curious blending of crude savagery with spiritual aspirations, was only one of a multitude of similar Oriental faiths which in the later days of paganism spread over the Roman Empire, and by saturating the European peoples with alien

XXXVII. Oriental Religions in the West

ideals of life gradually undermined the whole fabric of ancient civilisation. Greek and Roman society was built on the conception of the subordination of the individual to the community, of the citizen to the state; it set the safety of the commonwealth, as the supreme aim of conduct, above the safety of the individual whether in this world or in the world to come. Trained from infancy in this unselfish ideal, the citizens devoted their lives to the public service and were ready to lay them down for the common good; or if they shrank from the supreme sacrifice, it never occurred to them that they acted otherwise than basely in preferring their personal existence to the interests of their country. All this was changed by the spread of Oriental religions which inculcated the communion of the soul with God and its eternal salvation as the only objects worth living for, objects in comparison with which the prosperity and even the existence of the state sank into insignificance. The inevitable result of this selfish and immoral doctrine was to withdraw the devotee more and more from the public service, to concentrate his thoughts on his own spiritual emotions, and to breed in him a contempt for the present life which he regarded merely as a probation for a better and an eternal. The saint and the recluse, disdainful of earth and rapt in ecstatic contemplation of heaven, became in popular opinion the highest ideal of humanity, displacing the old ideal of the patriot and hero who, forgetful of self, lives and is ready to die for the good of his country. The earthly city seemed poor and contemptible to men whose eyes beheld the City of God coming in the clouds of heaven. Thus the centre of gravity, so to say, was shifted from the present to a future life, and however much the other world may have gained, there can be little doubt that this one lost heavily by the change. A general disintegration of the body politic set in. The ties of the state and the family were loosened: the structure of society tended to resolve itself into its individual elements and thereby to relapse into barbarism; for civilisation is only possible through the active co-operation of the citizens and their willingness to subordinate their private interests to the common good. Men refused to defend their country and even to continue their kind. In their anxiety to save their own souls and the souls of others, they were content to leave the material world, which they identified with the principle of evil, to perish around them. This obsession lasted for a thousand years. The revival of Roman law, of the Aristotelian philosophy, of ancient art and literature at the close of the Middle Ages, marked the return of Europe to native ideals of life

XXXVII. Oriental Religions in the West

and conduct, to saner, manlier views of the world. The long halt in the march of civilisation was over. The tide of Oriental invasion had turned at last. It is ebbing still.

Among the gods of eastern origin who in the decline of the ancient world competed against each other for the allegiance of the West was the old Persian deity Mithra. The immense popularity of his worship is attested by the monuments illustrative of it which have been found scattered in profusion all over the Roman Empire. In respect both of doctrines and of rites the cult of Mithra appears to have presented many points of resemblance not only to the religion of the Mother of the Gods but also to Christianity. The similarity struck the Christian doctors themselves and was explained by them as a work of the devil, who sought to seduce the souls of men from the true faith by a false and insidious imitation of it. So to the Spanish conquerors of Mexico and Peru many of the native heathen rites appeared to be diabolical counterfeits of the Christian sacraments. With more probability the modern student of comparative religion traces such resemblances to the similar and independent workings of the mind of man in his sincere, if crude, attempts to fathom the secret of the universe, and to adjust his little life to its awful mysteries. However that may be, there can be no doubt that the Mithraic religion proved a formidable rival to Christianity, combining as it did a solemn ritual with aspirations after moral purity and a hope of immortality. Indeed the issue of the conflict between the two faiths appears for a time to have hung in the balance. An instructive relic of the long struggle is preserved in our festival of Christmas, which the Church seems to have borrowed directly from its heathen rival. In the Julian calendar the twenty-fifth of December was reckoned the winter solstice, and it was regarded as the Nativity of the Sun, because the day begins to lengthen and the power of the sun to increase from that turning-point of the year. The ritual of the nativity, as it appears to have been celebrated in Syria and Egypt, was remarkable. The celebrants retired into certain inner shrines, from which at midnight they issued with a loud cry, "The Virgin has brought forth! The light is waxing!" The Egyptians even represented the new-born sun by the image of an infant which on his birthday, the winter solstice, they brought forth and exhibited to his worshippers. No doubt the Virgin who thus conceived and bore a son on the twenty-fifth of December was the great Oriental goddess whom the Semites called the Heavenly Virgin or simply the Heavenly Goddess; in Semitic lands she was a form of Astarte. Now

Mithra was regularly identified by his worshippers with the Sun, the Unconquered Sun, as they called him; hence his nativity also fell on the twenty-fifth of December. The Gospels say nothing as to the day of Christ's birth, and accordingly the early Church did not celebrate it. In time, however, the Christians of Egypt came to regard the sixth of January as the date of the Nativity, and the custom of commemorating the birth of the Saviour on that day gradually spread until by the fourth century it was universally established in the East. But at the end of the third or the beginning of the fourth century the Western Church, which had never recognised the sixth of January as the day of the Nativity, adopted the twenty-fifth of December as the true date, and in time its decision was accepted also by the Eastern Church. At Antioch the change was not introduced till about the year 375 A.D.

What considerations led the ecclesiastical authorities to institute the festival of Christmas? The motives for the innovation are stated with great frankness by a Syrian writer, himself a Christian. "The reason," he tells us, "why the fathers transferred the celebration of the sixth of January to the twenty-fifth of December was this. It was a custom of the heathen to celebrate on the same twenty-fifth of December the birthday of the Sun, at which they kindled lights in token of festivity. In these solemnities and festivities the Christians also took part. Accordingly when the doctors of the Church perceived that the Christians had a leaning to this festival, they took counsel and resolved that the true Nativity should be solemnised on that day and the festival of the Epiphany on the sixth of January. Accordingly, along with this custom, the practice has prevailed of kindling fires till the sixth." The heathen origin of Christmas is plainly hinted at, if not tacitly admitted, by Augustine when he exhorts his Christian brethren not to celebrate that solemn day like the heathen on account of the sun, but on account of him who made the sun. In like manner Leo the Great rebuked the pestilent belief that Christmas was solemnised because of the birth of the new sun, as it was called, and not because of the nativity of Christ.

Thus it appears that the Christian Church chose to celebrate the birthday of its Founder on the twenty-fifth of December in order to transfer the devotion of the heathen from the Sun to him who was called the Sun of Righteousness. If that was so, there can be no intrinsic improbability in the conjecture that motives of the same sort may have led the ecclesiastical authorities to assimilate the Easter festival of the death and resurrection of their Lord to the festival of the death and resurrection of another Asiatic god which fell at the same season. Now the

Easter rites still observed in Greece, Sicily, and Southern Italy bear in some respects a striking resemblance to the rites of Adonis, and I have suggested that the Church may have consciously adapted the new festival to its heathen predecessor for the sake of winning souls to Christ. But this adaptation probably took place in the Greek-speaking rather than in the Latin-speaking parts of the ancient world; for the worship of Adonis, while it flourished among the Greeks, appears to have made little impression on Rome and the West. Certainly it never formed part of the official Roman religion. The place which it might have taken in the affections of the vulgar was already occupied by the similar but more barbarous worship of Attis and the Great Mother. Now the death and resurrection of Attis were officially celebrated at Rome on the twenty-fourth and twenty-fifth of March, the latter being regarded as the spring equinox, and therefore as the most appropriate day for the revival of a god of vegetation who had been dead or sleeping throughout the winter. But according to an ancient and widespread tradition Christ suffered on the twenty-fifth of March, and accordingly some Christians regularly celebrated the Crucifixion on that day without any regard to the state of the moon. This custom was certainly observed in Phrygia, Cappadocia, and Gaul, and there seem to be grounds for thinking that at one time it was followed also in Rome. Thus the tradition which placed the death of Christ on the twenty-fifth of March was ancient and deeply rooted. It is all the more remarkable because astronomical considerations prove that it can have had no historical foundation. The inference appears to be inevitable that the passion of Christ must have been arbitrarily referred to that date in order to harmonise with an older festival of the spring equinox. This is the view of the learned ecclesiastical historian Mgr. Duchesne, who points out that the death of the Saviour was thus made to fall upon the very day on which, according to a widespread belief, the world had been created. But the resurrection of Attis, who combined in himself the characters of the divine Father and the divine Son, was officially celebrated at Rome on the same day. When we remember that the festival of St. George in April has replaced the ancient pagan festival of the Parilia; that the festival of St. John the Baptist in June has succeeded to a heathen midsummer festival of water: that the festival of the Assumption of the Virgin in August has ousted the festival of Diana; that the feast of All Souls in November is a continuation of an old heathen feast of the dead; and that the Nativity of Christ himself was assigned to the winter solstice in December because that day was deemed the Nativity of the Sun; we can hardly be thought rash or unreasonable in conjecturing that the other cardinal festival of the Christian church—the solemnisation of Easter—may have been in like manner, and from like motives of edification, adapted to a similar celebration of the Phrygian god Attis at the vernal equinox.

At least it is a remarkable coincidence, if it is nothing more, that the Christian and the heathen festivals of the divine death and resurrection should have been solemnised at the same season and in the same places. For the places which celebrated the death of Christ at the spring equinox were Phrygia, Gaul, and apparently Rome, that is, the very regions in which the worship of Attis either originated or struck deepest root. It is difficult to regard the coincidence as purely accidental. If the vernal equinox, the season at which in the temperate regions the whole face of nature testifies to a fresh outburst of vital energy, had been viewed from of old as the time when the world was annually created afresh in the resurrection of a god, nothing could be more natural than to place the resurrection of the new deity at the same cardinal point of the year. Only it is to be observed that if the death of Christ was dated on the twenty-fifth of March, his resurrection, according to Christian tradition, must have happened on the twenty-seventh of March, which is just two days later than the vernal equinox of the Julian calendar and the resurrection of Attis. A similar displacement of two days in the adjustment of Christian to heathen celebrations occurs in the festivals of St. George and the Assumption of the Virgin. However, another Christian tradition, followed by Lactantius and perhaps by the practice of the Church in Gaul, placed the death of Christ on the twenty-third and his resurrection on the twenty-fifth of March. If that was so, his resurrection coincided exactly with the resurrection of Attis.

In point of fact it appears from the testimony of an anonymous Christian, who wrote in the fourth century of our era, that Christians and pagans alike were struck by the remarkable coincidence between the death and resurrection of their respective deities, and that the coincidence formed a theme of bitter controversy between the adherents of the rival religions, the pagans contending that the resurrection of Christ was a spurious imitation of the resurrection of Attis, and the Christians asserting with equal warmth that the resurrection of Attis was a diabolical counterfeit of the resurrection of Christ. In these unseemly bickerings the heathen took what to a superficial observer might seem strong ground by arguing that their god was the older and therefore presumably the original, not the counterfeit, since as a general rule an original

XXXVII. Oriental Religions in the West

is older than its copy. This feeble argument the Christians easily rebutted. They admitted, indeed, that in point of time Christ was the junior deity, but they triumphantly demonstrated his real seniority by falling back on the subtlety of Satan, who on so important an occasion had surpassed himself by inverting the usual order of nature.

Taken altogether, the coincidences of the Christian with the heathen festivals are too close and too numerous to be accidental. They mark the compromise which the Church in the hour of its triumph was compelled to make with its vanquished yet still dangerous rivals. The inflexible Protestantism of the primitive missionaries, with their fiery denunciations of heathendom, had been exchanged for the supple policy, the easy tolerance, the comprehensive charity of shrewd ecclesiastics, who clearly perceived that if Christianity was to conquer the world it could do so only by relaxing the too rigid principles of its Founder, by widening a little the narrow gate which leads to salvation. In this respect an instructive parallel might be drawn between the history of Christianity and the history of Buddhism. Both systems were in their origin essentially ethical reforms born of the generous ardour, the lofty aspirations, the tender compassion of their noble Founders, two of those beautiful spirits who appear at rare intervals on earth like beings come from a better world to support and guide our weak and erring nature. Both preached moral virtue as the means of accomplishing what they regarded as the supreme object of life, the eternal salvation of the individual soul, though by a curious antithesis the one sought that salvation in a blissful eternity, the other in a final release from suffering, in annihilation. But the austere ideals of sanctity which they inculcated were too deeply opposed not only to the frailties but to the natural instincts of humanity ever to be carried out in practice by more than a small number of disciples, who consistently renounced the ties of the family and the state in order to work out their own salvation in the still seclusion of the cloister. If such faiths were to be nominally accepted by whole nations or even by the world, it was essential that they should first be modified or transformed so as to accord in some measure with the prejudices, the passions, the superstitions of the vulgar. This process of accommodation was carried out in after ages by followers who, made of less ethereal stuff than their masters, were for that reason the better fitted to mediate between them and the common herd. Thus as time went on, the two religions, in exact proportion to their growing popularity, absorbed more and more of those baser elements which they had been instituted for the very purpose of suppressing. Such spiritual decadences are inevitable. The world cannot live at the level of its great men. Yet it would be unfair to the generality of our kind to ascribe wholly to their intellectual and moral weakness the gradual divergence of Buddhism and Christianity from their primitive patterns. For it should never be forgotten that by their glorification of poverty and celibacy both these religions struck straight at the root not merely of civil society but of human existence. The blow was parried by the wisdom or the folly of the vast majority of mankind, who refused to purchase a chance of saving their souls with the certainty of extinguishing the species.

XXXVIII. The Myth of Osiris

In ancient Egypt the god whose death and resurrection were annually celebrated with alternate sorrow and joy was Osiris, the most popular of all Egyptian deities; and there are good grounds for classing him in one of his aspects with Adonis and Attis as a personification of the great yearly vicissitudes of nature, especially of the corn. But the immense vogue which he enjoyed for many ages induced his devoted worshippers to heap upon him the attributes and powers of many other gods; so that it is not always easy to strip him, so to say, of his borrowed plumes and to restore them to their proper owners.

The story of Osiris is told in a connected form only by Plutarch, whose narrative has been confirmed and to some extent amplified in modern times by the evidence of the monuments.

Osiris was the offspring of an intrigue between the earth-god Seb (Keb or Geb, as the name is sometimes transliterated) and the sky-goddess Nut. The Greeks identified his parents with their own deities Cronus and Rhea. When the sun-god Ra perceived that his wife Nut had been unfaithful to him, he declared with a curse that she should be delivered of the child in no month and no year. But the goddess had another lover, the god Thoth or Hermes, as the Greeks called him, and he playing at draughts with the moon won from her a seventy-second part of every day, and having compounded five whole days out of these parts he added them to the Egyptian year of three hundred and sixty days. This was the mythical origin of the five supplementary days which the Egyptians annually inserted at the end of every year in order to establish a harmony between lunar and solar time. On these five days, regarded as outside the year of twelve months, the curse of the sun-god did not rest, and accordingly Osiris was born on the first of them. At his nativity a voice rang out proclaiming that the Lord of All had come into the world. Some say that a certain Pamyles heard a voice from the temple at Thebes bidding him announce with a shout

XXXVIII. The Myth of Osiris

that a great king, the beneficent Osiris, was born. But Osiris was not the only child of his mother. On the second of the supplementary days she gave birth to the elder Horus, on the third to the god Set, whom the Greeks called Typhon, on the fourth to the goddess Isis, and on the fifth to the goddess Nephthys. Afterwards Set married his sister Nephthys, and Osiris married his sister Isis.

Reigning as a king on earth, Osiris reclaimed the Egyptians from savagery, gave them laws, and taught them to worship the gods. Before his time the Egyptians had been cannibals. But Isis, the sister and wife of Osiris, discovered wheat and barley growing wild, and Osiris introduced the cultivation of these grains amongst his people, who forthwith abandoned cannibalism and took kindly to a corn diet. Moreover, Osiris is said to have been the first to gather fruit from trees, to train the vine to poles, and to tread the grapes. Eager to communicate these beneficent discoveries to all mankind, he committed the whole government of Egypt to his wife Isis, and travelled over the world, diffusing the blessings of civilisation and agriculture wherever he went. In countries where a harsh climate or niggardly soil forbade the cultivation of the vine, he taught the inhabitants to console themselves for the want of wine by brewing beer from barley. Loaded with the wealth that had been showered upon him by grateful nations, he returned to Egypt, and on account of the benefits he had conferred on mankind he was unanimously hailed and worshipped as a deity. But his brother Set (whom the Greeks called Typhon) with seventy-two others plotted against him. Having taken the measure of his good brother's body by stealth, the bad brother Typhon fashioned and highly decorated a coffer of the same size, and once when they were all drinking and making merry he brought in the coffer and jestingly promised to give it to the one whom it should fit exactly. Well, they all tried one after the other, but it fitted none of them. Last of all Osiris stepped into it and lay down. On that the conspirators ran and slammed the lid down on him, nailed it fast, soldered it with molten lead, and flung the coffer into the Nile. This happened on the seventeenth day of the month Athyr, when the sun is in the sign of the Scorpion, and in the eight-and-twentieth year of the reign or the life of Osiris. When Isis heard of it she sheared off a lock of her hair, put on a mourning attire, and wandered disconsolately up and down, seeking the body.

By the advice of the god of wisdom she took refuge in the papyrus swamps of the Delta. Seven scorpions accompanied her in her flight.

XXXVIII. The Myth of Osiris

One evening when she was weary she came to the house of a woman, who, alarmed at the sight of the scorpions, shut the door in her face. Then one of the scorpions crept under the door and stung the child of the woman that he died. But when Isis heard the mother's lamentation, her heart was touched, and she laid her hands on the child and uttered her powerful spells; so the poison was driven out of the child and he lived. Afterwards Isis herself gave birth to a son in the swamps. She had conceived him while she fluttered in the form of a hawk over the corpse of her dead husband. The infant was the younger Horus, who in his youth bore the name of Harpocrates, that is, the child Horus. Him Buto, the goddess of the north, hid from the wrath of his wicked uncle Set. Yet she could not guard him from all mishap; for one day when Isis came to her little son's hiding-place she found him stretched lifeless and rigid on the ground: a scorpion had stung him. Then Isis prayed to the sun-god Ra for help. The god hearkened to her and staid his bark in the sky, and sent down Thoth to teach her the spell by which she might restore her son to life. She uttered the words of power, and straightway the poison flowed from the body of Horus, air passed into him, and he lived. Then Thoth ascended up into the sky and took his place once more in the bark of the sun, and the bright pomp passed onward jubilant.

Meantime the coffer containing the body of Osiris had floated down the river and away out to sea, till at last it drifted ashore at Byblus, on the coast of Syria. Here a fine *erica*-tree shot up suddenly and enclosed the chest in its trunk. The king of the country, admiring the growth of the tree, had it cut down and made into a pillar of his house; but he did not know that the coffer with the dead Osiris was in it. Word of this came to Isis and she journeyed to Byblus, and sat down by the well, in humble guise, her face wet with tears. To none would she speak till the king's handmaidens came, and them she greeted kindly, and braided their hair, and breathed on them from her own divine body a wondrous perfume. But when the queen beheld the braids of her handmaidens' hair and smelt the sweet smell that emanated from them, she sent for the stranger woman and took her into her house and made her the nurse of her child. But Isis gave the babe her finger instead of her breast to suck, and at night she began to burn all that was mortal of him away, while she herself in the likeness of a swallow fluttered round the pillar that contained her dead brother, twittering mournfully. But the queen spied what she was doing and shrieked out when she saw her child in

XXXVIII. The Myth of Osiris

flames, and thereby she hindered him from becoming immortal. Then the goddess revealed herself and begged for the pillar of the roof, and they gave it her, and she cut the coffer out of it, and fell upon it and embraced it and lamented so loud that the younger of the king's children died of fright on the spot. But the trunk of the tree she wrapped in fine linen, and poured ointment on it, and gave it to the king and queen, and the wood stands in a temple of Isis and is worshipped by the people of Byblus to this day. And Isis put the coffer in a boat and took the eldest of the king's children with her and sailed away. As soon as they were alone, she opened the chest, and laying her face on the face of her brother she kissed him and wept. But the child came behind her softly and saw what she was about, and she turned and looked at him in anger, and the child could not bear her look and died; but some say that it was not so, but that he fell into the sea and was drowned. It is he whom the Egyptians sing of at their banquets under the name of Maneros.

But Isis put the coffer by and went to see her son Horus at the city of Buto, and Typhon found the coffer as he was hunting a boar one night by the light of a full moon. And he knew the body, and rent it into fourteen pieces, and scattered them abroad. But Isis sailed up and down the marshes in a shallop made of papyrus, looking for the pieces; and that is why when people sail in shallops made of papyrus, the crocodiles do not hurt them, for they fear or respect the goddess. And that is the reason, too, why there are many graves of Osiris in Egypt, for she buried each limb as she found it. But others will have it that she buried an image of him in every city, pretending it was his body, in order that Osiris might be worshipped in many places, and that if Typhon searched for the real grave he might not be able to find it. However, the genital member of Osiris had been eaten by the fishes, so Isis made an image of it instead, and the image is used by the Egyptians at their festivals to this day. "Isis," writes the historian Diodorus Siculus, "recovered all the parts of the body except the genitals; and because she wished that her husband's grave should be unknown and honoured by all who dwell in the land of Egypt, she resorted to the following device. She moulded human images out of wax and spices, corresponding to the stature of Osiris, round each one of the parts of his body. Then she called in the priests according to their families and took an oath of them all that they would reveal to no man the trust she was about to repose in them. So to each of them privately she said that to them alone she entrusted the burial of the body, and reminding them of the benefits

XXXVIII. The Myth of Osiris

they had received she exhorted them to bury the body in their own land and to honour Osiris as a god. She also besought them to dedicate one of the animals of their country, whichever they chose, and to honour it in life as they had formerly honoured Osiris, and when it died to grant it obsequies like his. And because she would encourage the priests in their own interest to bestow the aforesaid honours, she gave them a third part of the land to be used by them in the service and worship of the gods. Accordingly it is said that the priests, mindful of the benefits of Osiris, desirous of gratifying the queen, and moved by the prospect of gain, carried out all the injunctions of Isis. Wherefore to this day each of the priests imagines that Osiris is buried in his country, and they honour the beasts that were consecrated in the beginning, and when the animals die the priests renew at their burial the mourning for Osiris. But the sacred bulls, the one called Apis and the other Mnevis, were dedicated to Osiris, and it was ordained that they should be worshipped as gods in common by all the Egyptians, since these animals above all others had helped the discoverers of corn in sowing the seed and procuring the universal benefits of agriculture."

Such is the myth or legend of Osiris, as told by Greek writers and eked out by more or less fragmentary notices or allusions in native Egyptian literature. A long inscription in the temple at Denderah has preserved a list of the god's graves, and other texts mention the parts of his body which were treasured as holy relics in each of the sanctuaries. Thus his heart was at Athribis, his backbone at Busiris, his neck at Letopolis, and his head at Memphis. As often happens in such cases, some of his divine limbs were miraculously multiplied. His head, for example, was at Abydos as well as at Memphis, and his legs, which were remarkably numerous, would have sufficed for several ordinary mortals. In this respect, however, Osiris was nothing to St. Denys, of whom no less than seven heads, all equally genuine, are extant.

According to native Egyptian accounts, which supplement that of Plutarch, when Isis had found the corpse of her husband Osiris, she and her sister Nephthys sat down beside it and uttered a lament which in after ages became the type of all Egyptian lamentations for the dead. "Come to thy house," they wailed. "Come to thy house. O god On! come to thy house, thou who hast no foes. O fair youth, come to thy house, that thou mayest see me. I am thy sister, whom thou lovest; thou shalt not part from me. O fair boy, come to thy house. . . . I see thee not, yet doth my heart yearn after thee and mine eyes desire thee. Come to her who loves thee, who loves thee, Unnefer, thou blessed one! Come to thy sister, come to thy wife, to thy wife, thou whose heart stands still. Come to thy housewife. I am thy sister by the same mother, thou shalt not be far from me. Gods and men have turned their faces towards thee and weep for thee together. . . . I call after thee and weep, so that my cry is heard to heaven, but thou hearest not my voice; yet am I thy sister, whom thou didst love on earth; thou didst love none but me, my brother! my brother!" This lament for the fair youth cut off in his prime reminds us of the laments for Adonis. The title of Unnefer or "the Good Being" bestowed on him marks the beneficence which tradition universally ascribed to Osiris; it was at once his commonest title and one of his names as king.

The lamentations of the two sad sisters were not in vain. In pity for her sorrow the sun-god Ra sent down from heaven the jackal-headed god Anubis, who, with the aid of Isis and Nephthys, of Thoth and Horus, pieced together the broken body of the murdered god, swathed it in linen bandages, and observed all the other rites which the Egyptians were wont to perform over the bodies of the departed. Then Isis fanned the cold clay with her wings: Osiris revived, and thenceforth reigned as king over the dead in the other world. There he bore the titles of Lord of the Underworld, Lord of Eternity, Ruler of the Dead. There, too, in the great Hall of the Two Truths, assisted by forty-two assessors, one from each of the principal districts of Egypt, he presided as judge at the trial of the souls of the departed, who made their solemn confession before him, and, their heart having been weighed in the balance of justice, received the reward of virtue in a life eternal or the appropriate punishment of their sins.

In the resurrection of Osiris the Egyptians saw the pledge of a life everlasting for themselves beyond the grave. They believed that every man would live eternally in the other world if only his surviving friends did for his body what the gods had done for the body of Osiris. Hence the ceremonies observed by the Egyptians over the human dead were an exact copy of those which Anubis, Horus, and the rest had performed over the dead god. "At every burial there was enacted a representation of the divine mystery which had been performed of old over Osiris, when his son, his sisters, his friends were gathered round his mangled remains and succeeded by their spells and manipulations in converting his broken body into the first mummy, which they afterwards reanimated and furnished with the means of entering on a new individual

XXXVIII. The Myth of Osiris

life beyond the grave. The mummy of the deceased was Osiris; the professional female mourners were his two sisters Isis and Nephthys; Anubis, Horus, all the gods of the Osirian legend gathered about the corpse." In this way every dead Egyptian was identified with Osiris and bore his name. From the Middle Kingdom onwards it was the regular practice to address the deceased as "Osiris So-and-So," as if he were the god himself, and to add the standing epithet "true of speech," because true speech was characteristic of Osiris. The thousands of inscribed and pictured tombs that have been opened in the valley of the Nile prove that the mystery of the resurrection was performed for the benefit of every dead Egyptian; as Osiris died and rose again from the dead, so all men hoped to arise like him from death to life eternal.

Thus according to what seems to have been the general native tradition Osiris was a good and beloved king of Egypt, who suffered a violent death but rose from the dead and was henceforth worshipped as a deity. In harmony with this tradition he was regularly represented by sculptors and painters in human and regal form as a dead king, swathed in the wrappings of a mummy, but wearing on his head a kingly crown and grasping in one of his hands, which were left free from the bandages, a kingly sceptre. Two cities above all others were associated with his myth or memory. One of them was Busiris in Lower Egypt, which claimed to possess his backbone; the other was Abydos in Upper Egypt, which gloried in the possession of his head. Encircled by the nimbus of the dead yet living god, Abydos, originally an obscure place, became from the end of the Old Kingdom the holiest spot in Egypt; his tomb there would seem to have been to the Egyptians what the Church of the Holy Sepulchre at Jerusalem is to Christians. It was the wish of every pious man that his dead body should rest in hallowed earth near the grave of the glorified Osiris. Few indeed were rich enough to enjoy this inestimable privilege; for, apart from the cost of a tomb in the sacred city, the mere transport of mummies from great distances was both difficult and expensive. Yet so eager were many to absorb in death the blessed influence which radiated from the holy sepulchre that they caused their surviving friends to convey their mortal remains to Abydos, there to tarry for a short time, and then to be brought back by river and interred in the tombs which had been made ready for them in their native land. Others had cenotaphs built or memorial tablets erected for themselves near the tomb of their dead and risen Lord, that they might share with him the bliss of a joyful resurrection.

XXXIX. The Ritual of Osiris

1. *The Popular Rites*

A useful clue to the original nature of a god or goddess is often furnished by the season at which his or her festival is celebrated. Thus, if the festival falls at the new or the full moon, there is a certain presumption that the deity thus honoured either is the moon or at least has lunar affinities. If the festival is held at the winter or summer solstice, we naturally surmise that the god is the sun, or at all events that he stands in some close relation to that luminary. Again, if the festival coincides with the time of sowing or harvest, we are inclined to infer that the divinity is an embodiment of the earth or of the corn. These presumptions or inferences, taken by themselves, are by no means conclusive; but if they happen to be confirmed by other indications, the evidence may be regarded as fairly strong.

Unfortunately, in dealing with the Egyptian gods we are in a great measure precluded from making use of this clue. The reason is not that the dates of the festivals are always unknown, but that they shifted from year to year, until after a long interval they had revolved through the whole course of the seasons. This gradual revolution of the festal Egyptian cycle resulted from the employment of a calendar year which neither corresponded exactly to the solar year nor was periodically corrected by intercalation.

If the Egyptian farmer of the olden time could get no help, except at the rarest intervals, from the official or sacerdotal calendar, he must have been compelled to observe for himself those natural signals which marked the times for the various operations of husbandry. In all ages of which we possess any records the Egyptians have been an agricultural people, dependent for their subsistence on the growth of the corn. The cereals which they cultivated were wheat, barley, and apparently sorghum (*Holcus sorghum,* Linnaeus), the *doora* of the modern fellaheen. Then as now the whole country, with the exception of a fringe on the

XXXIX. The Ritual of Osiris

coast of the Mediterranean, was almost rainless, and owed its immense fertility entirely to the annual inundation of the Nile, which, regulated by an elaborate system of dams and canals, was distributed over the fields, renewing the soil year by year with a fresh deposit of mud washed down from the great equatorial lakes and the mountains of Abyssinia. Hence the rise of the river has always been watched by the inhabitants with the utmost anxiety; for if it either falls short of or exceeds a certain height, dearth and famine are the inevitable consequences. The water begins to rise early in June, but it is not until the latter half of July that it swells to a mighty tide. By the end of September the inundation is at its greatest height. The country is now submerged, and presents the appearance of a sea of turbid water, from which the towns and villages, built on higher ground, rise like islands. For about a month the flood remains nearly stationary, then sinks more and more rapidly, till by December or January the river has returned to its ordinary bed. With the approach of summer the level of the water continues to fall. In the early days of June the Nile is reduced to half its ordinary breadth; and Egypt, scorched by the sun, blasted by the wind that has blown from the Sahara for many days, seems a mere continuation of the desert. The trees are choked with a thick layer of grey dust. A few meagre patches of vegetables, watered with difficulty, struggle painfully for existence in the immediate neighbourhood of the villages. Some appearance of verdure lingers beside the canals and in the hollows from which the moisture has not wholly evaporated. The plain appears to pant in the pitiless sunshine, bare, dusty, ash-coloured, cracked and seamed as far as the eye can see with a network of fissures. From the middle of April till the middle of June the land of Egypt is but half alive, waiting for the new Nile.

For countless ages this cycle of natural events has determined the annual labours of the Egyptian husbandman. The first work of the agricultural year is the cutting of the dams which have hitherto prevented the swollen river from flooding the canals and the fields. This is done, and the pent-up waters released on their beneficent mission, in the first half of August. In November, when the inundation has subsided, wheat, barley, and sorghum are sown. The time of harvest varies with the district, falling about a month later in the north than in the south. In Upper or Southern Egypt barley is reaped at the beginning of March, wheat at the beginning of April, and sorghum about the end of that month.

XXXIX. The Ritual of Osiris

It is natural to suppose that the various events of the agricultural year were celebrated by the Egyptian farmer with some simple religious rites designed to secure the blessing of the gods upon his labours. These rustic ceremonies he would continue to perform year after year at the same season, while the solemn festivals of the priests continued to shift, with the shifting calendar, from summer through spring to winter, and so backward through autumn to summer. The rites of the husbandman were stable because they rested on direct observation of nature: the rites of the priest were unstable because they were based on a false calculation. Yet many of the priestly festivals may have been nothing but the old rural festivals disguised in the course of ages by the pomp of sacerdotalism and severed, by the error of the calendar, from their roots in the natural cycle of the seasons.

These conjectures are confirmed by the little we know both of the popular and of the official Egyptian religion. Thus we are told that the Egyptians held a festival of Isis at the time when the Nile began to rise. They believed that the goddess was then mourning for the lost Osiris, and that the tears which dropped from her eyes swelled the impetuous tide of the river. Now if Osiris was in one of his aspects a god of the corn, nothing could be more natural than that he should be mourned at midsummer. For by that time the harvest was past, the fields were bare, the river ran low, life seemed to be suspended, the corn-god was dead. At such a moment people who saw the handiwork of divine beings in all the operations of nature might well trace the swelling of the sacred stream to the tears shed by the goddess at the death of the beneficent corn-god her husband.

And the sign of the rising waters on earth was accompanied by a sign in heaven. For in the early days of Egyptian history, some three or four thousand years before the beginning of our era, the splendid star of Sirius, the brightest of all the fixed stars, appeared at dawn in the east just before sunrise about the time of the summer solstice, when the Nile begins to rise. The Egyptians called it Sothis, and regarded it as the star of Isis, just as the Babylonians deemed the planet Venus the star of Astarte. To both peoples apparently the brilliant luminary in the morning sky seemed the goddess of life and love come to mourn her departed lover or spouse and to wake him from the dead. Hence the rising of Sirius marked the beginning of the sacred Egyptian year, and was regularly celebrated by a festival which did not shift with the shifting official year.

XXXIX. The Ritual of Osiris

The cutting of the dams and the admission of the water into the canals and fields is a great event in the Egyptian year. At Cairo the operation generally takes place between the sixth and the sixteenth of August, and till lately was attended by ceremonies which deserve to be noticed, because they were probably handed down from antiquity. An ancient canal, known by the name of the Khalíj, formerly passed through the native town of Cairo. Near its entrance the canal was crossed by a dam of earth, very broad at the bottom and diminishing in breadth upwards, which used to be constructed before or soon after the Nile began to rise. In front of the dam, on the side of the river, was reared a truncated cone of earth called the 'arooseh or "bride," on the top of which a little maize or millet was generally sown. This "bride" was commonly washed down by the rising tide a week or a fortnight before the cutting of the dam. Tradition runs that the old custom was to deck a young virgin in gay apparel and throw her into the river as a sacrifice to obtain a plentiful inundation. Whether that was so or not, the intention of the practice appears to have been to marry the river, conceived as a male power, to his bride the cornland, which was so soon to be fertilised by his water. The ceremony was therefore a charm to ensure the growth of the crops. In modern times money used to be thrown into the canal on this occasion, and the populace dived into the water after it. This practice also would seem to have been ancient, for Seneca tells us that at a place called the Veins of the Nile, not far from Philae, the priests used to cast money and offerings of gold into the river at a festival which apparently took place at the rising of the water.

The next great operation of the agricultural year in Egypt is the sowing of the seed in November, when the water of the inundation has retreated from the fields. With the Egyptians, as with many peoples of antiquity, the committing of the seed to the earth assumed the character of a solemn and mournful rite. On this subject I will let Plutarch speak for himself. "What," he asks, "are we to make of the gloomy, joyless, and mournful sacrifices, if it is wrong either to omit the established rites or to confuse and disturb our conceptions of the gods by absurd suspicions? For the Greeks also perform many rites which resemble those of the Egyptians and are observed about the same time. Thus at the festival of the Thesmophoria in Athens women sit on the ground and fast. And the Boeotians open the vaults of the Sorrowful One, naming that festival sorrowful because Demeter is sorrowing for the descent of the Maiden. The month is the month of sowing about the setting of the

Pleiades. The Egyptians call it Athyr, the Athenians Pyanepsion, the Boeotians the month of Demeter.... For it was that time of year when they saw some of the fruits vanishing and failing from the trees, while they sowed others grudgingly and with difficulty, scraping the earth with their hands and huddling it up again, on the uncertain chance that what they deposited in the ground would ever ripen and come to maturity. Thus they did in many respects like those who bury and mourn their dead."

The Egyptian harvest, as we have seen, falls not in autumn but in spring, in the months of March, April, and May. To the husbandman the time of harvest, at least in a good year, must necessarily be a season of joy: in bringing home his sheaves he is requited for his long and anxious labours. Yet if the old Egyptian farmer felt a secret joy at reaping and garnering the grain, it was essential that he should conceal the natural emotion under an air of profound dejection. For was he not severing the body of the corn-god with his sickle and trampling it to pieces under the hoofs of his cattle on the threshing-floor? Accordingly we are told that it was an ancient custom of the Egyptian corn-reapers to beat their breasts and lament over the first sheaf cut, while at the same time they called upon Isis. The invocation seems to have taken the form of a melancholy chant, to which the Greeks gave the name of Maneros. Similar plaintive strains were chanted by corn-reapers in Phoenicia and other parts of Western Asia. Probably all these doleful ditties were lamentations for the corn-god killed by the sickles of the reapers. In Egypt the slain deity was Osiris, and the name *Maneros,* applied to the dirge, appears to be derived from certain words meaning "Come to thy house," which often occur in the lamentations for the dead god.

Ceremonies of the same sort have been observed by other peoples, probably for the same purpose. Thus we are told that among all vegetables corn, by which is apparently meant maize, holds the first place in the household economy and the ceremonial observance of the Cherokee Indians, who invoke it under the name of "the Old Woman" in allusion to a myth that it sprang from the blood of an old woman killed by her disobedient sons. After the last working of the crop a priest and his assistant went into the field and sang songs of invocation to the spirit of the corn. After that a loud rustling would be heard, which was thought to be caused by the Old Woman bringing the corn into the field. A clean trail was always kept from the field to the house, "so that the corn might be encouraged to stay at home and not go wandering elsewhere." "Another curious ceremony, of which even the memory is now almost forgotten, was enacted after the first working of the corn, when the owner or priest stood in succession at each of the four corners of the field and wept and wailed loudly. Even the priests are now unable to give a reason for this performance, which may have been a lament for the bloody death of Selu," the Old Woman of the Corn. In these Cherokee practices the lamentations and the invocations of the Old Woman of the Corn resemble the ancient Egyptian customs of lamenting over the first corn cut and calling upon Isis, herself probably in one of her aspects an Old Woman of the Corn. Further, the Cherokee precaution of leaving a clear path from the field to the house resembles the Egyptian invitation to Osiris, "Come to thy house." So in the East Indies to this day people observe elaborate ceremonies for the purpose of bringing back the Soul of the Rice from the fields to the barn. The Nandi of East Africa perform a ceremony in September when the eleusine grain is ripening. Every woman who owns a plantation goes out with her daughters into the cornfields and makes a bonfire of the branches and leaves of certain trees. After that they pluck some of the eleusine, and each of them puts one grain in her necklace, chews another and rubs it on her forehead, throat, and breast. "No joy is shown by the womenfolk on this occasion, and they sorrowfully cut a basketful of the corn which they take home with them and place in the loft to dry."

The conception of the corn-spirit as old and dead at harvest is very clearly embodied in a custom observed by the Arabs of Moab. When the harvesters have nearly finished their task and only a small corner of the field remains to be reaped, the owner takes a handful of wheat tied up in a sheaf. A hole is dug in the form of a grave, and two stones are set upright, one at the head and the other at the foot, just as in an ordinary burial. Then the sheaf of wheat is laid at the bottom of the grave, and the sheikh pronounces these words, "The old man is dead." Earth is afterwards thrown in to cover the sheaf, with a prayer, "May Allah bring us back the wheat of the dead."

2. *The Official Rites*

Such, then, were the principal events of the farmer's calendar in ancient Egypt, and such the simple religious rites by which he celebrated them.

XXXIX. The Ritual of Osiris

But we have still to consider the Osirian festivals of the official calendar, so far as these are described by Greek writers or recorded on the monuments. In examining them it is necessary to bear in mind that on account of the movable year of the old Egyptian calendar the true or astronomical dates of the official festivals must have varied from year to year, at least until the adoption of the fixed Alexandrian year in 30 B.C. From that time onward, apparently, the dates of the festivals were determined by the new calendar, and so ceased to rotate throughout the length of the solar year. At all events Plutarch, writing about the end of the first century, implies that they were then fixed, not movable; for though he does not mention the Alexandrian calendar, he clearly dates the festivals by it. Moreover, the long festal calendar of Esne, an important document of the Imperial age, is obviously based on the fixed Alexandrian year; for it assigns the mark for New Year's Day to the day which corresponds to the twenty-ninth of August, which was the first day of the Alexandrian year, and its references to the rising of the Nile, the position of the sun, and the operations of agriculture are all in harmony with this supposition. Thus we may take it as fairly certain that from 30 B.C. onwards the Egyptian festivals were stationary in the solar year.

Herodotus tells us that the grave of Osiris was at Sais in Lower Egypt, and that there was a lake there upon which the sufferings of the god were displayed as a mystery by night. This commemoration of the divine passion was held once a year: the people mourned and beat their breasts at it to testify their sorrow for the death of the god; and an image of a cow, made of gilt wood with a golden sun between its horns, was carried out of the chamber in which it stood the rest of the year. The cow no doubt represented Isis herself, for cows were sacred to her, and she was regularly depicted with the horns of a cow on her head, or even as a woman with the head of a cow. It is probable that the carrying out of her cow-shaped image symbolised the goddess searching for the dead body of Osiris; for this was the native Egyptian interpretation of a similar ceremony observed in Plutarch's time about the winter solstice, when the gilt cow was carried seven times round the temple. A great feature of the festival was the nocturnal illumination. People fastened rows of oil-lamps to the outside of their houses, and the lamps burned all night long. The custom was not confined to Sais, but was observed throughout the whole of Egypt.

XXXIX. The Ritual of Osiris

This universal illumination of the houses on one night of the year suggests that the festival may have been a commemoration not merely of the dead Osiris but of the dead in general, in other words, that it may have been a night of All Souls. For it is a widespread belief that the souls of the dead revisit their old homes on one night of the year; and on that solemn occasion people prepare for the reception of the ghosts by laying out food for them to eat, and lighting lamps to guide them on their dark road from and to the grave. Herodotus, who briefly describes the festival, omits to mention its date, but we can determine it with some probability from other sources. Thus Plutarch tells us that Osiris was murdered on the seventeenth of the month Athyr, and that the Egyptians accordingly observed mournful rites for four days from the seventeenth of Athyr. Now in the Alexandrian calendar, which Plutarch used, these four days corresponded to the thirteenth, fourteenth, fifteenth, and sixteenth of November, and this date answers exactly to the other indications given by Plutarch, who says that at the time of the festival the Nile was sinking, the north winds dying away, the nights lengthening, and the leaves falling from the trees. During these four days a gilt cow swathed in a black pall was exhibited as an image of Isis. This, no doubt, was the image mentioned by Herodotus in his account of the festival. On the nineteenth day of the month the people went down to the sea, the priests carrying a shrine which contained a golden casket. Into this casket they poured fresh water, and thereupon the spectators raised a shout that Osiris was found. After that they took some vegetable mould, moistened it with water, mixed it with precious spices and incense, and moulded the paste into a small moon-shaped image, which was then robed and ornamented. Thus it appears that the purpose of the ceremonies described by Plutarch was to represent dramatically, first, the search for the dead body of Osiris, and, second, its joyful discovery, followed by the resurrection of the dead god who came to life again in the new image of vegetable mould and spices. Lactantius tells us how on these occasions the priests, with their shaven bodies, beat their breasts and lamented, imitating the sorrowful search of Isis for her lost son Osiris, and how afterwards their sorrow was turned to joy when the jackal-headed god Anubis, or rather a mummer in his stead, produced a small boy, the living representative of the god who was lost and was found. Thus Lactantius regarded Osiris as the son instead of the husband of Isis, and he makes no mention of the image of vegetable mould. It is probable that the boy who figured in the sacred drama played the part, not of Osiris, but of his son Horus; but as

XXXIX. The Ritual of Osiris

the death and resurrection of the god were celebrated in many cities of Egypt, it is also possible that in some places the part of the god come to life was played by a living actor instead of by an image. Another Christian writer describes how the Egyptians, with shorn heads, annually lamented over a buried idol of Osiris, smiting their breasts, slashing their shoulders, ripping open their old wounds, until, after several days of mourning, they professed to find the mangled remains of the god, at which they rejoiced. However the details of the ceremony may have varied in different places, the pretence of finding the god's body, and probably of restoring it to life, was a great event in the festal year of the Egyptians. The shouts of joy which greeted it are described or alluded to by many ancient writers.

The funeral rites of Osiris, as they were observed at his great festival in the sixteen provinces of Egypt, are described in a long inscription of the Ptolemaic period, which is engraved on the walls of the god's temple at Denderah, the Tentyra of the Greeks, a town of Upper Egypt situated on the western bank of the Nile about forty miles north of Thebes. Unfortunately, while the information thus furnished is remarkably full and minute on many points, the arrangement adopted in the inscription is so confused and the expression often so obscure that a clear and consistent account of the ceremonies as a whole can hardly be extracted from it. Moreover, we learn from the document that the ceremonies varied somewhat in the several cities, the ritual of Abydos, for example, differing from that of Busiris. Without attempting to trace all the particularities of local usage I shall briefly indicate what seem to have been the leading features of the festival, so far as these can be ascertained with tolerable certainty.

The rites lasted eighteen days, from the twelfth to the thirtieth of the month Khoiak, and set forth the nature of Osiris in his triple aspect as dead, dismembered, and finally reconstituted by the union of his scattered limbs. In the first of these aspects he was called Chent-Ament (Khenti-Amenti), in the second Osiris-Sep, and in the third Sokari (Seker). Small images of the god were moulded of sand or vegetable earth and corn, to which incense was sometimes added; his face was painted yellow and his cheek-bones green. These images were cast in a mould of pure gold, which represented the god in the form of a mummy, with the white crown of Egypt on his head. The festival opened on the twelfth day of Khoiak with a ceremony of ploughing and sowing. Two black cows were yoked to the plough, which was made of

XXXIX. The Ritual of Osiris

tamarisk wood, while the share was of black copper. A boy scattered the seed. One end of the field was sown with barley, the other with spelt, and the middle with flax. During the operation the chief celebrant recited the ritual chapter of "the sowing of the fields." At Busiris on the twentieth of Khoiak sand and barley were put in the god's "garden," which appears to have been a sort of large flower-pot. This was done in the presence of the cow-goddess Shenty, represented seemingly by the image of a cow made of gilt sycamore wood with a headless human image in its inside. "Then fresh inundation water was poured out of a golden vase over both the goddess and the 'garden,' and the barley was allowed to grow as the emblem of the resurrection of the god after his burial in the earth, 'for the growth of the garden is the growth of the divine substance.'" On the twenty-second of Khoiak, at the eighth hour, the images of Osiris, attended by thirty-four images of deities, performed a mysterious voyage in thirty-four tiny boats made of papyrus, which were illuminated by three hundred and sixty-five lights. On the twenty-fourth of Khoiak, after sunset, the effigy of Osiris in a coffin of mulberry wood was laid in the grave, and at the ninth hour of the night the effigy which had been made and deposited the year before was removed and placed upon boughs of sycamore. Lastly, on the thirtieth day of Khoiak they repaired to the holy sepulchre, a subterranean chamber over which appears to have grown a clump of Persea-trees. Entering the vault by the western door, they laid the coffined effigy of the dead god reverently on a bed of sand in the chamber. So they left him to his rest, and departed from the sepulchre by the eastern door. Thus ended the ceremonies in the month of Khoiak.

In the foregoing account of the festival, drawn from the great inscription of Denderah, the burial of Osiris figures prominently, while his resurrection is implied rather than expressed. This defect of the document, however, is amply compensated by a remarkable series of bas-reliefs which accompany and illustrate the inscription. These exhibit in a series of scenes the dead god lying swathed as a mummy on his bier, then gradually raising himself up higher and higher, until at last he has entirely quitted the bier and is seen erect between the guardian wings of the faithful Isis, who stands behind him, while a male figure holds up before his eyes the *crux ansata*, the Egyptian symbol of life. The resurrection of the god could hardly be portrayed more graphically. Even more instructive, however, is another representation of the same event in a chamber dedicated to Osiris in the great temple of Isis at Philae.

XXXIX. The Ritual of Osiris

Here we see the dead body of Osiris with stalks of corn springing from it, while a priest waters the stalks from a pitcher which he holds in his hand. The accompanying inscription sets forth that "this is the form of him whom one may not name, Osiris of the mysteries, who springs from the returning waters." Taken together, the picture and the words seem to leave no doubt that Osiris was here conceived and represented as a personification of the corn which springs from the fields after they have been fertilised by the inundation. This, according to the inscription, was the kernel of the mysteries, the innermost secret revealed to the initiated. So in the rites of Demeter at Eleusis a reaped ear of corn was exhibited to the worshippers as the central mystery of their religion. We can now fully understand why at the great festival of sowing in the month of Khoiak the priests used to bury effigies of Osiris made of earth and corn. When these effigies were taken up again at the end of a year or of a shorter interval, the corn would be found to have sprouted from the body of Osiris, and this sprouting of the grain would be hailed as an omen, or rather as the cause, of the growth of the crops. The corn-god produced the corn from himself: he gave his own body to feed the people: he died that they might live.

And from the death and resurrection of their great god the Egyptians drew not only their support and sustenance in this life, but also their hope of a life eternal beyond the grave. This hope is indicated in the clearest manner by the very remarkable effigies of Osiris which have come to light in Egyptian cemeteries. Thus in the Valley of the Kings at Thebes there was found the tomb of a royal fan-bearer who lived about 1500 B.C. Among the rich contents of the tomb there was a bier on which rested a mattress of reeds covered with three layers of linen. On the upper side of the linen was painted a life-size figure of Osiris; and the interior of the figure, which was waterproof, contained a mixture of vegetable mould, barley, and a sticky fluid. The barley had sprouted and sent out shoots two or three inches long. Again, in the cemetery at Cynopolis "were numerous burials of Osiris figures. These were made of grain wrapped up in cloth and roughly shaped like an Osiris, and placed inside a bricked-up recess at the side of the tomb, sometimes in small pottery coffins, sometimes in wooden coffins in the form of a hawkmummy, sometimes without any coffins at all." These corn-stuffed figures were bandaged like mummies with patches of gilding here and there, as if in imitation of the golden mould in which the similar figures of Osiris were cast at the festival of sowing. Again, effigies of Osiris, with faces of green wax and their interior full of grain, were found buried near the necropolis of Thebes. Finally, we are told by Professor Erman that between the legs of mummies "there sometimes lies a figure of Osiris made of slime; it is filled with grains of corn, the sprouting of which is intended to signify the resurrection of the god." We cannot doubt that, just as the burial of corn-stuffed images of Osiris in the earth at the festival of sowing was designed to quicken the seed, so the burial of similar images in the grave was meant to quicken the dead, in other words, to ensure their spiritual immortality.

XL. The Nature of Osiris

1. Osiris a Corn-god

The foregoing survey of the myth and ritual of Osiris may suffice to prove that in one of his aspects the god was a personification of the corn, which may be said to die and come to life again every year. Through all the pomp and glamour with which in later times the priests had invested his worship, the conception of him as the corn-god comes clearly out in the festival of his death and resurrection, which was celebrated in the month of Khoiak and at a later period in the month of Athyr. That festival appears to have been essentially a festival of sowing, which properly fell at the time when the husbandman actually committed the seed to the earth. On that occasion an effigy of the corn-god, moulded of earth and corn, was buried with funeral rites in the ground in order that, dying there, he might come to life again with the new crops. The ceremony was, in fact, a charm to ensure the growth of the corn by sympathetic magic, and we may conjecture that as such it was practised in a simple form by every Egyptian farmer on his fields long before it was adopted and transfigured by the priests in the stately ritual of the temple. In the modern, but doubtless ancient, Arab custom of burying "the Old Man," namely, a sheaf of wheat, in the harvest-field and praying that he may return from the dead, we see the germ out of which the worship of the corn-god Osiris was probably developed.

The details of his myth fit in well with this interpretation of the god. He was said to be the offspring of Sky and Earth. What more appropriate parentage could be invented for the corn which springs from the ground that has been fertilised by the water of heaven? It is true that the land of Egypt owed its fertility directly to the Nile and not to showers; but the inhabitants must have known or guessed that the great river in its turn was fed by the rains which fell in the far interior. Again, the legend that Osiris was the first to teach men the use of corn would be most naturally told of the corn-god himself. Further, the story that his

XL. The Nature of Osiris

mangled remains were scattered up and down the land and buried in different places may be a mythical way of expressing either the sowing or the winnowing of the grain. The latter interpretation is supported by the tale that Isis placed the severed limbs of Osiris on a corn-sieve. Or more probably the legend may be a reminiscence of a custom of slaying a human victim, perhaps a representative of the corn-spirit, and distributing his flesh or scattering his ashes over the fields to fertilise them. In modern Europe the figure of Death is sometimes torn in pieces, and the fragments are then buried in the ground to make the crops grow well, and in other parts of the world human victims are treated in the same way. With regard to the ancient Egyptians we have it on the authority of Manetho that they used to burn red-haired men and scatter their ashes with winnowing fans, and it is highly significant that this barbarous sacrifice was offered by the kings at the grave of Osiris. We may conjecture that the victims represented Osiris himself, who was annually slain, dismembered, and buried in their persons that he might quicken the seed in the earth.

Possibly in prehistoric times the kings themselves played the part of the god and were slain and dismembered in that character. Set as well as Osiris is said to have been torn in pieces after a reign of eighteen days, which was commemorated by an annual festival of the same length. According to one story Romulus, the first king of Rome, was cut in pieces by the senators, who buried the fragments of him in the ground; and the traditional day of his death, the seventh of July, was celebrated with certain curious rites, which were apparently connected with the artificial fertilisation of the fig. Again, Greek legend told how Pentheus, king of Thebes, and Lycurgus, king of the Thracian Edonians, opposed the vine-god Dionysus, and how the impious monarchs were rent in pieces, the one by the frenzied Bacchanals, the other by horses. The Greek traditions may well be distorted reminiscences of a custom of sacrificing human beings, and especially divine kings, in the character of Dionysus, a god who resembled Osiris in many points and was said like him to have been torn limb from limb. We are told that in Chios men were rent in pieces as a sacrifice to Dionysus; and since they died the same death as their god, it is reasonable to suppose that they personated him. The story that the Thracian Orpheus was similarly torn limb from limb by the Bacchanals seems to indicate that he too perished in the character of the god whose death he died. It is significant that the Thracian Lycurgus, king of the Edonians, is said to have been put to

XL. The Nature of Osiris

death in order that the ground, which had ceased to be fruitful, might regain its fertility.

Further, we read of a Norwegian king, Halfdan the Black, whose body was cut up and buried in different parts of his kingdom for the sake of ensuring the fruitfulness of the earth. He is said to have been drowned at the age of forty through the breaking of the ice in spring. What followed his death is thus related by the old Norse historian Snorri Sturluson: "He had been the most prosperous (literally, blessed with abundance) of all kings. So greatly did men value him that when the news came that he was dead and his body removed to Hringariki and intended for burial there, the chief men from Raumariki and Westfold and Heithmörk came and all requested that they might take his body with them and bury it in their various provinces; they thought that it would bring abundance to those who obtained it. Eventually it was settled that the body was distributed in four places. The head was laid in a barrow at Steinn in Hringariki, and each party took away their own share and buried it. All these barrows are called Halfdan's barrows." It should be remembered that this Halfdan belonged to the family of the Ynglings, who traced their descent from Frey, the great Scandinavian god of fertility.

The natives of Kiwai, an island lying off the mouth of the Fly River in British New Guinea, tell of a certain magician named Segera, who had sago for his totem. When Segera was old and ill, he told the people that he would soon die, but that, nevertheless, he would cause their gardens to thrive. Accordingly, he instructed them that when he was dead they should cut him up and place pieces of his flesh in their gardens, but his head was to be buried in his own garden. Of him it is said that he outlived the ordinary age, and that no man knew his father, but that he made the sago good and no one was hungry any more. Old men who were alive some years ago affirmed that they had known Segera in their youth, and the general opinion of the Kiwai people seems to be that Segera died not more than two generations ago.

Taken all together, these legends point to a widespread practice of dismembering the body of a king or magician and burying the pieces in different parts of the country in order to ensure the fertility of the ground and probably also the fecundity of man and beast.

To return to the human victims whose ashes the Egyptians scattered with winnowing-fans, the red hair of these unfortunates was probably significant. For in Egypt the oxen which were sacrificed had also to be red; a single black or white hair found on the beast would have disqualified it for the sacrifice. If, as I conjecture, these human sacrifices were intended to promote the growth of the crops—and the winnowing of their ashes seems to support this view—redhaired victims were perhaps selected as best fitted to personate the spirit of the ruddy grain. For when a god is represented by a living person, it is natural that the human representative should be chosen on the ground of his supposed resemblance to the divine original. Hence the ancient Mexicans, conceiving the maize as a personal being who went through the whole course of life between seed-time and harvest, sacrificed new-born babes when the maize was sown, older children when it had sprouted, and so on till it was fully ripe, when they sacrificed old men. A name for Osiris was the "crop" or "harvest"; and the ancients sometimes explained him as a personification of the corn.

2. *Osiris a Tree-spirit*

But Osiris was more than a spirit of the corn; he was also a tree-spirit, and this may perhaps have been his primitive character, since the worship of trees is naturally older in the history of religion than the worship of the cereals. The character of Osiris as a tree-spirit was represented very graphically in a ceremony described by Firmicus Maternus. A pine-tree having been cut down, the centre was hollowed out, and with the wood thus excavated an image of Osiris was made, which was then buried like a corpse in the hollow of the tree. It is hard to imagine how the conception of a tree as tenanted by a personal being could be more plainly expressed. The image of Osiris thus made was kept for a year and then burned, exactly as was done with the image of Attis which was attached to the pine-tree. The ceremony of cutting the tree, as described by Firmicus Maternus, appears to be alluded to by Plutarch. It was probably the ritual counterpart of the mythical discovery of the body of Osiris enclosed in the *erica*-tree. In the hall of Osiris at Denderah the coffin containing the hawk-headed mummy of the god is clearly depicted as enclosed within a tree, apparently a conifer, the trunk and branches of which are seen above and below the coffin. The scene thus corresponds closely both to the myth and to the ceremony described by Firmicus Maternus.

It accords with the character of Osiris as a tree-spirit that his worshippers were forbidden to injure fruit-trees, and with his character as a god of vegetation in general that they were not allowed to stop up wells of water, which are so important for the irrigation of hot southern lands. According to one legend, he taught men to train the vine to poles, to prune its superfluous foliage, and to extract the juice of the grape. In the papyrus of Nebseni, written about 1550 B.C., Osiris is depicted sitting in a shrine, from the roof of which hang clusters of grapes; and in the papyrus of the royal scribe Nekht we see the god enthroned in front of a pool, from the banks of which a luxuriant vine, with many bunches of grapes, grows towards the green face of the seated deity. The ivy was sacred to him, and was called his plant because it is always green.

3. *Osiris a God of Fertility*

As a god of vegetation Osiris was naturally conceived as a god of creative energy in general, since men at a certain stage of evolution fail to distinguish between the reproductive powers of animals and of plants. Hence a striking feature in his worship was the coarse but expressive symbolism by which this aspect of his nature was presented to the eye not merely of the initiated but of the multitude. At his festival women used to go about the villages singing songs in his praise and carrying obscene images of him which they set in motion by means of strings. The custom was probably a charm to ensure the growth of the crops. A similar image of him, decked with all the fruits of the earth, is said to have stood in a temple before a figure of Isis, and in the chambers dedicated to him at Philae the dead god is portrayed lying on his bier in an attitude which indicates in the plainest way that even in death his generative virtue was not extinct but only suspended, ready to prove a source of life and fertility to the world when the opportunity should offer. Hymns addressed to Osiris contain allusions to this important side of his nature. In one of them it is said that the world waxes green in triumph through him; and another declares, "Thou art the father and mother of mankind, they live on thy breath, they subsist on the flesh of thy body." We may conjecture that in this paternal aspect he was supposed, like other gods of fertility, to bless men and women with offspring, and that the processions at his festival were intended to promote this object as well as to quicken the seed in the ground. It would be to misjudge ancient religion to denounce as lewd and profligate the emblems and the ceremonies which the Egyptians employed for the purpose of giving effect to this conception of the divine power. The ends which they proposed to themselves in these rites were natural and laudable; only the means they adopted to compass them were mistaken. A similar fallacy induced the Greeks to adopt a like symbolism in their Dionysiac festivals, and the superficial but striking resemblance thus produced between the two religions has perhaps more than anything else misled enquirers, both ancient and modern, into identifying worships which, though certainly akin in nature, are perfectly distinct and independent in origin.

4. Osiris a God of the Dead

We have seen that in one of his aspects Osiris was the ruler and judge of the dead. To a people like the Egyptians, who not only believed in a life beyond the grave but actually spent much of their time, labour, and money in preparing for it, this office of the god must have appeared hardly, if at all, less important than his function of making the earth to bring forth its fruits in due season. We may assume that in the faith of his worshippers the two provinces of the god were intimately connected. In laying their dead in the grave they committed them to his keeping who could raise them from the dust to life eternal, even as he caused the seed to spring from the ground. Of that faith the corn-stuffed effigies of Osiris found in Egyptian tombs furnish an eloquent and unequivocal testimony. They were at once an emblem and an instrument of resurrection. Thus from the sprouting of the grain the ancient Egyptians drew an augury of human immortality. They are not the only people who have built the same lofty hopes on the same slender foundation.

A god who thus fed his people with his own broken body in this life, and who held out to them a promise of a blissful eternity in a better world hereafter, naturally reigned supreme in their affections. We need not wonder, therefore, that in Egypt the worship of the other gods was overshadowed by that of Osiris, and that while they were revered each in his own district, he and his divine partner Isis were adored in all.

www.ingramcontent.com/pod-product-compliance
Lightning Source LLC
LaVergne TN
LVHW051545070426
835507LV00021B/2421